This volume summarizes the key lessons of financial history for emerging markets and developing economies today, including the rise and role of central banks, debates on how to make banking secure and sound, the relative efficiency of universal banking compared with the Anglo-American commercial banking model, and the role of savings banks, nonbanks, and securities markets in development. Two lessons that should be kept in mind in reforming financial systems are the importance of incentives and diversification. Robust financial systems require incentive systems that reward prudent risk taking and encourage sound portfolio diversification. In addition, reputation has proved to be important: Central bankers must demonstrate anew why they have earned a reputation for noninflationary policies, and private intermediaries must similarly demonstrate again why they have earned a reputation for sound, as opposed to Ponzi, finance. Attempts to reform financial systems without due allowance for the time and effort to develop institutions, including their reputation, are likely to prove short-lived.

T0312096

Reforming financial systems

Reforming financial systems

Historical implications for policy

Edited by

GERARD CAPRIO, JR.
The World Bank

DIMITRI VITTAS
The World Bank

CAMBRIDGE
UNIVERSITY PRESS

CAMBRIDGE UNIVERSITY PRESS
Cambridge, New York, Melbourne, Madrid, Cape Town, Singapore, São Paulo

Cambridge University Press
The Edinburgh Building, Cambridge CB2 2RU, UK

Published in the United States of America by Cambridge University Press, New York

www.cambridge.org
Information on this title: www.cambridge.org/9780521581158

First published 1997
This digitally printed first paperback version 2006

A catalogue record for this publication is available from the British Library

Library of Congress Cataloguing in Publication data
Reforming financial systems : historical implications for policy /
edited by Gerard Caprio, Jr., Dimitri Vittas.
p. cm.
Includes index.
ISBN 0–521–58115–X
1. Finance – History – 20th century.   2. Banks and banking –
History – 20th century.   I. Caprio, Gerard.   II. Vittas, Dimitri.
HG171.R44   1997
332.1'09'04—dc20   96–38955
                                                         CIP

ISBN-13 978-0-521-58115-8 hardback
ISBN-10 0-521-58115-X hardback

ISBN-13 978-0-521-03281-0 paperback
ISBN-10 0-521-03281-4 paperback

Contents

Contents

Contributors

Michael Bordo
Rutgers University

Forrest Capie
Frobisher Crescent Barbican Centre London

Gerard Caprio, Jr.
The World Bank

Charles W. Calomiris
Columbia University

Randall S. Kroszner
University of Chicago

Frank Packer
Federal Reserve Bank of New York

Anthony Saunders
New York University

Richard Sylla
Stern School of Business

Dimitri Vittas
The World Bank

Eugene White
Rutgers University

Samuel H. Williamson
Miami University

Berry Wilson
Federal Communications Commission

Foreword

Until the early 1980s, developing country financial systems were widely regarded as passive funnels for external resources. Development banks, mostly
established with the help and encouragement of the World Bank, were expected to take the lead in identifying and financing major development projects in industry and infrastructure, as well as in supporting small-scale
farmers and the poor. When attention focused on the performance of development banks, it became clear that most of them were insolvent. The Bank
then quickly began using commercial banks as intermediaries, but it was soon
discovered that commercial banks were also mostly in financial distress.

In response to these problems, the main goal of the Bank's work in the
financial sector became the task of reforming finance and putting domestic
financial systems on a safe and sound footing. This initially involved ration-
alizing and deregulating interest rates and credit policies. The focus was then
widened to a restructuring, recapitalization, and privatization of banks, followed by a stronger emphasis on capital market development. More recently,
the strategy has been directed to what might be called the prerequisites of
sound financial systems: better infrastructure and better plumbing, that is,
better-defined property rights, more effective enforcement of contracts, improved information flows, and stronger supervision.

In refocusing the strategy, there is a wealth of historical experience from
which we can draw. However, attempting to transplant institutional structures
that are currently in fashion in OECD countries without sufficient regard
concerning their relevance for developing countries overlooks the lessons of
financial history. This book brings together a number of papers that were
presented at the seminar entitled Financial History: Lessons of the Past for
Reformers of the Present on May 23–25, 1994. The chapters address some
intriguing questions in financial sector development: What is the role of the
central bank? When, if ever, should sovereignty be sacrificed for currency
boards? If supervision cannot be effective, is there a case for ''free'' banking?
Is deposit insurance a good idea for developing countries? Does finance in
small economies need to be regulated differently than in larger neighbors?
What models of banking and financial structure should we look to for de-

veloping countries: Anglo-American, Japanese, or Continental? How can nonbanking financial intermediaries, including, in particular, thrift institutions and pension funds, contribute to development?

This book draws on the wealth of historical experience as reviewed by a group of eminent scholars in their field. It shows the many lessons that can be learned from history and also highlights some pitfalls that can be avoided. History cannot be transplanted, but it can shorten the distance to the future.

Gary Perlin
Vice President and Treasurer
The World Bank

CHAPTER 1

Financial history: Lessons of the past for reformers of the present

Gerard Caprio, Jr., and Dimitri Vittas

History teaches nothing, only punishes those who do not learn its lessons.
Charles Maurice de Talleyrand-Périgord (1754–1838)

Financial systems in many developing and transitional economies are in a state of flux, in many instances emerging from periods of significant repression and more recent episodes of financial reforms, with little to show for the changes. Indeed, financial crises or more silent forms of financial distress appear to be widespread, from Argentina, Mexico, and Venezuela, to many countries in Eastern Europe and the former Soviet Union, to those in Africa and parts of Asia. For a variety of reasons, financial reforms are difficult to manage, as they involve changing incentive systems and institutions. Also, finance – in particular, banking, the heart of developing and transitional economies' financial systems – is different from other sectors or industries in that failures can spread in a contagious fashion from one institution to another, with deleterious effects on the rest of the economy. And in part as an effort to cope with contagion, some or all of the liabilities of banks often carry an implicit or explicit government guarantee, creating a problem of moral hazard.

In addition, a major difficulty with attempts to reform finance, whatever the initial conditions, is that the reformers virtually always take as given the goal, namely, to move their financial systems toward the general model that has been adopted in most OECD countries today. This model, to the extent that one can generalize, is based on a safety net, in the form of government ''insurance'' for deposits, a prescribed minimum capital adequacy ratio, and government supplied supervision. Not only do these latter financial systems have unresolved problems of their own – for example, the significant bank insolvency problems in France, Japan, Scandinavia, and the United States during the 1980s and 1990s – but they require a rich institutional environment that cannot be transplanted to developing and transitional economics overnight or even in a few years, if at all. In particular, the upgrading of su-

1

pervisory systems to "world class" standards, without which government guarantees are dangerous, appears to be difficult and time consuming. It is also noteworthy that the prescribed capital ratios are low (8 percent) compared with those found in OECD countries during their industrializing period.[1]

Fortunately, the present OECD country experience is not the only one available to emerging markets today; modern banking has been in existence since the fourteenth century, and the late eighteenth century and especially the period of the nineteenth century through the 1920s are rich with the experience of financial systems that did not have much supervision or a government safety net, both of which began during and following the depression of the 1930s. This period is also relevant to developing and transitional countries today, because it is the era when OECD countries were moving from a reliance on agriculture and various commodities to industrial development. Given the relevance of these periods, the conference from which this chapter takes its title was organized to investigate various aspects of the evolution of financial systems and to draw out lessons for emerging economies today. This chapter summarizes the key lessons, including the following: the rise of central banks; debates on how to make banking safe, sound, and better able to fulfill its intermediary functions; the relative efficiency of universal banking (compared with the Anglo-American commercial banking model); and the role of savings banks, nonbanks, and securities markets in development. Section I concentrates on the lessons that have been deduced from a review of the rise of central and commercial banking. The principal questions posed are these:

- What is the role of the central bank and how have these institutions achieved greater independence?
- If financial regulation and supervision is so difficult, is free banking an option, and what does the most successful case of free banking teach us?
- How important is branching and other forms of bank diversification?
- Can varying liability limits help ensure safer banking?
- Is universal banking more efficient than the Anglo-Saxon separation of commercial and investment banking?

Unapologetically, this volume concentrates on banking, since in most developing and transitional economies, at least two-thirds of all financial system assets are in central and commercial banks, with this proportion rising to as much as 90 to 95 percent in the least-developed countries. Nonetheless, nonbanks can play a vital role in the provision of financial services. Nonbanks

---

[1] For example, in the United States capital–asset ratios routinely ranged from 15 to 35 percent in the latter part of the nineteenth century through the 1920s (Saunders and Wilson, chapter 6, this volume). According to Tilly (1966) even higher ratios – 25 to 50 percent – were recorded for German banks in the period 1830 to 1900.

provide a countervailing competitive force to banks, they reach segments of the population and economic sectors that may be neglected by banks, and they may help reform overstretched and unsustainable social security systems that may undermine macrofinancial stability and inhibit growth and development. Section II therefore addresses issues related to savings banks and nonbank finance. It asks:

- How did thrift institutions emerge and can they play an important role in developing and transitional economies?
- How did securities markets arise and how proactive must government policy be in order to stimulate their development?
- How did pension funds develop and become major forces in developed countries' financial systems?

Finally, Section III summarizes the editors' views of the most important lessons for developing and transitional country authorities.[2]

It should be noted that this chapter does not offer magic cures that, if taken, would alone suffice to ensure a dynamic and efficient financial system in which all deposits are safe, all loans are performing, all good investment projects are financed, and all bad ones rejected. If there had been such a successful model for finance, it would be clear from country experience – and although observers often have been quick to claim such merits for many financial systems, these claims rarely endure. Careful examination of cross-country and historical evidence can instead only lead one to conclude that recommendations for any country's financial system need to be "tuned" to the institutions and culture of the country. This volume was inspired by the many cases in which those engaged in financial reforms appeared either to ignore financial history or to proceed as if the lessons were clear and definitive. In the spirit of the this chapter's epigraph and as highlighted by Forrest Capie in Chapter 2, the temptation to draw lessons from history can be overdone. Sometimes history does not teach clear lessons, or stated differently, one has to be extremely careful in applying the so-called lessons. To the editors of this volume, a better acquaintance with history is a necessary ingredient in this endeavor.

That caveat notwithstanding, what are the general lessons? For government authorities, perhaps the two most important factors that should be kept foremost in mind in reforming financial systems are diversification and incentives. Regulators need constantly to verify that banks and other intermediaries can and do diversify their risks and that owners face incentives that will induce them to behave prudently. Although the latter is of prime im-

---

[2] The following chapters focus on lessons for developing countries, transitional economies – those in transition from socialism to a more capitalist system – and emerging markets (usually the often-changing subset of the two groups that attracts the attention of international investors). The editors believe that the chapters are relevant for all three groups. We will accordingly use "emerging market" to mean any of the developing or transitional economies.

portance, there are different ways of accomplishing this goal, which in turn provides the basis for some of the differences observed over time in financial systems. Another general theme concerns the importance of reputation, equally important for central bankers – their reputation for noninflationary policies – as for owners and managers of intermediaries – their reputation for sound, as opposed to Ponzi, finance.[3] Many of the following lessons put some flesh on these quite general recommendations and elaborate their consequences.

I   On the role of central and commercial banks

For several hundred years after the rise of banking during the Renaissance, banking systems functioned without a central bank, and these systems experienced serious inflationary and deflationary shocks associated with reserve flows, among other factors. Central banks emerged, as Forrest Capie explains in Chapter 2, to fulfill both the macro function of inflation control as well as the micro and macro role of ensuring banking system stability. Early central banks originated as national banks that were induced to assume more of a role as a lender of last resort, and it is this function that Capie notes was an important factor leading to their divestiture of commercial banking functions to avoid any conflict of interest. Also, it is often argued that it is difficult enough to excel at central banking functions, so one might suspect that central banks would perform better with fewer distractions.[4] Interestingly, transitional economies appeared to have relatively quickly separated commercial and central banking functions. However, the appearance of a move to a two-tier banking system is somewhat deceptive in economies where the central bank refinances a significant amount of credit by state-owned banks, a phenomena that has been occurring in some transitional economies.

Increasing central bank independence is intellectually fashionable in many parts of the world today, and Capie tells us why and how independence was achieved in the past. He notes that early central banks in effect had a special source for their independence: the absence of the notion that fiscal policy could be used to influence macroeconomic aggregates, such as employment and output. This notion did not become popularized until the Great Depression and the early post–World War II era. Without this presumption, and with a gold standard system, the few central banks in existence – the Bank of England and a dozen other institutions – were able to maintain a high

---

[3] Ponzi, or pyramid, schemes are those that often offer outrageously high rates of return, but pay them through the funds of new investors. "Ponzi finance" then refers to the tendency of intermediaries to take progressively greater risks to cover up for earlier losses.

[4] Hammond (1956) describes how the Second Bank of the United States – which, like the Bank of England, was a private institution – coped with this conflict of interest during the 1812–1932 period. As is easily imaginable, it is difficult to construct an incentive system for an institution with both commercial activities and central banking functions.

degree of independence.[5] Although many economists have long since concluded that changes in budget deficits will not have permanent real effects, the short-run orientation of many politicians, along with more widespread beliefs in the role of the state in providing an array of services and safety nets, has led to more regular attempts to use fiscal policy to influence macroeconomic aggregates. If authorities wish to increase the likelihood that the central bank will be able to resist pressures to accommodate future fiscal demands, then measures such as significantly lengthening the terms of office of central bank governors and making it difficult to remove them would tend to give monetary policy officials the longer-term view that, in effect, was formerly induced by the gold standard.[6]

A second lesson on central banking that is of importance to policy makers is that reforms take time. While it is fashionable to try to introduce market-determined interest rates and open market operations, Capie recounted in the seminar discussion period that the Bank of England took about fifty years to move from direct to indirect implementation of monetary policy. To be sure, as the first real central bank, in the sense of recognizing its lender of last resort functions, and the first one to make this shift, it is understandable that changes proceeded slowly. However, although this experience can help accelerate change in developing countries today, organizations and institutions still take time to change and acquire needed skills, such as the management of interest rate risk, and officials in particular need time to feel comfortable without direct controls. Since it is important that organizations competing in markets for funds be solvent, ensuring that the participants are and likely will remain solvent will also take some time. Thus, moving from direct to indirect implementation of monetary policy should be seen as a problem of financial development that will have to stretch over many years – say, a decade – and the lower the initial income level, the longer the expected time for this transition.

Finally, central bankers need to acquire credibility, or a reputation for noninflationary behavior, and this process also takes time. Given the role of the gold standard in helping to tie the hands of central bankers, Capie implicitly provides support for those advocating fixed exchange rates or, even more stringently, a currency board system for developing and transitional countries needing to establish such reputation quickly. The modern examples provided by Estonia and Argentina suggest that this is appreciated by some authorities today. History, however, also suggests that such arrangements are transitory, in part no doubt due to the well-known difficulty of persuading countries with surplus funding to adjust or to make fiscal transfers to weaker

---

[5] Of course, with a textbook gold standard, one might say that central bankers had little to do in terms of worrying about the growth of monetary aggregates. However, the gold standard was not quite an automatic textbook system, as suggested by Triffin (1964).

[6] Alcazar (1995) suggests that longer terms are more effective than other methods at increasing central bank independence.

6 Gerard Caprio, Jr., and Dimitri Vittas

parts of the currency zone.[7] Thus, authorities should look to additional ways to achieve reputation for their central banks, such as through long terms of office for their governors and budgetary independence from the rest of government.

Whenever central banks are criticized for their performance, or seem incapable of improving economic outcomes and possibly worsening them, inevitably there are calls to do away with these institutions and instead adopt free banking. This term can have many meanings. In the narrow sense, *free banking* means both free entry into banking and the ability of banks to issue their own paper, or notes. So conceived, free banking eliminates or appears to deny the need for a central bank, which is usually given a monopoly power on note issue and the ability to serve as a "gatekeeper" regarding entry into the system. The Scottish example (in the 150 years up to the Peel Act of 1844) comes the closest to satisfying the criteria for free banking, and it appears to be a successful case. During that period, Scotland was a rapidly industrializing country, starting from a low level and actually overtaking England. One of the fears of removing entry barriers in banking is that it might attract unsavory elements or, more kindly, those who are willing to engage in excessive risk taking. Kroszner makes clear in Chapter 3 that one important ingredient in the Scottish case was the unlimited liability of the owners of "free" banks. This feature likely led to the requirement of high levels of capital to protect the personal fortunes of bank owners. True, as with any regulatory requirement, its spirit can be evaded by having a part owner who is hard to find, but if laws dictate that locating reluctant owners is the duty of the other owners and the penalty for evading the law is high, such a requirement would likely be effective in motivating owners to ensure that their bank is prudently managed. In Scotland, reputation, rather than law, appears to have been more important in preventing such abuses. Diversification was also important in Scotland, in that free branching not only helped to increase competition and led to some of the innovations noted by Kroszner, but also contributed to the stability of banking.

If unlimited liability is more effective in inducing safe and sound banking, then one might expect to find lower losses and less evidence of contagion, and this is suggested by Kroszner, as well as by Saunders and Wilson in Chapter 6. Kroszner notes that the Scottish experience was not entirely without a lender of last resort, as there were three large banks with limited liability, as well as the Bank of England, to call on in times of crisis. So although it is possible to argue that unlimited liability reduced the threat of bank contagion, the presence of these other institutions, widespread branching, and the ability to suspend convertibility temporarily might have also

---

[7] Caprio, Dooley, Leipziger, and Walsh (1996) also note the difficulty in providing lender of last resort support in a currency board regime. Although various regulatory changes can help narrow the range of shocks that will buffet a banking system, there is no way to eliminate systemic risk, suggesting that currency board regimes will be transitional devices.

been factors. The case for unlimited liability is strengthened, however, by the fact that bank runs were more prevalent among English banks at the time, which of course also had the same Bank of England on which they could depend. To be sure, adopting free banking is not an all-or-none proposition: one could still have a central bank in charge of note issuance and yet have the higher liability limits and easy entry that allowed bank owners to reap the benefits. Free banking might be attractive where the ability to supervise banks effectively is limited – though some critics might contend that this is a wide sample indeed.

Saunders and Wilson also reviewed higher liability limits, in the form of the double liability limits in some states in the United States, a practice that came into existence at least in part following the experience, beginning in 1837, of free banking with limited liability (and the popular stories of "wildcat" banking). According to the double liability system, each owner was liable for a post-closure assessment of an amount equal to his or her capital, which would have already been drawn on to cover losses. As Saunders and Wilson indicate, this practice led to fewer involuntary closures, as well as more voluntary mergers, and appeared to have played an important role in insulating depositors against loss. Thus, some form of higher liability limits on bank owners appears to be worth consideration in emerging markets as a way of increasing owners' incentives to monitor their managers. As noted by Caprio (1995),[8] developing and transitional economies are risky environments, not just due to policy changes but even more so due to their small size. Hence, applying the same capital requirement – in the form of the Basle guidelines, which were devised for relatively large and diversified economies – to smaller and undiversified countries could be dangerous. Raising liability limits induces the owners, rather than officials, to set capital ratios, which may be convenient since it is difficult for officials to know how high capital ratios should be raised in different economies.

It is possible that raising liability limits too high might lead to a suboptimal supply of financial services. However, in neither the Scottish nor the U.S. case does this appear to have been a problem: both economies were the "miracle" economies of their era, and as Kroszner illustrates, even with unlimited liability there was notable innovation by the Scottish free banks, including a form of option contracts.[9] Thus, this drawback does not appear

---

[8] That paper also notes other methods to improve incentives facing bank owners, such as arbitrarily raising capital requirements, limiting entry to build up franchise value, free banking, and narrow banking. It should be recognized that all of these assume private owners. Joint liability, such as through participation in a clearinghouse association, would also improve private incentives. For state-owned banks, there is no clear evidence that any of these options would have an effect, as they assume owners that are motivated by profits.

[9] Interestingly, these option clauses represented a market solution to bank runs, in that they gave the issuing bank the right to defer payment on bank notes, so that holders would get either what they were due when they presented the note or, alternatively, that sum plus interest in six months. As Kroszner notes, these options were quite popular until banned, largely at

to be too severe, though it would be reassuring if there were more cases of higher liability limits on which a conclusion could be based. But for officials beset by financial instability and underdeveloped supervisory capacity, higher liability limits appear to be a potential solution ensuring safe and sound banking.[10] Completely free banking – including removing monopoly of note issuance – need not be adopted as part of the same reforms, though as more countries are willing to consider currency board arrangements, they might even consider this radical step. For now, a system of freely competing currencies appears to be an idea whose time has not yet come.

Officials intent on reforming their financial systems should keep in mind that most banks – and banking systems – encounter solvency problems (or bank crises) because they fail to diversify. To be sure, there are myriad reasons for bank failure, such as connected lending, regulatory restrictions, and an inability on the part of bank management to plan. Regulatory restrictions are the easiest for authorities to correct in principle. In the United States, the battle to keep as many regulatory powers as possible at the state level, coupled with a fear of concentrating of wealth and political power, led to the imposition of a prohibition on interstate branching, and in many states there were further restrictions limiting banks to a single branch. Calomiris (1992) has shown that states that permitted branch banking enjoyed more stable banks and lower losses per dollar of deposit than did unit banking states. Michael Bordo, Chapter 4, this volume, shows quite convincingly how branching restrictions led to a much higher failure rate in the United States than in Canada during the 1870–1980 period. Canada experienced the same shocks and was a smaller economy, yet had a much lower bank failure rate due to nationwide branching, which led to far fewer banks. Indeed, he notes that during the international business cycle contraction – most severe in the 1870s and 1890s – the contagion effect led to bank runs and a further contraction of output in the United States, but Canada, which was not spared the effects of international forces, did not suffer further contractionary effects because of its better-insulated banking system. Having a small number of banks also facilitates the merger process when one gets into trouble, as the remaining banks can clearly see the problems they might encounter if depositors at the insolvent bank suffer losses; having fewer banks also increases their incentive to supervise one another, as the costs of contagion are more clearly visible and the benefits from mutual oversight easier to appropriate.[11]

---

the behest of the large, limited liability banks, who were losing business, because the options made small banks' notes more attractive.

[10] The authors recognize that this suggestion may not be viewed as practical, given the current regime in industrial countries. Still, the greater risks and volatility in developing and emerging country markets may require different solutions than those in the OECD economies.

[11] Champ, Smith, and Williamson (1991) argue that a high degree of currency elasticity in Canada may also have figured prominently in explaining the greater degree of banking stability there. This may be the case, but the tendency of Canadian banks to issue banknotes

Thus, with fewer banks there may be a form of implicit joint liability, and Calomiris (1992, 1993) has substantiated these benefits in the case of U.S. clearinghouses, for which the joint liability feature was important.

It is likely that with the benefits of greater stability, there may be costs due to less competition. However, Canadian authorities appear to have offset this possible effect by keeping their economy open. Hence, this case might be useful for small emerging markets: for many countries the small size of their economies means that, even with national branching, their banks will still be concentrated, but then there is little choice, if stability is desired, but to permit these banks to hold assets overseas. Although many observers have noted that banks tend to make losses if they stray far from their home base, holding assets abroad need not mean lending there. Instead, banks in small developing countries could hold securities – such as shares in internationally diversified mutual funds – which would greatly limit their risk.[12] For example, Mexican banks were seriously weakened by the collapse of the peso in late 1994 and early 1995, and it is argued that the subsequent recession there will be worse due to the banks' weak condition. If Mexican banks had held, say, 50 percent of their portfolio in the form of internationally diversified mutual funds, they would be in much better condition today and would be better able to lend and thereby to support a recovery. Similarly, if Japanese banks had done the same in the 1980s, they would be in commensurably better shape at present.

As noted earlier, bank portfolios might be concentrated due to an inability to plan, as evinced in the failure to analyze and comprehend the extent to which various parts of their loan book – oil, land, and construction in the case of Texas banks – were correlated. Or they engaged in simpleminded forecasting,[13] such as the assumption, when asset prices or commodity prices rise, that the price rises would continue. This inability to plan should be understood not as an exogenous factor but rather as a consequence of poor incentives. If bank owners will reap a large reward from prudent bank practices, then that is the activity in which they will tend to engage. Thus, Caprio and Summers (1996) argue that as banks' franchise value declines, owners will invest less effort in ensuring safety and soundness, and Keeley (1990) links the declining franchise value of U.S. banks to lower capital ratios.

countercyclically was not sufficient to prevent Canadian authorities from having to step in and assume a more active role prior to the establishment of a central bank in 1935. Indeed, the concerns that currency elasticity was insufficient were important in mustering support for creating a central bank (Shearer, Chant, and Bond 1995).

[12] As should always be the case, attention should be paid to issues of asset liability management. Thus, banks with mostly short-term deposits would need to invest adequately in funds holding short-term, high-quality bills, while those with longer-term liabilities could hold some medium- and long-term bond funds.

[13] One could also classify interest and exchange rate mismatches as due to an inability to plan. De Juan (1987) describes in greater detail this process by which bankers descend along the path from being good bankers to bad.

Again, then, there appears to be a case for making sure that banking is profitable, and in emerging markets this usually means reducing the often excessive taxation of financial intermediaries. Attention to franchise value is also relevant in considering the role of fraud in bank failure. The temptation to "loot the bank" will grow the lower the franchise value is in relation to the short-run gains from looting (Akerlof and Romer 1993), and fraud is a popular form of looting. That fraud is often found when banks fail is thus not surprising, since when banks' net worth becomes either low or negative, there is less incentive for owners to police employees (or restrain themselves). This is especially true in a world in which cultures and legal systems place less importance on arms-length transactions and where the costs associated with a damaged reputation can be avoided by migration.

Insufficient diversification might also be due to connected lending, in which banks lend to related businesses – those that they own or are owned by – or to businesses owned by friends, family, or by those willing to pay a bribe for a loan. Even with proper regulations, history suggests that banks demand alert supervision to prevent these abuses, coupled with severe penalties in the case of transgressions. In nineteenth-century New England, insider lending was popular, yet the importance of maintaining a good reputation appeared to be a key factor in restraining abuses (Lamoreaux 1994). Regarding ownership links, it should be noted that banks often arose in connection with nonfinancial enterprises, as was the case of Japan in the last third of the nineteenth century. However, as Frank Packer reminds us in Chapter 8, this volume, as soon as these banks acquired some size, they went from being cost centers to specializing in short-term trade finance and became highly profitable. They later were split off from the commercial firms and – presumably because prudent banking was sufficiently profitable – functioned as independent banks, some of which failed in the 1920s, while others remained quite successful. The Japanese also adopted a "hard bankruptcy" policy that suspended transactions of firms that were unable to pay their notes. Thus, clear incentives matter. Also, when banks control firms – as in Japan and in Germany – excessive lending to related firms appears to be less of a problem than when firms control the banks, as in the case of Chile during the 1970s and early 1980s.

Should ownership links be severed and banks be constrained to commercial banking narrowly defined, or is universal banking the superior model? Research has not been able to answer this thorny, long-standing debate. Kennedy (1987) argues that in response to banking crises of the mid-nineteenth century, U.K. banks retreated to develop the most efficient short-term markets in the world but cut back on lending to industrial firms, whereas German universal banks continued this lending, in part due to their superior information and control over corporate clients, related to bank managers' ability to buy and underwrite securities including equity and their positions on corporate boards. Charles Calomiris, chapter 7, this volume, also shows convincingly that the German system permitted cheaper issuance of new shares than in the United States. This is an important comparison: Richard Sylla argues in Chapter 11 that inefficient regulation of U.S. banks – in particular the balkanization of this industry due to limits on branching – contributed directly to the development of U.S. securities markets, which he argues were deeper than those in the United Kingdom except for the period 1870–1920. Yet the fact that equity issuance was cheaper in Germany gave firms there an ability to expand quickly and to benefit from economies of scale, which makes the universal banking model attractive for newly industrializing countries. Although it is a theoretical possibility that lower transaction costs could reduce savings and growth (Bencivenga, Smith, and Starr 1995), there is no empirical support for this effect, and indeed the empirical evidence (Levine and Zervos 1996) favors a positive relationship between lower transaction costs and higher growth.

The major drawbacks to universal banking are, first, that these institutions are more complex to supervise than narrow commercial banks and, second, that they permit more transactions to take place outside of open markets. The first concern is genuine, but goes to the issue of how much reliance is placed on supervision versus incentives in trying to ensure safe and sound banking. If greater primacy is placed on the latter, then the supervisory concern might be lessened. Moreover, the efficiency gains noted by Calomiris might be sufficient to outweigh these concerns. The second objection is more one of culture and institutions. Some societies – often when they are relatively homogeneous or dominated by a relatively homogeneous group – are less concerned about the potential for a build up of wealth and influence. Others, being less homogeneous, are more concerned about level playing fields and avoiding undue concentrations of power. Thus, these "tastes" might figure prominently in determining whether or not to adopt the universal banking route. The evidence here suggests that if this model can be accommodated to other institutions in a country, there are some potential efficiency gains. Finally, for developing and transitional economies in which volatility is large, allowing banks some equity ownership may contribute to faster growth, since if banks can engage only in debt finance in a high-risk environment, they may retreat and do less lending than otherwise. An equity stake in their clients can (but does not necessarily) make them inside investors, with the hope that better information will offset higher volatility.[14]

To summarize, then, banking systems can be made more safe and sound by focusing on incentives facing bank owners, as well as by ensuring that banks are adequately diversified. History provides some useful lessons on both counts. More radical reforms, such as free banking and higher liability

---

[14] German banks own relatively little equity in industrial companies but have influence by being able to exercise the proxy for many shareholders and by having bank personnel on the supervisory boards of firms they loan to.

limits, may be viewed as impractical in many countries, though as experience with systemic banking problems spreads and grows in importance, as it has in the 1980s and 1990s in industrial and developing economies, officials may become more disposed to return to these experiments from the past. The reform that appears somewhat more practical is to legislate the ability of banks to diversify, and even to force this process in countries that are relatively small. Although diversification, especially when it entails sending resources abroad, can be perceived as reducing the supply of funds for local investment, the improvement in the viability of domestic financial institutions may increase the volume of savings intermediated by the formal financial system and reduce the fiscal cost of covering losses associated with bank insolvency. Solvent domestic banks may also stimulate foreign direct and portfolio investment, thus further increasing the supply of financial capital to the local economy.

Even though incentives are important for motivating bank owners and managers, banking licenses will naturally be attractive to a variety of unsavory elements, as well as to investors who will attempt to maximize short-run profits notwithstanding the increased risk. For this reason, improving supervision in most emerging market economies is important, especially where the existing system is geared more to a repressed regime and not a market-oriented one. Supervisory powers could be augmented by either imposing (or vesting supervisors with the ability to impose) limits on banks' growth, since rapidly expanding lending often precedes bank failure. Indeed, one could envisage a range of choices for banks, such as allowing highly capitalized banks more powers and faster growth, while banks with lower capital ratios are constrained to slower growth and more conservative investments. For banking systems, authorities in very risky economies could opt to approach 100 percent reserve banking – the so-called narrow banking model – though it may take several significant banking crises before authorities are willing to opt for this solution.

We should point out here, as suggested by Kennedy (noted earlier), that the goal is not to have just safe, but safe and sound, banking. Banks could be made safe by eliminating any risks that they take, but this would push the business – and problems – of term transformation elsewhere in the financial system, and it is not clear that the economy would enjoy any net benefit. Instead of ensuring safety at any cost, the goal is to ensure that bankers engage in prudent and well-diversified risk taking, otherwise known as sound banking. This will ensure that savings are allocated efficiently to a variety of low-, medium-, and high-risk ventures, which would yield a basket of investments producing a growth rate superior to one in which a large proportion of bank loans did not pay off.

In addition to developing central and commercial banks, financial systems can be made more stable by also developing savings and nonbank financial intermediaries, and it is now to the lessons from the history of these institutions that we turn.

II Savings and nonbank finance

Financial policy in developing countries, as well as in most developed countries until recently, has long been concerned with real or perceived gaps in national financial systems. An early and persistent manifestation of this concern related to the shortage of term finance and long-term financial markets that characterized most developing countries. Commercial banks were widely criticized for focusing on trade and working capital finance and neglecting the long-term needs of large industrial firms. In many countries, commercial banks were nationalized in an attempt to control their lending decisions, while development banks were created to channel (long-term) finance to industry.

Development banking and state ownership were institutional innovations of the twentieth century. With few exceptions, their performance was dismal: lending decisions were often based on political considerations rather than on economic criteria; loan supervision and recovery were very weak; and such innovations also suffered from high levels of overstaffing and large overheads.[15] Moreover, their main customers were often themselves state-owned enterprises, suffering from overmanning, high labor costs, and large losses. State-owned commercial and development banks were faced with the wrong incentives, and their failure to develop profitable and efficient operations resulted in a heavy tax burden on the rest of the financial system and the economy at large. In many developing countries and especially in transitional economies, tackling the financial problems of state-owned enterprises and state-owned banks seems to be a sine qua non for effective restructuring of each country's financial system.

Commercial banks were also widely criticized for neglecting the financial needs of farmers, artisans, and small traders, as well as low- and middle-income people, especially with regard to their needs for mortgage loans to finance the acquisition of houses. Specialized thrift deposit institutions, ranging from various types of savings banks to credit cooperatives and credit unions to housing finance institutions, were created or emerged spontaneously to fill these gaps in the financial system throughout the late eighteenth and nineteenth centuries in many European countries, as well as in the United States and Canada.

The creation of thrift deposit institutions was often promoted by individuals of substance and high integrity who were eager to transplant ideas and institutions that appeared to work well from one country to another. Thrift

---

[15] World Bank (1989) contains an extensive discussion of the failure of state-owned commercial and development banks in developing countries.

deposit institutions took many different forms. Some were state owned, for example, the postal savings banks. Others, for example, the savings banks in Germany, Switzerland, and other European countries, were set up by municipal authorities and benefited from their tutelage and guarantee. Most were set up as mutual institutions, "owned" by their members but with limited liability. And some, for example, the rural credit cooperatives, were established with unlimited liability among their members, a feature that endured only in small communities with a more equal distribution of wealth. The types of thrift deposit institutions that prospered in different countries reflected the structure of market gaps in the respective financial systems.

Thrift deposit institutions were stronger in countries where they developed a three-tier structure that combined the local character and autonomy of individual institutions with the geographic diversification, liquidity management, and auditing and control services of central regional and national institutions. In general, those that emerged spontaneously by local interests performed better than those that were created by government initiatives.

Thrift deposit institutions were an institutional innovation of the eighteenth and nineteenth centuries. Their record was in general more favorable than that of state-owned commercial and development banks. They experienced considerable growth in many countries and came to represent a substantial share, ranging from 20 to 40 percent, of total financial assets by the mid-1970s.

The success of thrift deposit institutions can be attributed to their generally low transaction and information costs. Postal savings banks provided a convenient place for saving for the poor. Credit cooperatives and credit unions offered their members credit rates that avoided the high spreads charged by moneylenders. Housing finance institutions developed long-term mortgage instruments that facilitated the spread of home ownership. Thrift deposit institutions relied on the simplicity and convenience of their savings facilities for attracting funds from low- and middle-income households, while their credit facilities benefited from the local nature of their operations and from the peer monitoring and pressure for loan repayment that were encouraged by the common links among their members. Savings banks played a limited part in financing industry, especially large-scale manufacturing, except for the mutual savings banks in New England and the municipally owned savings banks in Germany and other central European countries. Their record was mixed. Early success was followed by failure as a result of connected lending and excessive risk exposure to cyclical industrial downturns.[16]

The financial fortunes of all types of thrift institutions were affected by the same gyrations as those affecting commercial banks. Like commercial

---

[16] In Germany, saving banks survived to the modern era, despite their interest rate mismatch and bouts of hyperinflation, because they were supported by their municipal authorities. Despite being state owned, they avoided a heavy politicization of their operations.

banks, they suffered when they were faced with distorted incentives (e.g., the savings and loan debacle of the 1980s in the United States), and they also had their share of fraud and mismanagement throughout the nineteenth and twentieth centuries. However, they were able to prosper in the longer run, supported by financial and political stability, as well as by efficient financial and legal infrastructures.

As argued by Dimitri Vittas, Chapter 9, this volume, the heyday of thrift deposit institutions in OECD countries was probably the mid-1970s. Since then they have come under increasing pressure because of four main factors: changes in the size and distribution of financial wealth that imply a growing demand for pension and mutual funds, which can then meet the financial needs of housing and other markets through the use of securitized instruments; greater competition from commercial banks, which have been forced to reorient their operations toward retail financial services; changes in transaction and information technology that have undermined the past comparative advantage of thrift deposit institutions; and changes in financial regulation that have removed the barriers between different types of financial institutions. These changes have motivated the recent trend of diversification of financial services, as well as despecialization and the concomitant trend of "demutualization," that is, conversion of mutual institutions into joint-stock ownership.

Thrift deposit institutions were also created in many developing countries, but their record suffered from the problems caused by high inflation, negative real rates of interest, weak monitoring and enforcement mechanisms, and government interference. These factors helped to weaken and distort the incentives facing their managers, owners, and customers. Loan arrears undermined their soundness and caused large failures, government bailouts, or stagnation. This sorry experience helps to underscore the importance of financial stability and a sound financial infrastructure.

Could thrift deposit institutions play a big role in the future in the financial systems of developing countries? The recent changes in the technological and institutional environment facing thrift deposit institutions in developed countries suggest that their prospects and future role in developing and transitional countries will be rather limited. In particular, their role in financing large-scale industry and in providing a specialized circuit for housing finance will likely be circumscribed by the development of more efficient networks based on securities markets and institutional investors.

Nevertheless, they could still play a role in rural and retail finance, as they did in the nineteenth and early twentieth centuries in industrial economies. Thus, provided inflation is kept under control, postal savings banks could mobilize deposits from poorer areas, where there may be few commercial bank branches. Credit unions and credit cooperatives could encourage thrift among poorer households and among farmers, artisans, and small traders, and they could distribute credits to these groups in countries where commercial banks have small branch networks and are unlikely to be successful in accessing these markets. But an important lesson from the experience of developed countries is the creation of three-tier structures, consisting of local, regional, and national institutions: local units operating in a small geographic area and having small membership (and thus the ability to monitor the performance of local borrowers and to exert peer pressure for loan repayment); regional units providing liquidity, auditing, and monitoring services to the local units; and national entities linking these institutions with the money and capital markets, as well as representing their interests at the national level.

Low inflation and sound public finances are also essential preconditions for the development of securities markets. As explained by Sylla in Chapter 11, this volume, the securities markets in the United States prospered after the restoration of sound public finances in the aftermath of the American Revolution. A major funding and restructuring of U.S. government debt, which also included the generation of secure state revenues to service this debt, caused a very large increase in its market value within the spate of a few years. The sound public finances attracted foreign capital and established the foundations for a thriving government bond market. Other securities markets followed and were helped by the absence of restrictive regulations on the formation of corporations.

A second essential precondition for the growth of securities markets is the generation and dissemination of standardized information (see Demirguc-Kunt and Levine 1996). The development of U.S. securities markets lagged behind those of Britain between 1870 and 1920. Sylla attributes this to the earlier development of stock market regulation in Britain, which required corporations to issue prospectuses and publish audited reports. During this period, U.S. securities markets suffered from a scarcity of reliable public information and from endemic insider trading. However, during the 1930s and 1940s, the market regulation developed by the Securities and Exchange Commission and the mandated disclosure of standardized information surpassed the financial regulation imposed in Britain and contributed to the further development of U.S. stock and bond markets.

Many developing countries try to expand their securities markets by providing tax incentives to firms that list on the stock markets, by offering tax incentives to savers who invest in long-term instruments, or by requiring banks and other financial institutions to invest in government and mortgage bonds. The experience of the United States (and other developed countries) suggests that these measures may not be necessary. Once governments set their public finances in order, establish effective regulation of information disclosure, and remove tax and other obstacles to the development of markets, all they have to do is get out of the way and let the markets develop on their own.

But a major problem facing developing countries today is that it is much more difficult to set public finances in order because governments are more heavily involved in all types of expenditure programs and have large amounts of explicit and implicit liabilities that may not be as easy to restructure and downsize as was perhaps the case in the United States at the end of the eighteenth century. As already noted, governments in developing and transitional countries must tackle the problems of state-owned enterprises, including state-owned banks and insurance companies, and must restructure their tax systems and improve the administrative efficiency of tax collection. But they must also reform their social security systems, which evolved over many years of government involvement in the provision of social pensions and are placing a heavy burden on public finances. Restructuring pension systems by downsizing the public pensions paid by social security institutions and encouraging the development of private pension funds is likely to be a major financial and political challenge, but it could have significant beneficial long-term effects on public finances and on the structure of capital markets.[17]

Pension funds as financial intermediaries were not important in the nineteenth century because coverage was limited and few people lived for any significant time after retirement. Historically, pension funds initially emerged at the turn of the century as labor market institutions, essentially as personnel management tools used by large corporations to attract skilled workers, reward loyalty, and facilitate the retirement of older workers. As discussed by Williamson, Chapter 10, this volume, pension schemes in the United States grew to replace more traditional forms of life saving, especially "tontine" insurance, which was banned in 1906. Early pension schemes were noncontributory and unfunded, and they offered no vesting and portability rights. Their actuarial cost was low because the labor force was young and firms expected to provide pensions to a small minority of loyal workers who stayed with the same firm until they reached the mandatory retirement age.[18]

Over time the structure of pension funds experienced several changes. Some pension funds became contributory, which increased pressures for better vesting and portability rights. There was a also a growing need for funding by investing in marketable securities, a trend that was encouraged by tax incentives and by fiduciary standards. Coverage expanded over time, although it has never reached a universal level, as small-scale employers have refrained from introducing pension schemes and the basic retirement needs of low-income workers have been met by the development of social security pensions. A recent trend that is fueled by basic changes in industrial structure and employment patterns is the relative growth of defined contribution funds, which are based on individual capitalization accounts and are fully funded, fully vested, and fully portable.

---

[17] The feasibility of pension reform and its beneficial effects for the capital markets have been demonstrated by Chile, which implemented such a reform in 1981. See Diamond and Valdes-Prieto (1994) and Vittas and Iglesias (1992) on the early success of the Chilean pension reform.

[18] This pattern of development was also experienced in Britain (Hannah 1986).

Pension funds are now a major force in the capital markets of many developed countries, as well as a small number of developing countries that have reformed their social security systems (e.g., Chile) or avoided the creation of pay-as-you-go social schemes (e.g., Singapore and Malaysia). Their role as financial intermediaries has grown because their coverage has expanded, life expectancy has increased, and funding has become more widespread. However, their role in the capital markets and in corporate governance is still in its early stages of evolution. The progressive aging of the population of most developed countries suggests a bigger role for pension funds as institutional investors in the future.

Developing and transitional countries need to undertake a fundamental reform of their social security systems, to lessen the fiscal burden of unsustainable and unfunded liabilities, and to create the regulatory and financial conditions for the creation and growth of supplementary funding schemes, preferably based on full funding, vesting, and portability. There is some hope based on the Chilean experience that a move in this direction will also have a favorable effect on the level of savings, in addition to increasing the supply of funds available for longer-term investments.

III   Concluding remarks

There are clearly some important lessons from the earlier history of financial development, even though the environment within which financial institutions operate is much different now. The first lesson is the importance of macroeconomic stability, implying low inflation and sound public finances. This is important not only for creating the right incentives for banks, but also for facilitating the development of securities markets. High inflation and large fiscal deficits distort economic behavior in favor of short-term speculative projects and discourage long-term investment projects that are conducive to sustainable economic development. Central bank independence may contribute to macroeconomic stability. One way to increase central bank independence is by lengthening the term of office of central bank governors.

The second lesson is to ensure that bank owners face incentives that induce them to behave prudently. This implies that bank owners have capital that is commensurate with the risks they assume. Although unlimited liability and double liability limits may be less feasible now than in the past, the implication is clear: banks in developing countries that face higher risks should maintain higher capital ratios than banks in the more advanced OECD countries.[19]

A third lesson relates to the need for risk diversification. Historical ex-

---

[19] Caprio and Summers (1996) and Hellmann, Murdoch, and Stiglitz (1994) argue that, if capital is scarce, bankers' incentives can be improved by limiting entry and creating greater charter value, in the form of higher expected future profits.

perience shows clearly that banks face solvency problems because they fail to diversify. Often, this failure is due to regulatory restrictions, especially geographic restrictions. But it may also be caused by excessive connected lending or by genuine mistakes. Regulators must ensure that banks diversify their risks. This requires removal of geographic and sectoral restrictions, including any prohibition to hold foreign assets. But it also requires restrictions on connected lending.

Restrictions on connected lending, as well as higher capital requirements, imply an important role for regulators and supervisors in ensuring meaningful and effective compliance with such rules. Developing effective supervision is difficult and time consuming but is essential if prudential rules are to be enforced.

The difficulty of supervising universal banks and financial conglomerates more generally is an argument used against them in developing countries. But universal banks may generate efficiency gains since they can overcome the problems caused by the absence of reliable public information on industrial and commercial companies. Holding small equity stakes and being involved in corporate governance may produce beneficial effects. The risk of excessive lending to related firms is likely to be small when banks hold small stakes in industrial firms. In contrast, it is very high when firms control banks.

Effective supervision is also important for the development of securities markets. Apart from low inflation and sound public finances, the other major factor that explains the growth of securities markets seems to be timely and reliable public disclosure of financial information, as well as protection of small investors and minority shareholders.

Pension funds and other institutional investors have grown in importance in many countries over the past thirty years or so, directly as a result of longer life spans and longer retirement. Although these funds started as labor market institutions and personnel management tools, they have become very important financial intermediaries. For developing countries, pension funds offer an alternative both for restructuring their public finances and for promoting their capital markets.

Pension funds can in fact play the role that thrift deposit institutions – such as savings banks, credit cooperatives, and building societies – played in developed countries in the nineteenth century. But despite the changes that have taken place in the technological and institutional environment, thrift institutions can still make a positive contribution to financial and economic development by promoting thrift and facilitating credit in rural areas and among low-income groups. Their contribution will be stronger if they involve a three-tier structure that combines the benefits of local involvement and monitoring with centralized auditing and supervision.

Financial reformers in developing and transitional economies can also draw lessons from the recent experience of financial systems, especially the adverse effects of the heavy politicization of the financial system that has characterized many countries in recent decades. State ownership of banks and other financial institutions is an extreme form of politicization. This has potentially serious adverse effects when large sections of industry are also under state ownership. In these circumstances, banks are pressured to lend to unprofitable and bloated state companies. Restructuring and privatization of state-owned banks and industrial companies should therefore be a high priority in reforming countries. But privatization by itself is not sufficient, as suggested by the Mexican crisis of 1994–95. Developing effective and independent regulators is necessary to prevent private bankers from engaging in self-lending and excessively risky ventures, as well as relying on government bailouts in the event of failure.

REFERENCES

Akerlof, George A., and Paul M. Romer, 1993. "Looting: The Economic Underworld of Bankruptcy for Profit." *Brookings Papers on Economic Activity*, no. 2: 1–73.

Alcazar, Lorena. 1995. "Political Constraints and the Use of Seignorage: Empirical Evidence from a Cross-Country Sample." Mimeo, Washington University, St. Louis, and the Brookings Institution.

Bencivenga, Valerie R., Bruce D. Smith, and Ross M. Starr. 1996. "Equity Markets, Transactions Costs, and Capital Accumulation: An Illustration," *World Bank Economic Review* 10 (2):241–66.

Calomiris, Charles. 1992. "Regulation, Industrial Structure, and Instability in U.S. Banking: An Historical Perspective." In Michael Klausner and Lawrence J. White, eds., *Structural Change in Banking*. Homewood, Ill.: Irwin, pp. 19–116.

———1993. "Getting the Incentives Right in the Current Deposit Insurance System: Successes from the pre-FDIC era." In James R. Barth and R. Dan Brumbaugh, eds., *The Reform of Federal Deposit Insurance: Disciplining the Government and Protecting Taxpayers*. Armonk, N.Y.: Harper, pp. 142–78.

Caprio, Gerard, Jr. 1995. "Bank Regulation: The Case of the Missing Model." Paper presented at the Brookings/KPMG conference Sequencing of Financial Reforms. Washington, D.C.

Caprio, Gerard, Jr., and Lawrence H. Summers. 1996. "Financial Reform: Beyond Laissez Faire." In Dimitri Papadimitriou, ed., *Financing Prosperity into the 21st Century*. New York: Macmillan, pp.

Caprio, Gerard, Jr., Michael Dooley, Danny Leipziger, and Carl Walsh. 1996. "The Lender of Last Resort Function under a Currency Board: The Case of Argentina." Policy Research Working Paper no. 1648, World Bank, Washington, D.C., September.

Champ, Bruce, Bruce D. Smith, and Stephen D. Williamson, 1991. "Currency Elasticity and Banking Panics: Theory and Evidence." Working Paper no. 91–14, Center for Analytic Economics, Cornell University, August.

de Juan, Aristobulo. 1987. "From Good Bankers to Bad Bankers: Ineffective Supervision and Management Deterioration as Major Elements in Banking Crises." Washington, D.C.:World Bank, Financial Policy and Systems Division.

Demirguc-Kunt, Asli, and Ross Levine. 1996. "Stock Markets, Corporate Finance, and Economic Growth: An Overview," *World Bank Economic Review* 10 (2): 223–40.

Diamond, Peter A., and Salvador Valdes-Prieto. 1994. "Social Security Reforms."

In B. Bosworth, ed., *Chilean Economy: Policy Lessons and Challenges*. Washington, D.C.: Brookings Institution, pp. 396–432.

Hammond, Bray. 1956. *Banking and Politics in America from the Revolution to the Civil War*. Princeton, N.J.: Princeton University Press.

Hannah, Leslie. 1986. *Inventing Retirement: The Development of Occupational Pensions in Britain*. Cambridge University Press.

Hellmann, Thomas, Kevin Murdock, and Joseph Stiglitz. 1994. "Deposit Mobilization through Financial Restraint." Mimeo, Stanford University, Stanford, Calif.

Keeley, Michael C. 1990. "Deposit Insurance, Risk, and Market Power in Banking." *American Economic Review* 80 (5): 1183–2000.

Kennedy, William P. 1987. *Industrial Structure, Capital Markets, and the Origins of British Economic Decline*. Cambridge University Press.

Lamoreaux, Naomi R. 1994. *Insider Lending: Banks, Personal Connections, and Economic Development in Industrial New England*. Cambridge University Press.

Levine, Ross, and Zervos, Sara, 1996. "Stock Market Development and Long-Run Growth." *World Bank Economic Review* 10 (2):323–40.

Shearer, Ronald A., John F. Chant, and David E. Bond. 1995. *Economics of the Canadian Financial System: Theory, Policy, and Institutions*, 3rd edition. New York: Prentice-Hall.

Tilly, Richard. 1966. *Financial Institutions and Industrialization in the German Rhineland, 1815–1870*. Madison: University of Wisconsin Press.

Triffin, Robert. 1964. "The Myth and Realities of the So-Called Gold Standard." In Robert Triffin, ed., *The Evolution of the International Monetary System: Historical Reappraisal and Future Perspectives*. Princeton, N.J.: Princeton University Press, pp. 2–20.

Vittas, Dimitri, and Augusto Iglesias. 1992. "The Rationale and Performance of Personal Pension Plans in Chile." Policy Research Working Paper no. 867, World Bank, Washington, D.C.

World Bank. 1989. *World Development Report, 1989: Financial Systems and Development*. World Bank, Washington, D.C., and New York: Oxford University Press.

CHAPTER 2

The evolution of central banking

Forrest Capie

Different types of economists have different views on the establishment, reform, and shape of central banks. Some think first of issues such as time consistency and the trade-off between inflation and unemployment. Others would construct an index of independence (one of these exercises in spurious accuracy that Morgenstern warned against about forty years ago). Economists with a more political bent would talk about the need for accountability of central banks in a democracy. Economic journalists are inclined to find in the Maastricht Treaty the ideal model. But economists with historical leanings think of longer-term factors and of the circumstances in which institutions might have been effective. All approaches have their uses but this chapter emphasises the contribution of history.

In this exercise we seek to say something of the historical experience and the lessons that might be learned. However, it is important to say that lessons from history are not easily uncovered. One distinguished historian suggested that the only lesson to be learned from history is that there are no lessons. History at the very minimum encourages caution and perhaps produces skepticism. The quest for lessons produces tensions in historians. The "historian" in the economic historian is content to explain events as the unique outcome of a specific set of factors; while the "economist" in the economic historian is always looking for patterns, that is, pulled toward generalization. This temptation is understandable and although it carries dangers it will be succumbed to here. The good economic historian should remain alert for the contingent while keeping an eye on the systematic.

The central argument of this chapter is that a major obstacle to the successful transition to a market economy is inflation. (There are, of course, others, but this is the monetary problem.) The key to the working of the market economy lies in the signals given by prices. These signals are harder to discern in an inflationary environment, and particularly so when the market economy is becoming established. So a major objective is the control of inflation, and there is a role here for a well-behaved central bank. Furthermore, in the absence of well-defined and secure property rights – the basis for an efficient tax system – governments can be tempted to raise revenue by means other than taxes. The easiest and most common is monetary expansion and the inflation tax. Thus, the case for some independent body to look after monetary policy is strengthened.

This chapter first outlines some experience of inflation in countries in turmoil and hints at the lessons to be found there. It then comments on how central banks have operated historically and suggests how they should operate today. The questions of why they are needed and what they require in order to perform well are addressed. Consideration of their historical development reveals some of the tensions that have arisen.

Inflation

For economies in transition the need to reform the monetary sector derives from the danger of inflation, particularly great if, as is likely, there are expected to be tensions in the transition. An examination of the incidence of serious inflations (inflations in excess of 100 percent per year) before 1950 reveals some striking features (Capie 1986). First, there were remarkably few episodes, and most of them took place in the twentieth century. Second, they were all a result of monetary expansion necessitated by budget deficits. In most cases the principal cause of the deficit was great economic stress, and the potential for disorder was real because the government was weak or at least facing forces stronger than itself. The circumstances were therefore almost invariably civil war or revolution. The explanation behind these rapid inflations is then straightforward: serious social disorder provokes large-scale spending by the government in an attempt to placate or suppress the rebellious element, or else to resist it with force.

When this kind of tension exists, public revenue falls as the disaffected section withdraws its support. The need for extra support and the shrinking of the tax base force the government to print money to cover the budget deficit – in other words, it turns to the inflation tax. As Keynes put it in 1923, inflation is the form of taxation that the public finds hardest to evade, and even the weakest government can enforce it when it can enforce nothing else.

The proliferation of rapid inflations after 1950 would seem to have a similar explanation. And indeed a casual examination of the worst cases of inflation between 1950 and 1990 confirms that this stress is a common experience. Recent evidence provides further confirmation, with the worst examples coming from some parts of the former Soviet Union and former Yugoslavia.

Inflation arises not simply because of monetary expansion, but because of an unsustainable fiscal position. In the fiat monetary regimes that have characterized most countries for the last twenty-five years, the only backing for the currency has been government commitment to a sustainable fiscal position: that is, the stream of income from taxation is sufficient to cover proposed expenditure. In countries in transition, such a commitment is difficult to provide. Furthermore, in many of these countries price deregulation has meant that cash flow to the central government has been cut, especially cash from state-operated enterprises. With few if any alternative sources of tax revenue and a debt market in its infancy, budget deficits widen and the danger of monetization and inflation arises. Some countries such as Czechoslovakia, Hungary, and Poland have been able to cope with this stress quite well, but others have not. It is this danger of inflation appearing or worsening that produces the need for monetary reform.

A properly functioning market economy needs a stable currency. Regardless of how the currency came to be stabilized, it was in place before economic growth occurred in all modern industrial countries. Reforming countries, particularly those with command economies, must establish a proper legal framework that includes a comprehensive commercial code covering the operation of the monetary sector. In particular the code must specify the provision of the currency.

Development of central banking

The starting point for a central bank is that there is a banking system in place. It is the presence of the banking system that necessitates, if anything does, the central bank. The argument of this chapter is that central banking with very few exceptions (most notably the Bank of England) is essentially a twentieth-century phenomenon and emerged in order to deal with perceived or potential problems in the banking system. The Bank of England was established in 1694, but at that time there was no concept of central banking. Something close to a modern conception emerged by the end of the eighteenth century, and Henry Thornton in 1801 probably regarded the Bank of England as a central bank in a modern sense of the term, albeit recognizing some deficiencies in its behaviour. But there are others who would prefer to date the emergence of central banking from the acquisition of monopoly privileges in note issue, and others still who would date it from when the institution accepted its function as a lender of last resort – and so divested itself of commercial business to avert any a conflict of interest. This leaves the status of most other European "central banks" open for discussion. If we accept that all of these conditions are needed, then most European central banks during most of the nineteenth century were not central banks.

By the beginning of the twentieth century there were 18 institutions and all of them were central banks. Thereafter the concept was so thoroughly established and the institutions so widely desired that many independent countries established their own central banks, although there are still some cases where another institution carried out the function before the full-blown version came into being. By 1950, there were 59 central banks and this number had nearly trebled to 161 by 1990. Currently the numbers are rising and likely to go on doing so.

Central bank operations

What do central banks do? They have two functions: one macroeconomic, the preservation of price stability, and the other microeconomic, the preservation of financial stability. The main objective over their lifetime has been the maintenance of the (internal and external) value of the currency, or price stability. While maintaining the value of the currency has almost always been achieved via the same instrument, the central bank's discount rate, this objective has not always meant the same thing. Under the classical gold standard the objective was cast in terms of "metal convertibility." That is, the value of central bank notes was expressed in terms of their metal (gold) "content," which central banks attempted to maintain at stated levels over time. With the gradual erosion of the gold standard throughout the first half of the twentieth century and its replacement everywhere by a pure fiat standard in the third quarter of the century, the objective of central bank policy has been recast in terms of "price stability." That is, the value of central bank notes has come to be understood as the inverse of the price level – the price of a particular bundle of goods – and monetary authorities try to achieve (often implicit) price level or inflation targets. Comparisons between the classical gold standard period (1870–1913) and subsequent monetary regimes (see Bordo 1990) indicate that while none of them actually delivered price stability, the former system clearly outperformed all others in this respect.

Throughout the history of central banking there has been an inherent tension between the objective of maintaining the value of the currency and its function as banker to the (central) government. Central banks have almost invariably been established by legislation (e.g., a government charter) and have been designated as banker to the government. Governments have a natural preference for cheap finance from their own bank, particularly when there is a threat such as war. The government has both the power and the incentive to force the central bank to give priority to the government's immediate needs. Another tension arises in the exercise of the lender of last resort function, which may necessitate the Bank seeking agreement of the government.

Their second function is the micro one. The most widely accepted explanation of the need for central banks is the one that stresses the unique nature of the banking business. Banks hold deposits that are redeemable into monetary base on a first-come, first-served basis. In a fractional reserve banking system there can therefore be a run. That can produce a collapse in the money stock with disastrous results for the real economy. One way of preventing such a run is to have the banks' assets marked to market. But that proves impossible because there is no market for the bulk of the assets. In other words it is the peculiar nature of the assets that is responsible. Something is therefore needed to prevent bank failures or, more correctly, to prevent bank failures from spreading. So the argument is that central banks, the providers of the ultimate means of settlement, have a role to play in stabilizing the financial system and, therefore, the macro economy.

According to an authoritative source from the 1930s, "The very idea of a central bank presupposes that the commercial banks will deposit their cash resources, other than till money, with it, and that a system will be established under which the commercial banks will not counter the credit policy of the central bank by any actions on their part" (Kisch and Elkin 1932:106). And according to one recent view this was a perfectly sensible and natural evolutionary process. For just as individuals choose to place their deposits in banks, so banks place their own deposits in a safe bank, and ultimately they find their way to the safest of all banks, the government's bank (Congdon 1981). Further, Kisch and Elkin argued that since the central bank must on occasions enforce a credit policy unwelcome to merchants and commercial banks, it should not have private customers. This was, broadly speaking, the English tradition, but there were different traditions in the United States and Europe.

The character of the relationship between banks and the Bank is governed by the nature of the product. Banks in fractional reserve systems take deposits, make loans, and by doing so multiply the stock of money. Similarly, when they fail or take steps to reduce their assets, they reduce the stock of money, which, in the face of wage and price stickiness, has a deleterious impact on real output. The danger of one bank failure leading to others failing increases the danger of a major collapse in the stock of money and hence a severe collapse in the real economy.

Avoiding financial instability and the dangers it carries has been both an evolutionary process and the conscious application of some specific measures. An example of the former is the evolution of the banking system itself into a stable structure – a well-diversified and branched system. At the other end of the spectrum lies the suggestion of the 100 percent reserve rule. Short of that extreme position there is scope for action by the central bank or by the banks themselves.

Rescuer of the system

The role of lender of last resort is at the core of the discussion of central banking. The issue is much discussed but either much of the discussion has been at cross purposes or there is disagreement over how the role should be defined (Bordo, 1990). Usage of the phrase *lender of last resort* is taken by some to mean rescuing individual institutions in distress, whereas others use it to mean supplying the market as a whole with liquidity in times of pressure. The difficulty can be illustrated in the following way. Any commercial bank may, on occasion, extend additional loans to clients who are temporarily illiquid or possibly, by some accounting standards, insolvent. They may do so, even when the present expected return from the new loan itself is zero or negative, if the wider effects – for example, on their own reputation for commitment to clients or the knock-on effects of the failure of the first client on other customers – should warrant it. By the same token, a nascent central bank may "rescue" some client or correspondent bank, just as a commercial bank may support a business customer. But we would not want to describe such occasional and ad hoc exercises as involving a conscious assumption of a systematic lender of last resort function. Otherwise, for example, we would have to date the Bank of England as filling this role from a very early date, in the eighteenth century (Lovell 1957).

On the other hand, no central bank would want to precommit itself to giving special support to *any* individual bank that was running into liquidity problems. Especially with the development of efficient, broad interbank and other short-term money markets, a bank liquidity problem that is not caused by some technical problem (e.g., computer failure) is likely itself to be a reflection of some deeper (market) suspicions about solvency. Consequently, an unqualified precommitment to provide assistance would involve too much moral hazard.

My view is that the assumption by a central bank of the role of lender of last resort can be dated from the moment it accepts a responsibility for the stability of the banking system as a whole, and that should override any (residual) concern with its own private profitability. Thus, it is the rationale for providing such support, rather than the acts themselves, that determines whether the central bank has in fact become a lender of last resort. But while rescues can be clearly dated, shifts in mental perceptions are harder to date. The Bank of England's Court remained divided and uncertain over this issue at least until after the publication of Bagehot's *Lombard Street* (1873), and we have less insight into the appropriate date in other countries with institutions founded at quite early dates. By about 1900, however, this function was widely accepted as a core function, indeed almost a definition, of any newly established central bank.

A similar problem exists when central banks came to use open market operations. The early banks were often the largest or sole (special) commercial bank in the country. By extending or reducing their own loans and discounts, they found themselves able to influence market rates of interest and external gold flows. And they used this power to that end. Nevertheless, this behavior did not necessarily show that these bankers had a full understanding and command of open market operations. As the commercial banks in England and France increased in size relative to the respective central banks in the middle of the nineteenth century, the Banks often found that market rate diverged from Bank rate, and they worried how to make Bank rate effective. Sayers (1936) records in some detail how the Bank of England began to develop its understanding of how to use open market operations in this period in order to maintain day-to-day control over short-term interest rates under all (market) conditions. Again, our knowledge of similar learning processes among other early central banks is deficient.

Since the central bank has a crucial interest in, indeed an overriding objective of, financial stability (upon which economic stability is predicated), it will come to the rescue of the system by lender of last resort means. That leads on to two other features: the first is the cessation of commercial rivalry; the second is the possibility of the need to monitor and regulate the system.

In order for a central bank to act with the necessary detachment and objectivity, it should not conduct commercial activity on a scale that would lead it into competition with other banks. As Goodhart (1988) put it, "It was the metamorphosis from their involvement with commercial banking as a competitive profit-maximising bank among many to a non-competitive non-profit-maximising role that marked the true emergence and development of proper central banking" (p. 9). Before 1900 most European "central banks" failed this test.

Since the central bank has to provide for the stability of the system, it may be inclined to argue that in order to avoid or at least to minimize the need for rescue, it should lay down some guidelines for commercial bank behavior and monitor that behavior. In other words it should supervise and possibly regulate the system. These then are the key microeconomic functions of central banks: the lender of last resort, which is frequently associated with supervision and regulation. It should be said, though, that such a sequence has not been the historical pattern. Regulation and the accompanying supervision has almost always (perhaps always) been the consequence of crisis. Regulation was frequently in place before last resort practice and indeed is seen by some to be the cause of crisis on some occasions. Furthermore, as a result of crisis, new regulation is invariably carried out in haste. As a result it is less good than it might have been had it been more considered.

An independent institution

How then can central banks meet their goals? I shall argue that the evidence shows that independence is an advantage. But what is *independence*? I define it as *the right to change the key operating variable without consultation with or challenge from government.*

Defining independence in this way or, indeed, in any other that is operationally useful does not at a stroke remove the difficulties. It is still not possible to read the extent of independence from the statutes. This is made more difficult by the fact that these statutes were invariably modified frequently. Furthermore, the question of operating variable is seldom dealt with explicitly. And even if such policy were stated explicitly, it does not follow that it always or even normally prevailed. Categorization still requires a fairly intimate knowledge of the structure, organization, and working practices of the institution, to say nothing of the personalities in both the central bank and the government.

Several studies have examined the relationship between central bank independence and inflation. Using data from 1973 to the present – a period of floating exchange rates – Bade and Perkin (1988) found a close correspondence between independence and good price performance. A colleague and I ran the test for the period 1890 to 1990, during which there were several periods of floating rates, and our findings confirm the earlier results.

The nature of central bank independence

Institutions that were founded before the nineteenth century but were not yet central banks began acquiring central bank functions and behaving like modern central banks in the nineteenth century. Chief among these functions was responsibility for maintaining currency convertibility under the gold standard. It was in this period that central banking as we understand it today can be said to have emerged. A laissez-faire philosophy dominated much of the century and under its influence the state's role was a diminished one. It was natural therefore that such banks enjoyed a greater latitude then than at other times. World War I brought that to an end; and while there was a desire to return to independence and some movement in that direction after the war, it was hampered by (1) the Great Depression, (2) the perceived role that banking played in the depression, (3) World War II, and (4) the rise of the managed economy. Only in recent years has that trend begun to be reversed (Capie, Goodhart, Fischer, and Schnadt 1994).

The case for the Bank of England being considered as a central bank from around 1800 is that at that time the Bank dominated the monetary system and held the reserve of that system. Also, there are examples of the Bank acting as a lender of last resort in a restricted sense in the eighteenth century. Freed from the obligation to convert its notes after 1797, it was accused of being responsible for the falling exchange rate. The Bank rejected the idea that it had the power to influence the price level or, indeed, that it had public responsibilities. But the case was clearly developing that the Bank was something other than a private profit maximizing institution. It had many of the characteristics of a modern central bank, and it was being urged by people such as Henry Thornton to behave in keeping with that.

Even for nineteenth-century England, however, the situation is far from straightforward. The 1844 Act helped, but the exact nature of the relationship continued to be debated. In the financial crises of 1847, 1857, and 1866, there was a need either for the government to intervene or for the Bank to consult the government. In the first crisis, suspension of the 1844 Act was allowed, and in the latter two crises, suspension actually took place.

Independence was certainly not widespread in this age of economic liberalism. For example, even the Bank of France, which claimed considerable autonomy, was subject to considerable control from its birth in 1800 until the mid-nineteenth century. But with the increasing liberalism that followed, things were expected to change. The Ministry of Finance exercised considerable power, but if our definition of independence were insisted upon – control of a key operating variable – then there was surely a good measure of independence, or freedom of action, in the operation of monetary policy in France and in other countries in the nineteenth century.

Central European experience was somewhat different and undoubtedly owes something to the fact that the age of economic liberalism arrived there much later and barely had time to emerge and flourish before the end of the nineteenth century. Intervention was always more popular there. The story that is usually told of much of continental Europe derives from the work of Gerschenkron (1965). The original hypothesis was that because European countries had come to industrialization relatively late (in varying degrees), they needed to take actions that were not needed in Britain. It was this need that gave rise to the universal bank and a greater role for the state. The more backward the country, the greater was the need for intervention. This thesis has been under some challenge in recent years, particularly with respect to the contribution of the universal bank, but it is still useful as an explanation for the extent of intervention.

When the gold standard was disrupted and in effect abandoned at the outbreak of World War I and as governments sought greater control over resources, price levels soared almost everywhere. The nature of the relationship between the state and the central banks was sharpened. Irrespective of the degree of independence, either statutory or in practice, that obtained, in crises of this kind the state enforces its authority. When World War I broke out there was a stern test of Bank independence. In England the prime minister invited the governor of the bank to make a written promise: "that during the war the Bank must in all things act on the directions of the Chancellor of the Exchequer." The governor resisted but not for long. The same sort of thing was happening all around the world. The Federal Reserve, designed as an independent institution immediately before the war, lost that independence almost immediately when the United States entered the war.

After the war there was a widespread desire to return central banks to their prewar role. Furthermore, in the aftermath of the war and its inflationary experience there was widespread acceptance of the dangers inherent in political interference, and equally widespread desire to bring about central bank independence. At the Brussels Conference in 1920 a resolution was passed stating, "Banks and especially banks of issue should be freed from political pressure and should be conducted solely on the lines of prudent finance" (Resolution III, Commission on Currency and Exchange). The years until the Great Depression were characterized by this pursuit of independence as a result of the price experience of the years 1914–20 and reinforced by the hyperinflations of the early 1920s. It was a cardinal feature of the reconstruction schemes of the League of Nations. It was also true separately of Latin America.

The Bank of England returned to its independent status after World War I. Indeed, a principal complaint against the Bank at the time was that Montagu Norman as governor had the power to change the discount rate without consulting anyone either inside or outside the Bank (Pollard 1970). From the depression years onward there was a greater desire on the part of government, including the Treasury, to influence interest rates. The fact that the Bank rate remained unchanged at 2 percent from 1932 to 1939 is perhaps indicative of the growing influence of government. But if it remains difficult to sort out the issue for the Bank of England, how much more so is it for many other banks whose histories have not been researched so intensively and about which we know a great deal less?

It may be thought that if governments almost invariably set up central banks, then their relationship with them, at least at the time of origin, must have been close. That is not necessarily the case. In some periods, as noted, the call was for independence, and even though the central bank was the creation of the state, it may nevertheless have been set up to operate at arm's length and perhaps only later, not much later in some cases, to be brought under tighter control. At the end of the interwar period Plumtree wrote, "One of the primary tenets of accepted central banking thought has been the importance of keeping central banks politically independent" (1940:23). That view had been weakening for some years. The Great Depression of 1929–33 was regarded in many countries as a consequence of central and commercial bank failings. Reform was seen as urgently required, and an aspect of this was the removal of independence. Thus, Plumtree's view was effectively obsolete by the middle of the 1930s as confidence in liberal capitalism weakened. Three factors were primarily responsible. One was the worldwide drift to socialism and intervention. A second was the rise of Keynesian economics and economic management. The third, more or less coincident with the second, was World War II and its aftermath. Governments were therefore encouraged to return to interventionist policies. Nationalization of central banks was common as governments everywhere took a closer interest in monetary policy. Indeed it went much further, for monetary policy was conceived in a wholly different way. To quote Radcliffe: "More than that, monetary policy, as we have conceived it, cannot be envisaged as a form of economic strategy which *pursues its own independent objectives*. It is a part of a country's economic policy as a whole and must be planned as such" (Radcliffe Committee 1959:par. 767; italics added).

Then, in the 1940s, 1950s, and 1960s there was a great extension of national political independence. The birth of new states and the acquisition of sovereignty by former colonies resulted in the emergence of governments who sought control over their own affairs. Governments established central banks or took over or converted existing institutions (such as currency boards). Thus, the period from World War II until around 1970 was characterized by great growth in central banking, but during this period and for most of the nineteenth century the desired and pursued relationship with government was of relative closeness – dependence – unlike the earlier interwar years.

The inflationary experience of the two decades that followed – roughly the late 1960s to the late 1980s, when the world, for the first time ever, in a generally peaceful period, adopted fiat money – brought home again the clear relationship between expansionary monetary policy and inflation. The view developed that where central banks were less susceptible to government pressure, they delivered lower inflation. The desire was then for more independence, and now that desire is being put into practice.

The principal factors influencing autonomy over almost two centuries have been the prevailing political conditions (essentially peace/war), the dominant political/economic philosophy of the time (laissez-faire/dirigisme), and the exchange rate (fixed/floating). Thus, in the nineteenth century, peace, laissez-faire, and the gold standard encouraged the appearance of independence and sometimes allowed a considerable measure of it. After what has been called "the end of the intermission in mercantilism" that arrived with World War I, things changed. Crises provoke government intervention. But the experience of wartime inflation and the return to peace of a kind saw independence enjoy a brief return. Greater changes came in the new dirigiste environment following the Great Depression and the rise of the managed economy that came with World War II. In the current climate, where market solutions have been in the ascendancy and intervention has fallen out of favor, and following more inflation, the pendulum has swung again. Thus, as in much of economic life, there has been an alternating pattern, in this case of relative dependence and independence. And it is worth emphasizing that whatever was on the statute book, personalities had a powerful part to play in practice.

Concluding comments

Where does this history leave us in terms of advising economies in transition? Currently, new countries are being formed as old empires and some countries break up. For the foreseeable future the major monetary issue in these circumstances will be the control of inflation. The question is, how can it be achieved? Under fiat money regimes, the money supply is under the control of the domestic monetary authorities. But have the authorities got what it takes to control monetary growth? Previous and current records are not encouraging. And even if the authorities have good intentions, will they be believed – an essential element in the process? Credibility cannot be achieved easily, certainly not where there is a poor record and where there continue to be tensions in the society.

One prominent suggestion has been the revival of currency boards. Currency boards act like the ultimate independent central bank. Domestic currency is tied to a strong foreign currency and 100 percent reserves are held. The historical experience of these arrangements has been very successful. The vast majority of cases were sterling-based in a period when sterling for the most part was strong. But more than that, in the majority of cases the great bulk of foreign trade was with Britain or conducted in sterling. It may be that it was these particular circumstances that allowed such successful functioning. Apart from that there are drawbacks. Currency boards require a considerable sacrifice of sovereignty. It is therefore unlikely to appeal to countries that are only beginning to recover lost sovereignty (Schwartz, 1992).

What have we learned from this history of central banking? The institutions that we know as central banks frequently emerged or were established as commercial banks or government banks. Their evolution into central banks came from their acquisition of the monopoly of note issue and their related ability to provide for the stability of the financial system by means of last resort action to the system as a whole. There was a conflict of interest as long as they carried out commercial business on a significant scale, and that therefore had to go. There was also an obstacle to achieving their best performance as long as they were dependent on government. However, establishing the degree of dependence/independence is difficult, and it is subject to change abruptly in times of crisis. Independence is important. Among other things it helps in the establishment of reputation. Reputation is everything in banking and by definition it cannot be acquired overnight.

There is surely a lesson to be learned from history in the treatment/maltreatment of central banks. They perform best when left alone to provide for the long-term stability of the price level. Countries in transition should surely resist the temptation to coerce central banks into monetary expansion for possible short-term gains.

REFERENCES

Bade, R., and M. Perkin. 1988. "Central Bank and Monetary Policy." Working Paper, Western Ontario, University.

Bagehot, W. 1873. *Lombard Street*, 14th edition. London: Paul Kegan.

Bordo, Michael D. 1990. "The Lender of Last Resort, Alternative Views and Historical Experience." *Federal Reserve Bank of Richmond Review* 76(1):18 – 21.

Capie, F. H. 1986. "Conditions in Which Very Rapid Inflation Has Appeared." *Carnegie – Rochester Conference Series on Public Policy* 24 (Spring): 115–68.

Capie, F. H., C. A. E. Goodhart, S. Fischer, and N. Schnadt 1994. *The Future of Central Banking*. Cambridge University Press.

Congdon, T. 1981. "Is the Provision of a Sound Currency a Necessary Function of the State?" *National Westminster Quarterly Review*. (August):2–21.

34   Forrest Capie

Gerschenkron, A. 1965. *Economic Backwardness in Historical Perspective*. Cambridge University Press.
Goodhart, C. A. E. 1988. *The Evolution of Central Banks*. Cambridge, Mass: MIT Press.
Kisch, C. H., and W. A. Elkin. 1932. *Central Banks*. London: Macmillan.
Lovell, Michael. 1957. "The Role of the Bank of England as Lender of Last Resort in the Crises of the Eighteenth Century." *Explorations in Entrepreneurial History* 10 (1):8–21.
Plumtree, A. F. W. 1940. *Central Banking in the British Dominions*. Toronto: University of Toronto Press.
Pollard, S., ed. 1970. *The Gold Standard and Employment Policies between the Wars*. London: Methuen.
[Radcliffe Committee] Committee on the Working of the Monetary System. 1959. Report. London.
Sayers, R. S. 1936. *Bank of England Operations, 1890–1914*. London: King and Son.
Schwartz, A. J. 1992. *Do Currency Boards Have an Interest?* London: Institute of Economic Affairs.

DISCUSSION

Question: I recently heard a presentation by Adam Posen on the independent relationship between central bank independence and inflation. Are you familiar with that presentation, and if so would you comment on it? In particular, please comment on one of his conclusions: he believed that the influence of the banking sector (measured by concentration) is just as important as the legal independence of central banks. His line of argument held that it was in the banking sector's interest that inflation not get out of control.

Prof. Capie: And more independence is gained the greater the degree of concentration?

Comment: Yes, and lower inflation is maintained the greater the degree of concentration.

Prof. Capie: Yes, I am familiar with Posen's view on this relationship. I don't know how extensively he has investigated that particular issue. I am more taken with his first point, in which he says that we should be very skeptical of the independence–inflation relationship because we haven't identified the direction of causality. For example, the culture of the country is likely to be just as important as central bank independence. If citizens are generally opposed to inflation, then the central bank will try to keep inflation low. This position seems to be very sensible. Independence is certainly not a panacea, even if it could be guaranteed. Our own long-term study showed that Sweden, for example, got just as good price performance from the dependent bank as it got from the independent version of the Riksbank.

Prof. White: With the emphasis on central bank independence as a springboard for maintaining price stability, periods of instability do arise. Thus, historically, there have been periods of price instability and high inflation. But isn't instability really related to the fact that there are well-understood rules that aren't written in central bank charters that allow a departure from price stability in times of crisis, and that this flexibility is an important part of having a central bank? The problem is that it is very hard to design a system that will allow for such flexibility.

Prof. Capie: I'm not sure. It depends mostly on credibility. And of course the Bank of England had a long history of being the most sober institution. When World War I broke out in 1914, the bank lost its independence and prices started rising steeply. By the end of the period there was about 20 to 25 percent inflation. More surprising, budget deficits rose to around 60 percent of GDP, and yet there wasn't any collapse in belief on the part of the public. In fact, there was a very widespread acceptance that as soon as the war was over, inflation and deficits would simply be reversed. And indeed, they were reversed. Within two and a half years of the war's end, Britain returned to Gladstonian finance with government revenue barely in excess of government expenditure. But this case points to the importance of reputation. It can't be acquired quickly, and therefore any act that would promote it should be welcome, including independence.

Question: If you asked central bankers in any industrial country which is more important, price stability or economic growth, I am sure they would answer price stability. They believe that high economic growth at the expense of price stability is not sustainable. But if you ask the same question to central bankers in developing countries, particularly those in East Asia, their answer might be slightly different. Intellectually, they understand that price stability is very important. But at the same time economic growth is also important. To them stability and tolerable inflation with a comfortable economic growth rate is the most ideal situation. What do you think about this opinion?

Prof. Capie: I thought that we all accepted that there was no trade-off between inflation and the real economy in the long run or medium run. It seems to me that there is not much getting away from that.

Comment: It is obvious to central bankers living in the modern world that there is no trade-off between the short-term goal and the long-term goal. But if you look at recent history, for example, the high growth period of the Japanese economy in the 1950s, "high stability" was not achieved. Instead, they experienced double-digit inflation even though the real economic growth rate was very high.

Prof. Capie: No one would surely suggest that one was the cause of the other.

Comment: Well, that kind of divergence from the long-term goal could be allowed in the transition period if there is a mechanism that will ensure that the central bank and the government make more prudent policies when they become more comfortable with the rate of economic growth or overall economic conditions.

Prof. Capie: I don't know what kind of divergence you might expect. I have a certain sympathy with the view that you are expressing. I think that it has always been the case that people have been more optimistic when prices have been rising gradually rather than declining. Of course, in the nineteenth century when prices were falling, it indicated that the economy was moving toward a depression; when they were rising, the economy was going to enjoy a boom. But in the longer term, although the same kind of principle might hold to some extent, it is dangerous to start talking about the kind of inflation that the economy could sustain in order to enjoy a higher rate of economic growth.

Comment: On this point, I agree with Professor Capie that there isn't any trade-off between price stability and growth. But inflation is a distributional issue. It involves shifting resources from one side to the other. If you look at the United States in the nineteenth century, there were very high growth rates, yet very good price stability after the Civil War, in fact a little price deflation. But some interest groups wanted higher inflation and growth because they were interested in distributional issues. And thus I suppose that one concern would be that inflation is being used as a distributional device, rather than more direct policies.

Dr. Sato: We had a very interesting conference attended by many East Asian central bank governors. Central bankers from Australia, Japan, New Zealand, and the Republic of Korea emphasized price stability, whereas central bank governors from India, Indonesia, Malaysia, and Thailand recognized the importance of price stability but did not have the luxury of emphasizing it too much. To them, economic growth is also important. They also understand that inflation might have an adverse effect on distribution, but if high growth is achieved, distortions can be dealt with later. How would you interpret this?

J. Caprio: It seems to me that although we might agree on what is appropriate in the long run, policy makers and central bankers live in the short run. And it is difficult to reconcile short-term goals with longer-term pricing goals. But that's where we move away from any type of science and into the real art of central banking. That central bankers make judgments about how long the economy might deviate from price stability or that the Fed decides how long the economy can keep interest rates at 3 percent can make people a little nervous. It is possibly the "unwritten rule" Eugene White was discussing and just as surely depends, as Professor Capie said, on credibility. I don't know what history could teach other than that there have been a lot of dangerous errors made in overestimating how long the economy could maintain a stimulative policy.

Question: You described the evolution of the Bank of England into a central bank. Were there arguments against this evolution? What were the arguments against the creation of the central bank in the United States? What types of institutional or historical forces pushed it in different directions?

Prof. Capie: There was resistance from the Bank of England itself. For a long time it denied that it had any control over the price level. It denied that it was responsible for the falling exchange rate when convertibility was suspended in 1797. So there was resistance. But I think that the only case put up against it was the free banking case. The Bank of England gradually acquired power and accepted public responsibility in the middle of the nineteenth century, particularly during the financial crises that flared up. The Bank never made an explicit statement that it was taking on that public responsibility, but it's clear that, from the 1870s, particularly after Bagehot's *Lombard Street*, it did assume these responsibilities.

Prof. Calomiris: I want to take your discussion away from comparing different central banks to the issue of having a central bank compared with not having a central bank. I think the interesting question to which I do not have the answer is whether history tells us that, on average, choosing to charter a central bank is a choice of rules over discretion versus discretion over rules. Let's take the U.S. experience. In the Civil War the United States did not have a central bank, but it did bail out the banking system in December 1861, and it did coordinate with consortia banks on loans to the government as part of an implicit and explicit agreement to help the banking system. And going all the way back to the first bank of the United States, there was a clear relationship between a set of chartered banks and the government. And you can take this relationship back 1,961 years to Emperor Tiberius, who bailed out the Roman banking system with a huge interest-free loan from the Roman treasury when the banking panic accompanying the commercial crisis in the Roman Empire struck. So, isn't chartering a central bank in some sense avoiding discretion? If the central bank is chartered, then in some sense a set of rules is adopted. If the central bank is not chartered, the government will fulfill the same roles: acting as a lender of last resort, controlling inflation during wartime, and so on. But it will not do so in any well-defined, "rules-related" context. So I don't know the answer. What do you think?

Prof. Capie: I'm not quite sure what you mean. I think you said that if a central bank is chartered a set of rules is laid down in a sense. Yet Sayers, thinking of the Bank of England, said that the essence of central banking was discretion.

Prof. Calomiris: My point is that if the government doesn't charter a central bank, it will have to act as a central bank – inflating occasionally, bailing out private institutions occasionally. So, in some sense there will be fewer rules if a central bank isn't chartered.

Prof. Capie: I don't believe that need be the case. Also, it is conceivable that a completely discretionary institution could be chartered.

Prof. Calomiris: Yes. Let me rephrase the idea. Suppose that I am a strong advocate of rules and that I want to create as little discretion as possible. Of course, I could charter a currency board. But a currency board is only as good as the government that charters it. I could impose a fixed-exchange-rate gold standard, but that policy is only as credible as the government that institutes it. And all of these policies are subject to change. In the nineteenth century governments were able to adapt rules with some discretion. But I'm not sure that for countries in Eastern Europe, if I wanted to avoid discretion and I'm really worried about time inconsistency, whether chartering a central bank will solve the problem.

Prof. Capie: I think I am in agreement with you, but aren't you focusing on central banks' macroeconomic function when you think in these terms? It is a key function, but an equally important function may be the preservation of financial stability.

Prof. Calomiris: I'm saying that it is not clear how to categorize the decision to charter a central bank with explicit or implicit powers to help finance a war effort or bail out institutions. If a bank is not chartered, these powers are still implicit in the government.

Question: Doesn't part of this question also hinge on who's deciding how insulated from political pressures the bank would be?

Prof. Bordo: I'd like to play devil's advocate. About thirty years ago Milton Friedman wrote an essay making a case against central bank independence. He was about to publish his book with Anna Schwartz on the monetary history of the United States, and his reading of history was that the Great Depression, during which the money supply fell by 33 percent and U.S. GNP fell by a third, was a result of the failure of monetary policy. The Fed did not act to avert the banking panics. He concluded that independent monetary policy in the United States was a disaster. He advocated that the Fed should be subordinated to the Treasury (a recommendation that he may not agree with today) and a constant rate of money growth rule. Milton was writing before the literature on time inconsistency emerged, which is where the new interest in central bank independence comes from. The new interest in central bank independence also comes from the example of Germany and the good behavior of the Bundesbank. I wonder, being the devil's advocate, if one could look at world economic history from Milton Friedman's perspective, focusing not just on recent inflation, but on other kinds of mistakes involving fine tuning. Would you really come up with the view that Milton did thirty-three years ago?

Prof. Capie: Wouldn't it be fair to say that the current discussion on central banking has picked up on some of these issues and defined them to some extent so that independent central banks are designed to be open and accountable? And they are given an objective, which is some rate of price growth. If they don't achieve that objective, heavy penalties must be paid. So whether the danger is inflation or a collapse of the money stock, banks have to report their procedures and can be overruled.

Prof. Bordo: I agree, but ultimately you still need precommitment, which can be achieved only through an ironclad rule like a currency board. There is still the problem of returning to the commitment mechanism.

Question: What would happen if there was a currency board, and a financial panic ensued?

Prof. Capie: That is a different issue. If money is stable, then financial crises will be fewer. If a stable money rule is being followed and if there is a properly functioning lender of last resort, then contagion problems that we've observed in the past should not arise. With a stable money rule and other mechanisms such as branch banking, deposit insurance schemes, and incentive mechanisms in private and financial markets, then a lender of last resort, or any kind of agency, may not be needed. But if there is some form of agency, the possibility for discretion arises.

Comment: But there was a monetary growth rule in England in the nineteenth century and there were financial crises.

Prof. Capie: The Peel Act called for 100 percent reserves and the separation of the Bank of England into a currency and a banking department. And yet, in writing about it Overson said in effect, "Well, of course, though, when a crisis happens, we recognize that we're going to relax that rule." It is very hard to know what constitutes a rule. England had a money growth rule, but it was a contingent rule; the central bank and the government together decided when to relax it. It's not clear, as Charles Calomiris has said, how we define *rule* with respect to central banking and, hence, to resolve the rules versus discretion debate.

Prof. Bordo: To take a bottom line on this issue, I think the literature on central banking says, "It depends." There may always be a problem with discretion – a rule may be needed for optimal performance. And central banking independence is not a rule. I think there are two sets of people who advocate central banking independence. Some take a conservative view and really do believe in price stability, taking a Bundesbank view: every country should have a conservative central banker. Others believe in government intervention and discretion. They are using this literature to justify their original belief: we central bankers know what to do. There are some countries – Switzerland and Germany – that have really done it right, even though historically they didn't always do it right. Germany had the worst case of hyperinflation ever. I'm not criticizing the paper, but we must be very cautious in taking the central banking independence view and saying that this is the route for the whole world.

J. Caprio: I would add that central banking independence might not be possible if countries don't have democratic governments. Some transition and developing countries are not democratic at all. As a result we should try to push for some type of rule, such as a currency board, rather than pushing for independence in advance of a well-established democracy.

Prof. White: I want to get back to the issue of independence. In the 1820s and 1830s the big fight between Nicolas Biddle and President Jackson led to the demise of the Second Bank of the United States. As Charles Calomiris pointed out, it survived until 1913 partly because the British were investing in the Second Bank. Today, is it wise to support central banks in transition countries? It wasn't wise in the United States because of the political climate.

The Bank's demise resulted in the Treasury creating a system that worked for a long time.

Prof. Capie: Even though independence may have many desirable features, for the countries that we are thinking about, the prospects of instituting it are slim and the chances of it being successful are low.

Prof. Honohan: Do you have any enthusiasm for regional or international arrangements such as currency zones? It is one approach to independence (similar to appointing a foreigner as your central bank governor). By having a regional cooperative arrangement, the impact of any one government is diluted. But in practice this arrangement hasn't worked well. In Africa and in the Ruble Zone it has resulted in an international power play; governments haven't left it to run itself. On the other hand, it is the model that Europe is supposedly moving toward.

Prof. Capie: The currency zone that I am most familiar with is the EMS [European Monetary System]. The concept of a central bank that I've set out suggests that it does not make much sense to talk about a European central bank until there is a single currency issued by central bank. It doesn't make sense because the central bank has to be the ultimate source of means of payment in order to be the lender of last resort. If Europe had wound up with a single currency, such as the deutsche mark or the ECU [European Currency Unit], then I suppose there would be a case for a European central bank. But there would be a lot of headaches over the kind of price index that it should follow to pursue price stability.

CHAPTER 3

Free banking: The Scottish experience as a model for emerging economies

Randall S. Kroszner

The notion of free banking is at least as difficult to define as the notion of central banking. Rather than enumerate the principles that must be met in order for a financial system to be characterized as a "free banking" system, this chapter focuses on the features of a relatively unregulated banking system that operated in Scotland during the eighteenth and nineteenth centuries. Although U.S. banking during the mid-nineteenth century is often described as "free banking," the banking system was much more regulated than in Scotland. Other countries, such as Sweden, had experiences similar to Scotland's during the nineteenth century. Allegedly, a Swedish clergyman visited Scotland, observed the wonders of its banking system, and proselytized its virtues back in Sweden, where it was eventually adopted.

Although I am certainly no clergyman, I will nonetheless attempt to convince you that a relatively unregulated system is a reasonable option to consider for emerging markets today. I am somewhat critical of some aspects of this type of system – it definitely has impurities. I also wish to avoid defining *pure freedom* or *complete lack of regulation*. When considering the financial system, we must look beyond the explicit regulation of the banking and financial sectors to consider broader issues of, for example, contractual innovation and contractual enforcement.

In this chapter I first argue that emerging market economies today share many important features with the eighteenth- and nineteenth-century Scottish economy. Certainly there is much variation across transition economies, but at least some aspects of the Scottish economy are relevant for thinking about policies for these economies.

In the second part of the chapter I describe how the Scottish free banking system operated. The discussion will highlight how specific institutions emerged, identify the private incentives that led to their development, and show how they performed. In particular, I will focus on competition among the note-issuing banks, the innovative note contracts that became widespread, the emergence of a private clearing system, the stability of the banking system, and the role of bank branching. To evaluate performance, England provides a useful benchmark because England and Scotland experienced highly correlated macroeconomic shocks but had different banking systems. England, for example, had many restrictions on the size and expansion of banks and many protective regulations for the Bank of England, which was emerging as the central bank. Scotland had no such regulations. Rather, it had relatively free entry into banking and into the private issuance of bank notes. Currency competition in Scotland was more vigorous than in England, although both countries were on the gold standard for most of the period. The final section concludes with lessons for financial reform in emerging markets today.

Scotland as an emerging market economy

While Scotland of 200 years ago may not immediately come to mind when considering emerging market economies today, it is quite relevant for current development policy. The initial conditions and challenges faced by Scotland closely parallel those that many emerging economies are now grappling with. In particular, they share six common elements: an initial low level of GDP per capita compared with industrial countries, legal uncertainty over financial contracts, lack of experience with financial services, a large role for international trade in the economy, the dominance of a neighboring financial center, and substantial macroeconomic shocks, including wars (Kerr 1918; Cameron 1967; Checkland 1968, 1975; Munn 1981; White 1984; Cowen and Kroszner 1989, 1992).

In the beginning of the eighteenth century, Scotland was much poorer than England. The GDP per capita in Scotland was roughly half of that in England in the mid-eighteenth century. By the mid-nineteenth century, however, Scotland's GDP per capita nearly equaled that of England. The relative poverty of many emerging countries is similar to Scotland's initial position in the 1700s, although the disparity in GDP per capita may be wider today. The example of Scotland gives us hope that many developing countries can reach Western European and U.S. standards of living if appropriate policies are pursued.

One of the most intriguing parallels between eighteenth-century Scotland and many developing countries today concerns the infancy of contract law and the difficulties of enforcing contracts. The common law of contracts was still in its early stages of development in the early eighteenth century, becoming what we think of as the common law only in the nineteenth century. During the eighteenth century a rich variety of contracts and enforcement mechanisms were tried, and new forms evolved. The legal form of the business enterprise was problematic. Following the Bubble Act of 1720, special grants from the Crown or acts of Parliament were necessary to get a limited liability corporate charter, the form of incorporation that is the standard structure for most enterprises today. Instead, during this period the vast majority of banks as well as most other business enterprises were organized as partnerships; however, it was often very difficult and costly to bring an enforcement action against a partnership because action would have to be taken against each partner. Sometimes businesses made sure that at least one of the partners was difficult to find – perhaps living in a colony – thereby delaying and making it more expensive to take action against the partnership.

Even if taking action against an enterprise or business person did not involve such travails, many financial contracts had emerged only recently or were being used in new ways. Because so much of the law was new, people could not rely on an extensive body of common-law decisions to interpret precisely what each contract promised. At this time, for example, privately owned banks issued their own bank notes. The law was struggling to determine whether a bank note was a promissory note or a debt contract and which obligations were associated with such a contract. The Scottish case is thus relevant because we see many of the same problems in emerging markets today. Contract law was uncertain and evolving rapidly. There was much experimentation with forms and obligations. Even though having the law in such a state of flux was not an ideal situation, many different types of contracts were used and successful contracts emerged from this process, as I discuss in the next section.

The rapid changes were posing challenges for the law and lawyers, as well as for ordinary citizens. Financial contracts and markets were new to the Scottish population during the free banking era, much as they are to the average person in many of today's transition and developing economies. Aspects of the financial system now considered commonplace, such as bank notes and checkable deposits, simply did not exist in Scotland before the eighteenth century. Financial innovations occurred quite rapidly, but the population was able to adapt successfully to them. No equivalent of the Securities and Exchange Commission stood by to ensure full and fair disclosure beyond the standard antifraud aspects of the common law. While some may argue that the public has trouble adjusting to these types of rapid innovations, in Scotland competition provided a substantial amount of discipline and information to this market. When one bank or firm created a new type of instrument or included a new type of clause, competitors often responded by publicly questioning the innovation in advertisements: ''Stick with our tried-and-true product because the new one has the following flaws . . .''

International trade played an important role in the Scottish economy, subjecting it to numerous external shocks. Scotland was, for example, heavily involved in the international tobacco trade. Typically, emerging countries today are closely tied to developments in the international economy (and many wish to be even more involved in international trade).

The domestic financial market of Scotland was not isolated from other financial markets. Economic historians have investigated and debated the extent of the integration of European capital markets during the 1700s and 1800s. Nonetheless, it is clear that Scotland was greatly influenced by activ-

Table 3.1. *Time line of selected events during the Scottish free banking era, 1716–1845*

1716	Bank of Scotland monopoly of note issue ends
	Entry of Royal Bank of Scotland and British Linen Company, "note dueling"
1750s/1760s	"Option clause" note develops and becomes widespread
1765	Option clause notes and small denomination notes outlawed
1770s	Note exchange and clearing system develop
1797	Suspension of gold convertibility (Napoleonic Wars)
1819	Resumption of gold convertibility at prewar par
1820s	Restrictions on entry by limited liability partnerships eased
1844–45	Peel's Banking Acts end free entry into note issuance

ities in London – the Bank of England certainly exercised some control over the Scottish financial system and economy. The key question concerns the extent of that control. Such questions are raised currently, for example, about the role that Tokyo plays in emerging financial markets in Asia; London or Frankfurt, in the markets of the former Soviet Union and Eastern Europe; and the United States, in many markets, such as those in Latin America.

As in many emerging markets today, the Scottish economy was subject to major macroeconomic and financial disruptions during its transition from a developing to an industrial economy. For Scotland, England, and Wales, this period was not one of perfectly smooth growth. Several wars were fought, perhaps the most important being the Napoleonic Wars in the long-term struggle against the French. This war caused a major disruption in the financial system. The United Kingdom had been on the international gold standard until 1797, when it was suspended for roughly twenty years. Public debts rose sharply during wartime and subsequently had to be repaid. The six common elements outlined in this section demonstrate that eighteenth- and early-nineteenth-century Scotland is not merely a historical curiosity; it has strong parallels in emerging markets today.

Operation and performance of the Scottish free banking system

The free banking era in Scotland began with the end of the Bank of Scotland's monopoly on note issue in 1716 and ended in 1844–45 with Peel's Banking Act. Table 3.1 provides a brief time line of important developments during this period. The legislative changes in 1844–45 effectively shut down free entry and effectively cartelized the industry by limiting private note issues by incumbent banks, thereby cartelizing the Scottish banking industry and making it much more like the English system. This act brought the banking system of Scotland formally under the control of the Bank of England. At the beginning of the period only one bank, the Bank of Scotland, was issuing currency. Two other banks then entered – the Royal Bank of Scotland (1727) and the British Linen Bank. The British Linen Bank (1746) began as a linen trading company, and banking functions developed naturally from its merchant activities. These three banks had charters from the Crown or special grants from Parliament that made them limited liability corporations. Other banks that subsequently entered during the free banking era did so as unlimited liability partnerships (although there was a bit more flexibility beginning in the 1820s). The three big limited liability banks were a very important part of the financial system, initially holding the majority of Scotland's banking assets but gradually losing market share.

Private note issue

These banks freely competed in note issuance. The notes were denominated in pounds, and the pound was defined as a certain amount of specie. The notes were obligations of the individual banks, which competed vigorously to try to get people to take their notes rather than those of a rival bank. The transaction technologies were not well developed. At the beginning of this era, for example, there were no checking accounts per se, and people relied primarily on coins and notes for most transactions. The equivalent of checkable deposits and automatic overdraft facilities developed later. The banks paid interest on deposits. For larger transactions businesses used instruments called "bills of exchange," which were similar to negotiable commercial paper and were relatively large in denomination.

In an environment with this type of transaction technology, the banks focused on trying to deliver their notes to the public and on having the public hold them for as long as possible, before bringing them in to be redeemed in specie. The banks would benefit when individuals deposited specie, which they would then issue notes on. Banks also benefited when someone brought a bill of exchange or some other instrument for discount, which they exchanged for bank notes. The notes they issued were non-interest-bearing, at least in normal times. The profitability of issuance was thus directly related to the length of time that the public would hold the notes without demanding redemption. With less frequent redemptions, banks could hold lower gold reserves. The banks earned returns by holding interest earning assets, such as government securities and commercial paper equivalents, or by making loans or other investments.

Competition among note issuers led each bank to try to demonstrate how solid and reliable it was relative to other banks, and this competition effectively regulated the specie reserves held in the banking system. Banks wanted to economize on the amount of specie they had to hold for a given level of note issue, but also had to maintain the public's confidence that they could redeem the notes. High demand for note redemption could cause a liquidity problem – and a general loss of confidence – for a bank unless it held high specie reserves, which would, of course, reduce the profitability of note issuance. The banks, realizing this, would keep a check on the liquidity ratios of their competitors through a process called "note dueling."

The Royal Bank of Scotland, for example, would attempt to gather up as much of the outstanding note issue as possible from its rival, the Bank of Scotland. The bank hired people called "note pickers" to collect the rival's notes, and sometimes offer a little reward to individuals who would exchange their Bank of Scotland notes for the Royal Bank's notes. The note pickers would then simultaneously converge upon the Bank of Scotland and demand, "Redeem these notes as you promised, give us the gold now." The threat of a redemption attack by rivals thus was the market disciplining force that prevented the banks, operating on a fractional reserve basis, from excessively reducing their reserves. This mechanism was used by both large and small banks. Competitive rivalry thus had the salubrious effect of leading the Scottish banks to maintain reasonable reserve ratios. This important aspect of sound banking practice emerged naturally, without regulatory oversight or encouragement (Hayek 1978; Vaubel 1984).

The development of the option clause

This rigorous competition also generated a significant contractual innovation, known as "the option clause" (White 1984; Cowen and Kroszner 1989, 1990, 1992, 1994). Figure 3.1 illustrates a note, issued by the Bank of Scotland in the 1750s, that would pay the note holder one pound on demand or, at the option of the directors, one pound and six pence at the end of six months, which is about a 5 percent rate of return – exactly the usury ceiling. The Bank of Scotland implicitly was saying:

> It is costly for us to hold very high amounts of reserves. To insulate ourselves against the note attacks (which might be considered a form of a bank run), we will pay you if we can, but if too many people come in the door demanding redemption, we are going to hold off. Instead of having to liquidate our assets immediately, which might push us into bankruptcy, we will try to liquidate our assets in a more gradual and orderly fashion. Although you will not get your gold immediately, you will receive it in six months, plus some interest for any inconvenience you might have experienced.

In response, the Royal Bank handed out leaflets and took out advertisements in the newspapers describing this innovation as an outrage: "How can you trust the Bank of Scotland? Don't accept their notes because you might

Figure 3.1. Bank of Scotland note with option clause (Graham 1911).

not get your money back. We do not have such an option clause so you can depend on our notes.'' Also, there was uncertainty about the enforceability of this type of contract because it was a real innovation in note contracts. The rival bank thus found it in its own self-interest to help educate the public about this contractual innovation.

After much debate the banks and the public found that such a clause involved a reasonable trade-off. The loss from the inconvenience of (possibly) not having immediate specie redeemability was compensated in three ways. The first was the direct payment of interest during the period of suspended convertibility. Second, if individuals deposited their money at the Bank of Scotland, the Bank of Scotland might be able to pay them higher interest. Competition had already forced banks to pay interest on deposits.

Third, and most interesting, the option clause reduced the likelihood that a bank would experience a liquidity crisis, which could cause the bank to collapse, thereby decreasing the riskiness of the bank and its note issues (Diamond and Dybvig 1983). The option clause can be considered an endogenous market response to the classic ''runs'' problem, which plagues all fractional reserve banking systems in which demandable debt is issued. The more complicated debt contract, which gave the bank more time to deal with negative liquidity shocks, addressed the core problem of bank instability that

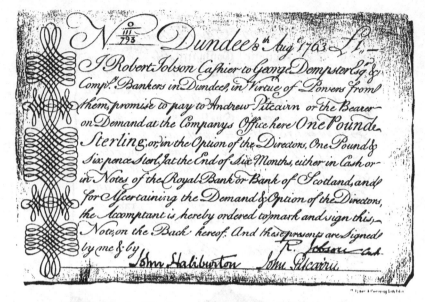

Figure 3.2. Bank of Dundee note with option clause (Graham 1911).

can arise from immediate redeemability of bank debts. Here was a competitive contractual response to one of the standard reasons for establishing central banks' role as a lender of last resort (see Capie, Chapter 2, this volume).

Notes with the option clause became widely accepted in Scotland. Almost all note issuers added the clause to their notes by the early 1760s. There was also a further development. The Bank of Dundee in 1763 offered payment of one pound or one pound and six pence at the end of six months in cash (specie) or in the notes of the Royal Bank of Scotland (Figure 3.2). This type of option clause with multiple redemption alternatives represented a move away from using gold as the sole reserve currency. People appeared to have had sufficient confidence in the Royal Bank of Scotland to accept this note from the Bank of Dundee knowing that in six months they might not get the specie, but a note from the Royal Bank of Scotland. The Royal Bank of Scotland notes, of course, contained the option clause permitting them to delay specie payments for another six months. A variety of redemption schemes thus evolved as innovative private contractual attempts to respond to problems that provide common rationales for the lender of last resort function of central banks.

The Banking Act of 1765 ended these contractual experiments by outlawing the option clause and effectively requiring immediate redeemability. Rather than letting the market set the value of innovations, the bigger banks turned to the government to impose regulations that would put new competitors at a disadvantage. The option clause had helped to facilitate entry, particularly for small banks for which the liquidity insurance offered by the option clause would be highly valued. The major banks did not like the increased entry of small banks and lobbied Parliament to restrict it. There was also concern that multiple options were not fully consistent with common law.

The Act of 1765 also outlawed small notes, defined as those less than one pound sterling (Graham 1911).[1] The ability to issue small notes had also facilitated entry on a small scale. If the bank must have at least one pound of gold or specie available to meet any redemption demand (after the banning of the option clause), then the minimal scale of operation grows. In addition, arguments were made about the immorality or irresponsibility of using paper rather than specie, which was seen as especially problematic for the peasant and working classes. The Act of 1765 thus greatly restricted the competitive innovative process, causing the Scottish banking system to evolve toward the English type of system.

The private clearing house system and the check on overissue

Another fascinating development in the Scottish banking system occurred in 1770–71 with the creation of a note exchange and clearing system (Munn 1975). These functions are typically associated with central banks today, and it is often argued that a government has a comparative advantage in setting uniform standards and coordinating different actors. In Scotland the note exchange system developed voluntarily.

Banks' private profit incentives led them to develop a payment mechanism that was beneficial to both the banks and individuals. During the free banking era there was currency competition: each bank was competing to expand its note issue at the expense of the others. In the first half of the eighteenth century, banks would frequently refuse to accept notes from other banks because acceptance might promote liquidity and hence the demand for the rivals' notes. Refusal to accept others banks' notes, however, was inconvenient to bank customers. Banks began to experiment with bilateral acceptance agreements. The first bilateral exchanges were made in Edinburgh in the 1760s; some of the smaller provincial banks also provided note acceptance services and set up some bilateral exchanges. Eventually, by 1771, the three big banks, all of which were headquartered in Edinburgh, were willing to bring the provincial banks into their main note clearing system. A private clearing system thus emerged without government intervention or encouragement.

The note clearing system was based in Edinburgh and involved weekly meetings. Banks would net their balances against each other. The Royal

---

[1] One pound then would be worth roughly $250 today (Wallace 1984).

Bank, for example, would produce 1,000 pounds of Bank of Scotland notes, and the Bank of Scotland produce 900 pounds of Royal Bank notes. They would then exchange the notes, and the Bank of Scotland would transfer 100 pounds, either in specie, securities, or deposits to the Royal Bank.

The increased acceptance of bank notes was particularly important for the smallest banks because the largest banks – the Bank of Scotland, the Royal Bank, and the British Linen Bank – were already very well known and accepted. If a Bank of Dundee note would be accepted at the British Linen Bank or the Royal Bank, the note became much more valuable.

Why, then, would the big banks want to include the little banks if, by doing so, they might be conferring large benefits on the little banks? The key reason is that this system helped keep their notes in circulation for a longer average period before redemption. If customers could go to any bank to redeem a note, then they would accept a Royal Bank of Scotland note, for example, and hold it longer. The Edinburgh bank notes could thus be used more easily at greater distances from the head offices, where redemption would take place. All banks wanted to increase their note circulation since their notes (as long as the option clause was not invoked) were non-interest-bearing. The private note exchange and clearing system that developed in Scotland is not an isolated example. In the United States during the nineteenth century a similar private system developed – the Suffolk system in New England.

In addition to the convenience for both the users of notes and the banks from the weekly netting of claims, the note exchange and clearing system put an important check on excess note growth by any of the individual issuers. The "law of reflux" is how the Scots described the mechanism by which this system restrains note growth. Consider a case in which the Bank of Dundee began to issue a lot of notes relative to its gold reserves or the amount of good assets they might be able to turn into gold. What will happen at the weekly meeting? The Bank of Dundee will begin to have adverse clearings because all other banks will be holding a lot of Bank of Dundee notes relative to the amount of their notes that the Bank of Dundee is holding. At the weekly meeting the other banks will demand specie, London deposits, or securities from the Bank of Dundee. The Bank of Dundee will then have to reduce its note issue or face bankruptcy.

Still, there were attempts to inflate away the value of one bank's notes. The spectacular collapse of the Ayr Bank is one example. The Ayr Bank began to have adverse clearings and delayed, claiming that the funds were on their way up from London, but the funds never arrived. The Ayr Bank dramatically overissued and went bust. While this example illustrates that the note clearing system was not perfect, the Ayr Bank's overissue was detected early, and the losses to noteholders and depositors were fairly limited.[2] Ayr Bank is the only significant instance of overissue during the period.

---

[2] As noted earlier, all except the three large chartered banks in Edinburgh had unlimited liability, so this was another mechanism that helped to protect the holders of Ayr Bank notes. For the

In order to be accepted into the note exchange system, a bank would have to be reputable. The clearinghouse did not set up explicit liquidity requirements or explicit capital requirements, and there was no government supervision or regulation of these matters. Members simply had to be able to meet the regular netting payments by the end of the week. Adverse clearings would signal to the other members that something may be wrong, and exclusion from the system was possible. The clearing system thus turned into a one of prudential private regulation because being in the note exchange system was sending a clear signal to the public that if these other banks, who best knew what was going on within the bank, were willing to accept these notes, then an ordinary person might be willing to accept them also. It thus performed an important information function. No system of prudential regulation, publicly or privately created and enforced, is without flaws, but this system was relatively successful.

The note exchange system also had some beneficial effects on the efficiency of the fractional reserve system's ability to conserve on specie holdings and maintain stability. After the option clause was outlawed, banks had to increase their specie reserves substantially, typically holding about 50 percent of their demandable liabilities in their own specie or directly available specie through their correspondents in London. Through time, however, the clearing arrangement helped them to reduce the ratio of gold to demandable liabilities to roughly 2–3 percent. The conveniences of the note exchange system helped customers to become more accepting of these notes and more confident in the system.

Competition was pushing the banks to reduce reserves so that they could provide higher interest rates or more services to their depositors. The relatively low reserve ratio worked fairly well because the Scottish system was more stable than the English system, which did not have this sort of note clearing system, but instead the Bank of England's (protected) dominance of note issuance. The English had relatively small banks that were restricted in how large they could grow because the Bank of England did not want to face competition. Using bank failure rates as a measure of relative stability, the banking system in Scotland was much more stable. Fewer failures occurred even though the Scottish banks were holding relatively low ratios of specie. People had great confidence in the system, and the system was run very well, so that it survived several shocks without important disruptions.

One major shock that affected both the English and Scottish systems was the Napoleonic Wars. The Scottish system followed the English system in

Ayr Bank, there was roughly between a fivefold and a tenfold assessment on each share; that is, if an owner had a share worth one pound par value, that person would then have to pay to the creditors between five and ten pounds for the losses that occurred. Eventually the noteholders of the Ayr Bank did receive most of their nominal value, although they did have to wait before getting their money back (Hamilton 1956).

suspending all specie payment in 1797 (even though initially they had no legal basis for doing so), when the Bank of England suspended redemption on its notes. This example shows the importance of London as a financial center for Scotland because the Scottish banks relied heavily on their correspondents in London for access to specie. The Bank of England had secured a regulation preventing any bank operating an office within a certain distance of London from issuing notes. The Scottish banks thus did not open branches in London because they would have lost their right to issue notes, so the Scottish banks relied on these correspondent relationships.

During the twenty-year suspension period, the Scottish note exchange system operated but without the anchor of gold. In Scotland, as in England, the price level did not rise rapidly until the end of this period. When the Bank of England resumed gold redemption, the pound was returned to its presuspension level, and thus the price level returned to its previous level. During the suspension the note exchange helped to prevent wild overissue, even though there was no explicit requirement of redemption in gold, because notes required redemption in other assets – bills of exchange, government securities, and so on.

Resumption of the gold standard was followed by some banking problems in England during the 1820s. These problems sparked legal changes that permitted some partnerships to have limited liability. This change allowed some larger partnerships to form and compete more directly with the Bank of Scotland, the Royal Bank, and the British Linen Bank. The competition with respect to note issue, however, ended in the 1840s with Peel's Bank Act. This act also marked the end of the Scottish free banking era. Free entry was no longer allowed, and a cap was put on note issuance. This regulation effectively created a cartel among existing note issuers. Also, the Scottish banks became much more directly controlled by the Bank of England.

Unrestricted branching as a substitute for deposit insurance

An important aspect of the Scottish system during the free banking era was the unrestricted ability to set up branches. Branching helped make the system stable by allowing regional diversification and thereby acted as a substitute for deposit insurance. While Scottish banks were concentrated in the main financial center of Edinburgh, entry did occur in secondary cities and towns (Table 3.2). Through time, both the public banks (limited liability) and the others increased their number of branches, but the public banks' branching networks were far more extensive (Table 3.3). In the 1820s the public banks had almost fifteen branches each, whereas the other banks had an average of three branches each. The three public banks also tended to be much larger than the other banks and were branched throughout the country; they could take deposits from and make loans in many different areas and, consequently, were relatively well diversified. The smaller banks did diversify geographi-

Table 3.2. *The number of banks in Scotland in selected years*

District	1772	1810	1830
Edinburgh	21	13	12
Glasgow	5	4	5
Secondary burghs	4	12	15
Lesser burghs	1	8	4
Total	31	37	36

Sources: Carr and Matthewson (1988), Checkland (1975).

cally, although not to the extent of the public banks. In the absence of a deposit insurance system, banks naturally diversified their deposit and lending base through branching.

A comparison of the English and Scottish banking systems

Before drawing lessons from the Scottish experience, I will contrast some aspects of the banking system in the emerging market of Scotland with its more-developed southern neighbor. Comparing some rough proxies of how well each system provided financial services to individuals and firms is useful since I am arguing that the Scottish banking system helped Scotland catch up rapidly to England.

The English system was more heavily regulated due to the Bank of England's dominance, the restrictions on note issuance by banks located within a certain number of miles of London, and, importantly, the prohibition on entry with more than six partners. The last regulation forced the English banks to remain fairly small. Clearly, the restrictions were directed at shielding the Bank of England from competition.

The density of banking, as measured by the number of banking offices per ten thousand inhabitants, was greater for Scotland at the turn of the nineteenth century, when it was still developing relative to England (Table 3.4, panel A). By the end of the free banking era, however, the figure for Scotland had grown by roughly 250 percent, whereas in England it had increased by less than 50 percent. The Scottish system thus offered far more opportunities for banking activities.

Banking depth is a measure often used in the development literature to determine how successful the banking system is at intermediating and whether it is playing an important role. Comparing per capita banking assets in pounds sterling, in 1802 this number was approximately 20 percent greater

Table 3.3. *Bank size in Scotland in selected years*

	Average for the three "public" banks		Average for unlimited liability banks	
Year	Mean total assets (in pounds per bank)	Mean number of branches per bank	Mean total assets (in pounds per bank)	Mean number of branches per bank
1772	220,000	1.3	88,000	0.07
1802	2,215,000	12.3	200,000	0.86
1825	3,754,000	14.7	398,000	2.82

Sources: Carr and Matthewson (1988), Checkland (1975).

in Scotland than in England (Table 3.4, panel B). The turn-of-the-century numbers are particularly striking considering that the Scots were less wealthy and consequently had fewer assets per capita at that time. By the middle of the nineteenth century, banking assets per capita in Scotland had grown to be more than twice that of England. These brief comparisons underscore the success of the Scottish system.

One of the innovations made during the Scottish free banking era, which also may have contributed to the rapid development of the Scottish economy, was the "cash credit overdraft" system, which is analogous to a system of automatic overdraft on a checking account today. The Scots may have been the first to create a line of credit that a firm or merchant could obtain in advance. This overdraft ability gave great flexibility to those who wished to take advantage of immediate purchasing opportunities or to industrialists who might not be able to predict exactly their cash needs months in advance. Such innovations may have facilitated investment and industrialization in Scotland, and they were much less common in England.

Finally, note that both of these systems were concentrated initially. Open entry is not inconsistent with dominant players (Table 3.4, panel C). There is not as dramatic a contrast as one might have originally thought between the market share of banking assets in Scotland held by the three public banks and the Bank of England's share in England. The three Scottish banks and the Bank of England began the century with a majority of banking assets held in their respective countries, but saw their market shares erode by the middle of the century. The large role of the three public banks in Scotland, however, differs from that of the Bank of England because the Scottish banks were competing and the Bank of England had many monopoly protections. In addition, the Bank of England enjoyed a much closer relationship with the government.

Table 3.4. *Contrasts between banking in Scotland and in England*

A. Banking density (number of bank offices per 10,000 inhabitants)		
Year	Scotland	England
1802	0.56	0.48
1845	1.41	0.71
B. Banking depth (banking assets per inhabitant in pounds sterling)		
Year	Scotland	England
1802	7.46	5.97
1845	18.05	9.00
C. Banking concentration (percentage of bank assets held by three public banks and the Bank of England)		
Year	Scotland	Bank of England
1802	54	58
1845	33	36

Sources: Checkland (1975), Munn (1981), and Slaven and Aldcroft (1982).

Lessons for reformers today

I have argued that this fascinating historical episode does hold lessons for current reformers. The situation of eighteenth- and nineteenth-century Scotland resembles that in many emerging markets today: an initially low level of GDP per capita relative to other countries, an uncertain legal environment for contractual enforcement, an initial inexperience with many financial services and contracts, an important economic dependence on international trade, the dominance of a neighboring financial center, and frequent and substantial macroeconomic shocks. Given these parallels, I believe that the Scottish free banking experience can inform the policy making process.

What are the lessons then that can be drawn for current policy (see Table 3.5)? I will group them into three related sets. The first set concerns private institutions and monitoring, which is typically thought to be the responsibility of central banks. Two issues arise: the feasibility of privately developing and operating a clearing system and the feasibility of privately developing and enforcing capital and liquidity standards. As the Scottish case illustrates, financial institutions have strong private incentives to create their own clearing system, which would benefit both the banks and the public. In creating such a system, the financial institutions develop standards for capital, liquidity, and prudential management that will become requirements for membership in the system. Illustrations of these incentives at work today are the private clearing houses set up by the Chicago Board of Trade and the Chicago Mercantile Exchange, which enforce such requirements on their members (Kaufman and Kroszner 1985). A related lesson is that competition is generally

Table 3.5. *Lessons from the Scottish free banking experience*

Feasibility of private clearing system
Feasibility of private development and enforcement of capital and liquidity standards
Competition that is compatible with prudence and coordination
Branching and portfolio diversification as a substitute for deposit insurance
"Extended" liability as a substitute for deposit insurance
"Option clause" and equity-like contracts as substitutes for deposit insurance
Feasibility of sophisticated note and deposit contracts
Importance of free entry to promote innovation
Is any role left for a central bank as lender of last resort?

---

compatible with stability and coordination, although the excessive note issue by the Ayr Bank demonstrates that the system did not eliminate all rogues. The Ayr Bank is the only major exception to the smooth operation of the private clearing and monitoring system in more than a century, and the system helped to contain the problems from this bank's collapse. The system worked well in fulfilling the roles typically thought to be the domain of a central bank.

The next set of lessons concerns private alternatives to deposit insurance or to a central bank to maintain confidence in, and foster the stability of, the financial system. We learn that bank branching and portfolio diversification can contribute to the stability of the banking system. In addition, some form of extended liability beyond simple limited liability of the shareholders might give depositors and noteholders some assurance that a bank could withstand a negative shock. Notes issued by both limited and unlimited liability banks successfully competed against each other during the free banking era, so it is unclear from this experience whether one is clearly superior to the other. Another important lesson is that the option clause and other contingent or equity-like contracts can solve or minimize the problems of bank runs that can destabilize a fractional reserve banking system. Even in the relatively unsophisticated financial environment of eighteenth-century Scotland, where the law was unsettled, clever contractual solutions to problems of instability, like the option clause, developed and became widely accepted. Exploring such alternatives could hold great promise for emerging and transition economies.

The final set of lessons concerns broad features of competition in the financial system. In Scotland we witnessed the feasibility of new and sophisticated bank liability contracts created through competition, even if people had no experience with such instruments before. The final lesson, closely related to the preceding, establishes the great importance of free entry for promoting innovation and providing information. Competition gave rise to the option clause innovation, and rivals made the public aware of the consequences of the new contract. What may seem like a great idea to policy makers may not survive the market test, and this test is fundamental for any financial innovation (Kroszner 1996).

I will end with a question: Is there thus any need for a central bank acting as a lender of last resort to the financial system? There has been controversy about the role of the Bank of England in the Scottish system. The Bank of England certainly had no legal obligation to intervene in the Scottish system. In fact, it was not even explicitly obligated to intervene in the English system during this period. To some extent (mostly after resumption of the gold standard in 1819) the Bank of England did operate like a shadow central bank, particularly in times of trouble, and provide loans to some large lenders and some large borrowers. As Forrest Capie discusses in Chapter 2, central banking functions can evolve without explicit passage of regulations. The Bank of England may be an example of a bank that has no requirements to intervene, particularly in Scotland, but occasionally provided some extra support to the system in times of stress. An explicit central bank may not be needed, but rather mechanisms to provide added liquidity during distress, perhaps through the clearing system, may evolve in its place.

REFERENCES

Cameron, R. 1967. *Banking in the Early Stages of Industrialization*. New York: Oxford University Press.
Carr, J., and F. Mathewson. 1988. "Unlimited Liability as a Barrier to Entry." *Journal of Political Economy* 96 (June): 766–84.
Checkland, S. G. 1968. "Banking History and Economic Development: Seven Systems." *Scottish Journal of Political Economy* 15: 144–66.
1975. *Scottish Banking: A History, 1695–1973*. Glasgow: Collins.
Cowen, T., and R. S. Kroszner. 1989. "Scottish Banking before 1845: A Model for Laissez-Faire?" *Journal of Money, Credit, and Banking* 21: 221–31.
1990. "Predictions of the New Monetary Economics: Perspectives on Velocity." *Journal of Policy Modelling* 5 (Summer):265–79.
1992. "Scottish Free Banking." In J. Eatwell, M. Milgate, and P. Newman, eds., *New Palgrave Dictionary of Money and Finance*. London: Macmillan, pp. 398–400.
1994. *Explorations in the New Monetary Economics*. Cambridge, Mass.: Blackwell.
Diamond, D., and P. Dybvig. 1983. "Bank Runs, Deposit Insurance, and Liquidity." *Journal of Political Economy* 91 (June):401–19.
Graham, William. 1911. *The One Pound Note in the History of Banking in Great Britain*, 2nd edition. Edinburgh: J. Thin.
Hamilton, H. 1956. "The Failure of the Ayr Bank, 1772." *Economic History Review* 8 (April):405–17.
Hayek, F. A. 1978. *Denationalisation of Money: An Analysis of the Theory and Practice of Currency Competition*, 2nd edition. London: Institute of Economic Affairs.
Kaufman, George G. and R. S. Kroszner. 1996. "How Should Financial Institutions and Markets Be Structured? Analysis and Options for Financial System Design." Unpublished manuscript, University of Chicago.
Kerr, A. W. 1918. *History of Banking in Scotland*, 3rd edition. London: A&C Black.

Kroszner, R. S. 1996. "The Evolution of Universal Banking and Its Regulation in Twentieth Century America." In A. Saunders and I. Walter, eds., *Financial System Design: Universal Banking Considered.* New York: Irwin, pp. 70–99.

Munn, C. W. 1975. "The Origins of the Scottish Note Exchange." *Three Banks Review* 107:45–60.

———. 1981. *The Scottish Provincial Banking Companies, 1747–1814.* Edinburgh: John McDonald.

Slaven, A., and D. Aldcroft, eds. 1982. *Business, Banking, and Urban History: Essays in Honour of S. G. Checkland.* Edinburgh: John McDonald.

Vaubel, R. 1984. "The History of Currency Competition." In P. Salin, ed., *Currency and Monetary Union.* The Hague: Martinus Nijhoff, pp. 59–73.

Wallace, N. 1984. "Do We Need a Special Theory for 'Money'?" Unpublished manuscript, University of Minnesota, Minneapolis.

White, L. H. 1984. *Free Banking in Britain: Theory, Experience, and Debate, 1800–1845.* Cambridge University Press.

DISCUSSION

Question: What would be the differences between free entry and other restrictions? You said there were no legal capital requirements, but was there a difference that was observed in terms of how much capital these different types of bank hold?

Prof. Kroszner: Unfortunately, I do not have those numbers at my fingertips. Even if I did, however, such comparisons would not be straightforward because there are both scale and liability effects on capital choices. Recall that the largest banks had limited liability and the other banks, which were typically much smaller, had unlimited liability. Generally, larger banks have more diversified portfolios and hence can hold lower levels of capital (for a given level of risk) than smaller banks. It would be difficult to disentangle the two effects. In addition, it is difficult to measure the effective capitalization of the unlimited liability partnerships, due to both data availability and problems in valuing the ability to call on the partners of the bank.

Question: Do you have any idea how inflationary the Scottish system was?

Prof. Kroszner: Scotland was on a gold standard and so was England, and that really helped to keep inflation in check. The most interesting time to look at is the suspension period of 1797 to roughly 1820. There doesn't seem to be much evidence of an increase in the price level of Scotland relative to the price level of England. Certainly the price level was rising – the English were using the excessive printing of bank notes as seigniorage in their war finance effort. But there is no evidence that Scotland's pound floated against the English pound. So there didn't seem to be any excess of note issuance. Part of the reason behind this restraint is that it could only be coordinated through all the banks together because of the exchange clearance system. If they coordinated their activities, there wouldn't be any net clearings against any one bank. I think part of the reason they didn't do that was because they realized that eventually they would return to the gold standard, which would then bankrupt them all. But there was not a greater tendency for inflation in Scotland than in England.

Question: How important was the gold standard in giving credibility and stability to the system? If a country were to experiment with such a system today, would it need to anchor its currency with the dollar or another currency?

Prof. Kroszner: Certainly in some countries choosing the dollar as an anchor is politically risky, so another currency or another real asset may be more appropriate. I think that it was certainly useful for the operation of the system to have some sort of real anchor back then. But I think today we've developed further and could use other types of instruments as the backing for these note issuances – perhaps something akin to a mutual fund that would own a set of shares in the financial assets of real enterprises. During this time the anchor of the gold standard was certainly helpful overall. But some of the banks did try to deviate and put out more notes than others. They were eventually checked from doing so.

M. Long: Would you speculate why free banking might not be appropriate? What brought it to an end in the nineteenth century? Which financial services would be constrained by having such a system?

Prof. Kroszner: Why did it come to an end? There is very rich political economy behind any banking regulation act, and I think there was a strong desire on the part of the Bank of England to gain complete control over the banking system. Also, implicitly, the government wanted to have more direct control if it was going to engage in seigniorage. Some people actually argue that Peel simply bought some of the scribblings of some long-dead economists, but there was an ideological change that also took place. But I think there was a strong desire on the part of the Parliament to transfer control from Scotland to London. It didn't like the competition.

M. Long: What might not be appropriate to have in a free banking system?

Prof. Kroszner: The Scottish populace was relatively unsophisticated with respect to financial services. Remember, notes were brand new, demand deposits and other types of deposits were relatively new, contract law was unsettled, and England, Wales, and Scotland were involved in many foreign hostilities. The system proved resilient to both an initial lack of information and external shocks. The only situation in which I see this system as being inappropriate is if contracts cannot be trusted at all. Reputational development is very important. If you cannot rely on contracts in six months or six years, then a system like this is not going to function very well. But even in relatively tumultuous circumstances, like wars, bad harvests, and great variation in the business cycle, the Scottish system did extremely well relative to the English system and relative to the Continental system. It may not be optimal, but it was better in most of these circumstances than the other systems that were around at that time.

J. Caprio: You said that banks were able to diversify their portfolios. A lot of the countries that we work with are very specialized. They might have one crop or commodity that accounts for 20 to 50 percent of GNP. In the case of Texas, oil was only 12 percent of GNP and still brought down a lot of banks. Were Scottish free banks really able to invest in assets all over

England and internationally? And were they doing so because they functioned within a tiny economy, and if they had concentrated portfolios, they would have been a lot more fragile?

Prof. Kroszner: Perhaps I exaggerated the extent to which these banks fully diversified. They were certainly able to diversify within Scotland without any trouble, and they were able to hold some of the government debt from England, so they were able to diversify their assets that way. A lot of trade financing was for international trade. So not everything was localized, although the majority of their portfolio was held within Scotland, so they weren't fully diversified – far from it – but they were relatively well diversified.

Question: Was there a limitation on the kinds of financial services that banks could provide?

Prof. Kroszner: It seems like they provided a lot, given the innovations in that period. To be able to predict whether and when the exact innovation would occur in other places is very difficult. But I think it shows that, in this setting, where there were few financial innovations, they were the first to do a lot of things, like create this note exchange and the cash credit system and provide interest on deposits. So they were helpful on the depositor side as well as on the lender side. A lot of people would argue, although it is very difficult to show, that part of the reason that Scotland's GDP grew from half of England's in the 1700s to the equivalent of England's in the mid-1800s was the efficiency of its financial system.

Prof. White: Let me put what you said in a more general context and explain why you're talking about Scotland and not about a number of free banking episodes. There was a brief free banking period in the United States and a short period in France, but Scotland's was the best-designed, best-functioning free banking system that we know of. Scotland had a very simple economy, devoted to agricultural exports. It was not highly diversified, but growing over time. The banking system helped to expand the economy's range of activities. There is one limitation to this system that sticks in my mind. I would say that this system was designed primarily for businesses because of the limitation on small notes. This is a very important qualification. The people who received these notes, the public, didn't monitor the banks in the same way that people in business monitored bigger banks. There was a fear that smaller banks would overissue and collapse. But it is not clear that political economy was the whole story. Given that qualification, it was a well-functioning system – the best of the free banking system. There were no capital requirements, no reserve requirements – none of these things that central bankers and regulators have come to think of as absolutely essential.

Prof. Calomiris: The point that I was going to raise was that there is a book that I worked on called *If Texas Was Chile*, and, to get to Jerry Caprio's point, in the essay I wrote for that book I made the point that the United States in the 1920s is a nice example because there wasn't interstate branching. The states that allowed branching allowed it only within state, and some of those states had very undiversified economies. South Carolina is a good example. And yet, it seemed to do very well – much better than unit banking states – as a result of branching. So, surprisingly, branching seems to help, even in very undiversified economies.

Now, to the point I wanted to raise. I agreed with 99 percent of what you said, and I think that in terms of policy ramifications, you and I are on the same wavelength. But I do want to express some skepticism about your interpretation of the demise of the option clause. I think that there is a real economic demand for immediacy, liquidity, and demandability, and although there may be some deterrence and entry stories that can be told about Scotland in general, this demandability was chosen economically throughout the world. You could have had bills of exchange instead of checking accounts – those were standard. There were post notes in the United States. There were many examples of deferred payment, debt obligations, or equity obligations, and I think that throughout the world these simply were not the vehicle of choice for banking transactions. So you have to be careful in saying, "Gee, if Scotland hadn't gotten rid of option clauses, it never would have developed an economic reason for demandable debt and, therefore, the policy problems concerning bank runs."

In the United States, bankers got around this because although they had a strong motivation for demandable debt, they recognized that they needed occasionally to relax demandability. Virginians, for example, passed a law in 1858 saying: "We didn't realize that we could run into the problems we ran into in 1857. From now on, if a bank is called on to deliver gold, it can deliver New York bank notes instead. Because, through no fault of our own, the New York banks suspended, and we couldn't pay up in gold because all of our gold was in New York." Georgia and other states had laws that explicitly gave the governor power to say, "There's a systemic problem – we'll suspend." So, again, you don't necessarily need deposit insurance, but I don't think your argument sits on solid ground.

Prof. Kroszner: In some sense you did have true competition in demandable debt between the Bank of Scotland notes and the Royal Bank notes. One bank had the option clause and the other didn't, and it seems that the option clause won out. It is curious that in every case where something like this pops up – like the option clause in the United Kingdom or post notes in New York – a law always seems to come in and outlaw this activity.

Prof. Calomiris: There was not any law outlawing trading bills of exchange for time deposits as opposed to demand deposits in banks, and there are other explanations as to why those laws come about that have to do with the economies of standardization or externalities.

Prof. Kroszner: I think that it is very interesting to look at the emergence of different types of contracts. I put it on the floor because I want people to think about alternative types of contracts that can solve these fundamental problems. If you're going to have demandable debt, then you might want to change the asset side of your bank to have it be more like a narrow bank or hold 100 percent reserves, if either is feasible. Then you no longer need a lender of last resort. But given these alternatives, even in this relatively unsophisticated economy, competition among these different types of instruments arose.

D. Vittas: I'm not so sure that I understand. What was the unlimited liability that the partnership banks had? Were there joint and several liabilities in the community or otherwise? And was there a change in partnership – could people move in and out of partnership, and were the partners all equal, or were there senior and junior partners?

Prof. Kroszner: If a partner wanted to leave or if a partner died, the bank or the institution had to be formally liquidated and then reconstituted. So if someone died or wanted to leave, the procedure was like that of a prepackaged bankruptcy. It was fairly cumbersome. It was very difficult to get out of the unlimited liability obligation. In the Ayr Bank there hadn't been any recent changes in partnerships. At some of the smaller banks, creditors would go after people who had been partners of the banks. This system operated with some degree of certainty in that you could get after these people. Whether you could get all of your money back is not clear. It was something closer to joint and several liability.

D. Vittas: But there was still one type of bank that was not allowed – near banks with unlimited liability.

Prof. Kroszner: It was only at a later time that they started coming in. After the 1820s a hybrid between a joint-stock bank, the three public banks, and these unlimited partnerships emerged.

D. Vittas: And they could take over these unlimited liability banks?

Prof. Kroszner: No, the unlimited banks would have to be formally liquidated so they would attract more partners, making them something between partners and shareholders in these new entities. Thus, they could bring in hundreds of "partners" who were very close to being shareholders, but they would still have some excess liability following them around. If they sold their shares six months before the bank collapsed, they still might be accessed.

D. Vittas: It seems that these free banking periods are always limited in time. Would you say that there is a historical necessity that could predict the end of these systems?

Prof. Kroszner: Well, there's certainly pressure that often leads the government to increase its control over things like the banking industry, and so it does seem that in the past we have not seen a free banking system last, although this one lasted for almost 150 years. So, that's a fair amount of longevity. However, I see this as having waves of regulation and waves of deregulation. As Forrest Capie mentioned – I think that during much of this century we seem to have had a wave of regulation within the financial system. Regulation is much more detailed than was ever thought possible in the nineteenth century. But I think we're starting to see a backlash against this regulation because it has not bought us much. It bought us the savings and loan crisis in the United States. It bought us the collapses of banking systems throughout Scandinavia and elsewhere. I think people are starting to realize that all these regulations are not necessary. And so there can be a sufficient constituency among other users of the system, not just the central government itself, that may think they get more votes by trying a less reg-ulated system because it will provide interest on deposits. It will provide better services to individuals and industry, which could potentially generate more tax revenues down the line. So although I agree that we have seen a wave of regulation over the past 100 or 150 years, I think people might consider a free banking relationship once again.

Question: That statement really leads into the question I want to ask. Is it really the desire of governments to regulate and monopolists to control? You said the system worked well in Scotland but not elsewhere. Why did it evolve in Scotland? Why did it work well there and not elsewhere? And thinking about the policy implications, why do you look at the outlier? Why didn't you look at the average experience?

Prof. Kroszner: The phrase *free banking* is used for all kinds of systems that I would consider very far from free. I've avoided giving a very specific definition of free banking. It's a combination of a lot of the factors that were in Scotland – I don't want to say exactly which ones are necessary. The ex-periences in the United States are quite different because if you wanted to enter as a so-called free bank and issue notes, you had to buy the state government's debt. Your fortunes were tied to the state government's for-tunes, and there were a lot of state governments that got into trouble, and their banking systems got into trouble. It's a bit problematic to use the term *free banking* for other experiences that have special features that undermine their stability.

I wouldn't say that all banking in the eighteenth and the nineteenth centuries was like that in Scotland. I think it was perceived at the time as one of the most successful systems and one that Sweden tried to imitate for about fifty years (and had a relatively successful experience with it). Other countries didn't take it nearly as far. At least we have an example of how things can work right. But I agree, this is not the typical experience of eighteenth- and nineteenth-century banking (although it was generally a lot less regulated than that in the twentieth century).

Question: One of the main reasons given for why note issuance was restricted in private banks was to enable governments to draw the seigniorage. Where did the seigniorage go in this system? Partly to competition, but how was the provident element in note issue eliminated if no interest was paid on the note, especially after 1770? Was the seigniorage dissipated in small bank branches after the enormous growth in branches beginning in 1770?

Prof. Kroszner: Well some of it was dissipated through this note clearing system. But also during this period, we saw an increasing importance of deposit liabilities and checkable deposit liabilities relative to notes. Unfortunately, I didn't reproduce that information here, but you have made an excellent point. All the different types of debt liabilities outstanding were notes in the mid-1700s. Then checks became more frequently used. The laws about what a check is and how checking could be enforced were worked out in the late eighteenth century and the early nineteenth century. People started to use alternative forms and earn interest on their demand deposits. This period saw people switching into holding more deposit-type liabilities and the banks having to pay more in interest. The banks wanted keep as many notes out as possible, but people were moving in a new direction.

Question: I think that there is some confusion about the definition of seignorage. Seigniorage in a fiduciary money system is just the difference between the nominal value of the notes and the real value of the reserve backing times the interest that could be earned on alternative assets. Banks weren't paying interest on notes. Therefore, there was seigniorage. Where did it go? That was my point and the answer is that there was a lot of interest paid in the system.

Prof. Kroszner: Competition was forcing them to pay market rates of interest on the equivalent of demand deposit liabilities. Accounts that didn't have a set time element associated with them typically paid less than the time deposit, just as we see today.

CHAPTER 4

Regulation and bank stability: Canada and the United States, 1870–1980

Michael Bordo

This chapter compares the banking systems in Canada and the United States between 1870 and 1980.[1] The comparison is interesting to policy makers, economic historians, and macroeconomists because it presents two countries that have much in common – comparable levels of economic development and similar cultural, political, and social traditions. But although Canada and the United States are probably as similar as any two countries in the world, one important difference persists: they have and always have had very different banking systems.

Throughout its history the United States has had, by and large, a unit banking system. True, many states allow branch banking or limited branch banking. But until 1994, when the U.S. Congress removed the prohibitions on interstate branch banking, the practice was prohibited nationwide and within many states. This prohibition led to a system characterized by a large number of small banks. In 1990 there were about 12,000 banks, perhaps the largest number of any country, and there were as many as 30,000 banks in the early part of the century.

Compare this system with that of Canada. Canada is a much smaller country – approximately one-tenth or one-eleventh the size of the United States in every dimension (except geographically). And Canada has always had unlimited branching. As a result a small number of very large nationwide banks emerged in this century. From 1920 until 1980 there were approximately eleven. But other differences persist as well. The countries' regulatory systems differ: the United States has had a long tradition of reserve requirements, whereas Canada did not mandate these until the 1930s. In addition, capital requirements have been much higher in Canada than in the United States, and Canada requires new banks to obtain a charter – a difficult task until 1967.

---

[1] The research for this chapter was carried out with Angela Redish and Hugh Rockoff. See Bordo, Redish, and Rockoff (1994, 1995, 1996).

A formal comparison

In this chapter we review two pieces of research related to the banking systems in Canada and the United States that are of great importance for developing and transition economies. The first focuses on the years from 1920 to 1980, the period during which the two banking systems had the greatest contrast. Between 1920 and 1980 Canada had only eleven banks and the structure of the banking market changed very little. In the United States the dual banking system – of state and national banks – had been operative for about fifty years. The period under study ends in 1980, a year in which major changes in banking regulations in both countries began breaking down their regulatory differences. In the United States barriers to branching began to crumble, while in Canada barriers to competition from near banks and foreign banks were reduced.

If our comparison shows that one banking system performs better (as defined later) than the other, we argue that the cause resides with the regulatory system rather than with another part of the economic and social environment.

The second study focuses on Canada's first fifty years, from 1870 to 1920. We want to determine if our conclusions about banking in the twentieth century hold up in the nineteenth century. In this fifty-year period the Canadian banking system was evolving from a more primitive state, having a larger number of banks, while the U.S. banking system was not that different from the one prevailing in 1920. Lessons from Canada's early experience are very relevant to developing or newly emerging countries because even in the third quarter of the nineteenth century, Canada was still a developing country and the United States had not yet reached full maturity as an industrial power. For both periods we compare the stability and efficiency of the two systems, measuring stability by the incidence of bank failures and efficiency by the rate of return on equity. We held a prior belief that the Canadian system would prove to be more stable than the U.S. system, but less efficient. This belief was based on the fact that the Canadian banking industry has long been viewed as a highly concentrated oligopoly. Instead, we found that in the later period (1920–80), the Canadian system was superior to that of the United States according to both criteria, whereas in the nineteenth century the U.S. system was more stable and just as efficient.

The Canadian system was superior in the twentieth century because of the stability afforded by branch banking – the ability to diversify portfolios across regions. This ability allowed Canadian banks to hold more profitable portfolios than their U.S. counterparts. But in the earlier period the Canadian system suffered major bank failures and earned no higher return to equity than the U.S. system. Why? We argue that the Canadian system was undergoing a transition in which the competitive forces of free entry and the ab-

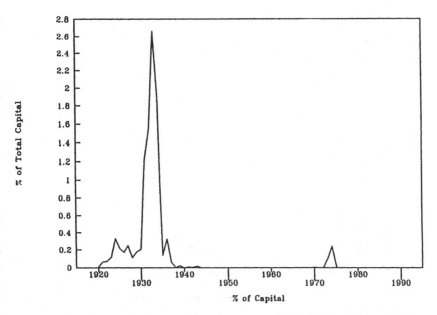

Figure 4.1. Percentage of capital: Insolvent national banks (Bordo, Redish, and Rock-off 1994).

sence of barriers to branching led to substantial losses before reaching (on the eve of World War I) a stable equilibrium.

Stability and efficiency: 1920–1980

For the 1920–80 period we compared the Canadian chartered banks and the U.S. national banks.[2] The U.S. national banks were closer in size and function to Canadian banks than were U.S. nonnational banks – state banks and private banks – which tended to be smaller and have lower capital requirements.

First, consider the data on stability. Between 1920 and 1980 only one major Canadian bank failed, the Home Bank in Winnipeg. It failed in 1923, holding $2.5 million of capital, more than 1 percent of total bank capital at the time. But this lone failure, although not small, was insignificant compared with those in the United States. The percentage of capital held by insolvent national banks was much larger in the United States, where a considerable number of banks failed in the 1920s, and one-third of all banks (not only national banks) failed during the Great Depression (Figure 4.1). We argue that the difference between the performances of the two systems can be ex-

[2] See Bordo, Redish, and Rockoff (1994, 1995).

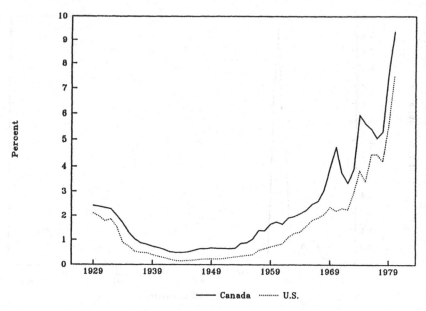

Figure 4.2. Interest rate on deposits: Canada versus United States (Bordo, Redish, and Rockoff 1994).

plained by the advantages of nationwide branching, a system that allows banks to diversify their portfolios across regions.

Our results on efficiency were very surprising. The popular assumption held that oligopolistic banks would charge higher interest on loans, pay lower interest on deposits, and generally be less efficient than those functioning in a more competitive system. Examining the data over the whole period (ignoring some of the differences within periods), we observe that the rate of interest paid on deposits is higher in Canada than in the United States, and the rates charged on loans are very similar (Figures 4.2 and 4.3). The rates of return on securities portfolios of the two banking systems were also not very different. But this result is not surprising because the securities held by the banks in both countries are typically traded in highly competitive domestic and international markets, so arbitrage can be expected to iron away any differences. It was even difficult to detect a country risk premium. Thus, the evidence produced in this comparison seemed to go against our original priors.

We then turned to the bottom line and compared the net rate of return on equity on banks in the two countries and found a striking result (Figure 4.4). Except for the late 1950s and 1960s, Canadian rates of return to equity were generally higher than the rates in the United States. This finding revealed a paradox. Although there is very little evidence of monopoly power in the

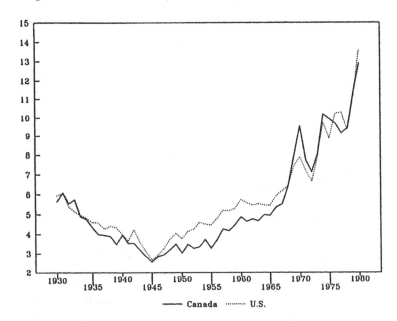

Figure 4.3. Return on loans: Canada versus United States (Bordo, Redish, and Rock-off 1994).

Canadian loan and deposit markets compared with U.S. markets, Canadian banks generally earned higher net returns on equity than U.S. banks. And this difference did not appear to have anything to do with the interest rates.

To explain this result we examined the balance sheets of the two banking systems. The rate of return on equity depends on the interest rate on deposits, loans, and securities and on four balance sheet ratios: the capital–asset ratio, the loan–asset ratio, the securities–asset ratio, and the deposit–asset ratio.[3]

To see how much of the difference in the rates of return on equity could be explained by prices and how much could be explained by the balance sheet, we constructed two counterfactual measures. First, we calculated what the gap between the rates of return on equity would be if we imposed Canadian interest rates on the U.S. data and if we imposed Canadian balance sheet ratios on U.S. data. We called the first gap the price gap and the second

---

[3] The rate of return on equity is determined according to:

$$ROE = (A/K)[rl(L/A) + rs(S/A) - rd(D/A) - x]$$

where ROE is the rate of return on equity, A is total assets, K is total equity, rl is the rate of return on loans, rs is the rate of return on securities, L is total loans, S is total securities, rd is the rate paid on deposits, D is total deposits, and x is the residual costs and earnings per dollar of assets.

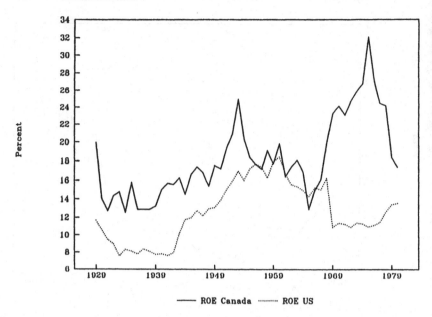

Figure 4.4. Return on equity: Canada versus United States (Bordo, Redish, and Rockoff 1994).

gap the balance sheet gap. The results are striking. The balance sheet gaps greatly favor the Canadian banks (Figure 4.5). That is, if the U.S. banking system had used the same balance sheet ratios as Canadian banks, it would have had a much higher rate of return on equity because Canadian banks had much higher loan-asset ratios. They also had much higher leverage ratios (lower capital–asset ratios) than their U.S. counterparts (Table 4.1).

When we imposed the Canadian interest rates on the U.S. balance sheet, the opposite picture emerged – the price gap favored the United States. What may really be going on, then, is that the balance sheet gap outweighs the price gap and explains much of the difference between the rates of return on equity.

We offer three explanations for the persistent difference in the countries' portfolios. First, regulatory differences affected the portfolios: the United States had higher reserve requirements than Canada. This gap may be related to stability in that U.S. regulations (reserve requirements) were imposed to counter instability. The second argument, the standard argument, holds that a large nationwide branching system is able to take advantage of economies of scale and scope. Although this explanation is plausible, a wealth of evidence suggests that it may not be that important – a banking

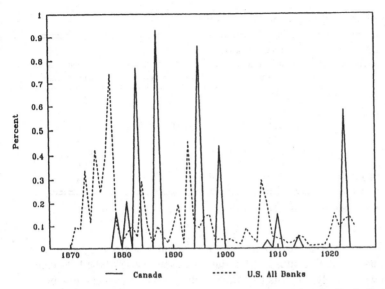

Figure 4.5. Deposit losses, 1870–1925 (percent of total deposits; Bordo, Redish, and Rockoff 1996).

system or an individual bank need not be that big to take advantage of economies of scale.[4]

We arrive at the third explanation: the low risk of failure in Canada might have made it possible for the Canadian banks to hold smaller amounts of non-interest-bearing assets and to arrive at higher equity–asset ratios. In other words, because the Canadian banking system was stable, banks did not have to maintain high liquidity ratios to convince the public that the banking system was stable. External regulations were unnecessary; the banking system became stable endogenously. We believe that this factor was the most important. By reducing the threat of failure, branch banking allowed banks to maintain low reserve ratios and to increase leverage without alarming their customers or provoking regulatory restrictions. The difference in rates of return might have been a return to the unmeasured component of the capital of Canadian banks, a return on their reputation for soundness.

Stability and efficiency: 1870–1920

Having reached this conclusion for performance in the twentieth century, now let us look back to the period from 1870 to 1920.[5] Do the same the results hold? In the earlier period both countries were still developing, and Canada's

[4] See Boyd and Graham (1991).
[5] See Bordo, Redish, and Rockoff (1996).

Table 4.1. *Key asset ratios, 1920–1980*

Year	U.S. loans-to-assets ratio (percent)	Canadian loans-to-assets ratio (percent)	U.S. assets-to-capital ratio	Canadian assets-to-capital ratio
1920	53.1	72.1	8.7	11.6
1930	51.2	69.1	7.2	10.2
1940	27.2	41.9	10.6	13.4
1950	32.6	43.6	14.5	27.4
1960	45.7	63.6	12.6	17.0
1970	50.9	61.2	13.7	21.6
1980	54.9	72.1	18.1	33.4

Source: Bordo, Redish, and Rockoff (1994).

banking system was moving from a large number of banks – about fifty – toward its twentieth-century equilibrium – eleven. By 1870 the U.S. banking system was already set in its twentieth-century mode, a dual and unit banking system in which state and national banks were governed by state and federal regulatory agencies.

In the second study we compared the two systems based, again, on stability and efficiency. But we obtained different results. The Canadian system was neither more stable nor more efficient than its U.S. counterpart – the twentieth-century results did not hold up.

First, we turn to the evidence on stability. We compared deposit losses as a fraction of all deposits from 1868 to 1920 for U.S. national banks and all Canadian banks. U.S. national banks incurred losses in virtually every year, whereas Canadian banks operated through long stretches without any losses (Figure 4.6). But when failures did occur in Canada, they often included a much larger fraction of total deposits than were seen in the United States.

Because this result may have reflected our focus on the national banks, we compared Canadian banks with all U.S. banks (Figure 4.7). The picture that emerged is somewhat different. Nonnational banks, mainly small state banks, had a considerably higher loss ratio than both the national banks and the Canadian banks, and thus on balance the Canadian banks had a lower loss ratio than U.S. banks. Breaking the data down into subperiods, we see that the Canadian banking system enjoyed greater overall stability, but between 1880 and 1900 Canada's losses were larger than those of the United States (Table 4.2).

However, a closer look at the data reveals an important difference between the two countries. Many of the big losses in the United States were concentrated around banking panics – in 1873, 1893, and 1907. During these crises the public would attempt to convert its deposits into currency, spreading a fear across the whole banking system that banks might fail and depositors

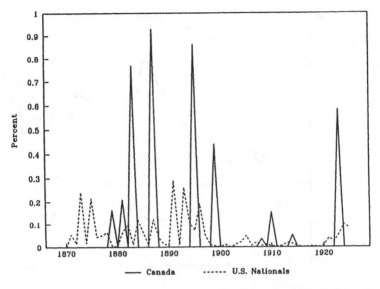

Figure 4.6. Deposit losses, 1870–1925 (percent of total deposits; Bordo, Redish, and Rockoff 1996).

would lose their money. This contagion effect led to the failure of otherwise sound banks. Each crisis was ended by a citywide or nationwide decree freeing banks from having to redeem their deposits into currency.

None of these crises occurred in Canada. Moreover, all of these episodes occurred during international business cycle contractions. Canada was not spared the contractions, but because it didn't have the banking panics, real output in Canada did not fall as much as in the United States. This fact suggests that although the U.S. banking system was nominally more stable than the Canadian system, a true measure of instability, which accounts for the effect of banking crises on the real economy, reveals the opposite.

Explaining the bank crisis experiences in Canada and the United States

The different experiences with banking crises of the two countries may be explained in part by the prohibition of branch banking in the United States and the resultant inability to absorb major shocks without massive bank failures. Indeed, the great strength of the Canadian banks was their ability to absorb regional shocks, such as the declines in wheat prices that hurt both western Canada and the United States in the 1880s and 1920s. They were able to absorb shocks because of their ability to offset losses in one region with gains in another and then transfer reserves from the head office in To-

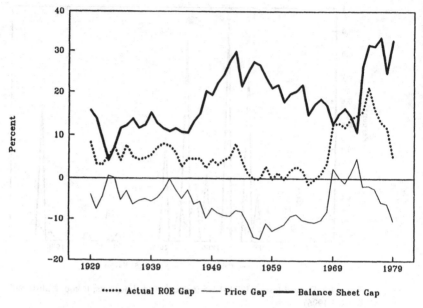

Figure 4.7. Determinants of the ROE gap (Bordo, Redish, and Rockoff 1994).

ronto or Montreal to losing branches. Even Canadian banks that didn't have nationwide branches were still partly protected from regional shocks by the merger market for banks. If a regional shock imposed heavy short-term losses in one part of the country, a small bank could seek a merger with a larger bank that had branches throughout the country.[6]

In the United States, by contrast, banks faced two constraints. First, unit banks were not able to diversify their portfolios across regions or more easily obtain funds from outside the region. And second, the laws that prohibited branching prevented the development of an interregional and in many cases an interstate or intrastate market for distressed banks. There was no market mechanism to deal with the problems associated with local shocks. Moreover, in the face of an external shock that affected the whole economy (such as a gold drain from the banks in New York or Montreal induced by a withdrawal of foreign capital), the Canadian system of branching, by allowing the quick pooling of bank reserves nationwide, was superior to the U.S. unit banking system, which had a regional correspondence network.[7]

---

[6] See Carr, Mathewson, and Quigley (1994).

[7] It would be an oversimplification to say that the banks in the United States were islands unto themselves. They had interregional correspondence networks, where they held deposits with banks in different cities, which they could obtain quickly. They could also receive loans from these other banks.

Table 4.2. *Losses on deposits*

Years	Canada	U.S. national banks	All U.S. banks
1865–1880	.01[a]	.06	.21
1881–1900	.16	.08	.15
1901–1920	.01	.01	.05

[a] This figure is for 1867 (Confederation) to 1880. In 1866 there was a major failure: the Bank of Upper Canada. If this failure were included, the Canadian average for 1865 to 1880 would be about .07. See Breckenridge (1910: 79–80) for a discussion of this failure.
Sources: Canada and U.S. National Banks, see text. All U.S. banks; U.S. FDIC, Annual Report (1940: 69).

Unlike the Canadian system, in the U.S. national banking system, under what was called the "inverted pyramid of credit," national banks would hold a sizable fraction of their reserves in large national reserve city banks in New York City. These city banks would in turn hold their reserves in the call loan market, and the call loans were used to finance the stock market.[8] If a major shock hit (such as a stock market crash at home or abroad), regional banks would have difficulty repatriating reserves from the central reserve city banks, which were liquidity-constrained, having invested the funds in the stock market. Thus, U.S. national banks would not be able to access their network as well as a branch of the Canadian bank would be able to access its head office.[9]

But not all of the financial instability in the United States can be blamed on limited branching. There was also an ongoing debate over cheap money, particularly silver. The threat that the silver forces would gain the upper hand and take the United States off the gold standard, by undermining expectations, may have contributed to the crisis of 1893.

A related problem concerned the function of lender of last resort. Canadian banks may have been more successful in avoiding crises because they had a better lender of last resort. However, neither country had a central bank. The Federal Reserve was not established until 1914, and Canada set up the Finance Act – a liberal discount facility – in 1914 and founded the Bank of Canada only in 1935. But during the period in question neither country had formal lender of last resort mechanisms. Thus, this explanation does not seem plausible, although one could argue that an incipient panic was averted in 1907 after the government of Canada stepped in and provided assistance to the chartered banks.

[8] See Bordo, Rappoport, and Schwartz (1992).
[9] That these shocks – sometimes mild but occasionally quite severe – often stemmed from some foreign disturbance should serve as a reminder that the 1994–95 Mexican crisis had ample historical precedence.

Table 4.3. *Canadian bank concentration measures, 1895–1927*

	Percentage of total bank assets			
Year	Top 3 banks	Top 5 banks	Top 10 banks	Herfindahl index
1895	34.19	43.85	64.07	.0648 (15)
1900	37.81	48.46	69.08	.0754 (13)
1905	37.39	46.03	68.64	.0775 (13)
1910	38.08	48.56	69.70	.0786 (13)
1915	44.14	55.89	78.86	.0891 (11)
1920	51.95	66.11	86.51	.1128 (9)
1925	65.90	78.91	98.31	.1656 (6)
1927	68.61	81.99	99.78	.1793 (6)

Source: Beckhart (1929: 30–3).

A central question remains – what explains the relative instability in Canadian banking before 1920? Two factors were at work. First, most of the failures were a result of fraud and mismanagement. Also, because Canadian banks had more freedom to expand than U.S. banks, the failure of a Canadian bank affected a larger fraction of the total system. The second reason, related to the first, is the birth of the merger movement. The Canadian Bank Act was revised in 1900, allowing banks to acquire the assets of other banks without an act of Parliament. Merging became much easier. Consequently, many large banks acquired smaller banks and their branching networks. The number of banks declined from approximately thirty in 1900 to eleven in 1920, making the banking system very concentrated very quickly. Several measures reveal a huge increase in concentration between 1895 and 1920 (Table 4.3). Also, in 1895 the share of the top ten banks in Canada was about six times as great as the share of the top ten banks in the United States. Thus, although the Canadian banking system was always more concentrated than the U.S. banking system, it became even more concentrated just after the turn of the century.

In the merger process some banks made mistakes and incurred very big losses. Mistakes were easy to make: a bank would acquire another bank with a branch network in another part of the country without obtaining full information on the riskiness of its portfolio. And when mistakes were made, the failure would be substantial, representing, for example, 2 percent of total bank assets. This process of consolidation, with occasional failures, continued in Canada until 1920.

The merger movement, by reducing the system to a small number of very large banks, may explain the absence of bank failures after 1923. Contributing to stability was the Canadian banks' promotion pyramid within the large nationwide branch networks. The pyramid was very difficult to scale. Incom-

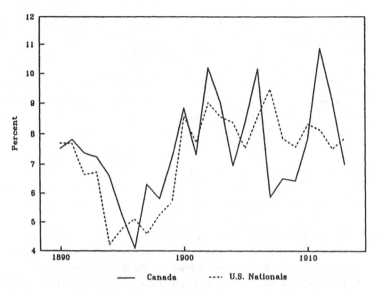

Figure 4.8. Rates of return to equity: Canada and the United States, 1890–1913 (Bordo, Redish, and Rockoff forthcoming).

petent managers were weeded out before they reached senior management, where their decisions could have endangered the entire institution. The large chartered banks hired young men after graduation from high school and assigned them to minor branches in different regions of Canada. Those who did well would be given larger branches to manage and after a number of years would be brought back to the head office in Montreal or Toronto. After years of service they would eventually be given major responsibilities. In this way the banks developed a core of managers who felt they owed all of their professional success to their bank and who responded with institutional loyalty. The chartered banks also had a very sophisticated system, replete with fail-safe devices, to audit and control their branches, making it very difficult for individuals to do much damage.

Although we did not have sufficient data to compare directly the rates of return on deposits and loans in the two countries during the period 1870–1920, we were able to construct a fairly crude measure of the rate of return on equity during the period 1890–1913 (Figure 4.8). This rate was no higher in Canada than in the United States. Moreover, although the loan–asset ratio was higher in Canada than in the United States (again this reflects lower reserve requirements – in fact Canada had no reserve requirements, just a voluntary reserve ratio) and the securities–asset ratio higher in the United States (reflecting the bond security provision of the national banking system), Canada's debt–equity ratio was lower.

Table 4.4. *Bank balance sheets, Canada and the United States, 1870–1919*

	1870–79	1880–89	1890–99	1900–09	1910–19
Canada					
Loan–asset	.717	.706	.696	.722	.640
Security–asset	.013	.021	.071	.087	.110
Debt–equity	1.458	1.914	2.796	4.232	6.876
United States					
Loan–asset	.487	.563	.589	.546	.567
Security–asset	.253	.169	.117	.164	.168
Debt–equity	1.826	2.334	2.620	4.184	5.352

Sources: U.S.: U.S. Comptroller of the Currency, Annual Report; Canada: Curtis (1931).

This evidence suggests that a lengthy and painful transition was required before the Canadian system reached a state of equilibrium (in the 1920s). At that point it was able to take advantage of its stability and create a more efficient portfolio (raise its debt–equity ratio). The United States, on the other hand, hobbled by its restrictions on branching, could not follow the same path (Table 4.4).

Policy implications

The key lesson coming from our research is that for the Canadian banking system, the transition process from a system of many small banks to the nationwide banking system was crucial. This process was protracted, and at times losses from bank failures were very heavy. On some occasions imprudent entrepreneurs took advantage of the freedom to branch and merge and expanded their institution too rapidly. But judging from the contrast between Canadian and U.S. banking, once a stable system was reached in Canada, it would have been a mistake to try to reverse the consolidation process, as some suggested, in response to the huge failures.

The Canadian banking experience reveals that once an industrywide equilibrium is achieved, it enjoys both stability and efficiency. But a note of caution should be made. The experience of the United Kingdom suggests that the outcome could have been different. In the United Kingdom, once the merger movement slowed (by World War I), the big five banks formed a cartel with the government's tacit assistance. According to Capie (1995) and Hannah (1995) the system became very inefficient. Protected by exchange and capital controls and legal restrictions on competition from other financial intermediaries, only a major change in legislation in 1971 (the Competition and Credit Control Act) and the removal of external exchange controls rectified the situation.

We can speculate that the Canadian banking system did not go the British route because of less intrusive government intervention and the proximity of competition – the U.S. financial system, which was not restricted by extensive controls on capital movements. This is not to say that the comparison between the systems in the United States and Canada is interesting only because it compares branch and unit banking. Other variables were held constant. A comparison could be made between the U.S. and U.K. systems, revealing the U.K. banks to be less efficient.

What sort of lessons can we pass on to transition economies and developing countries? One conclusion is that restricting nationwide branch banking is a mistake; the benefits of long-run stability and efficiency outweigh the cost of concentrated economic power. Efficiency can be promoted by permitting competition from foreign banking systems, as well as domestic and foreign nonbank financial intermediaries. As in Canada, it may take time to develop extensive branch networks. Some of the former Soviet republics and other transition economies have inherited a unit banking system, which was designed to finance particular functions of the economy, for particular sectors, and in certain regions. It might take time to move from these unit banks to a nationwide branch banking system. Institutions should be encouraged to develop correspondent networks and ultimately to branch their networks. Advisers should encourage these countries to move in the direction of the Canadian system, which is also the system of many other successful countries.

As a final note, the conclusion that the Canadian banking system was both more stable and more efficient than the U.S. system raises a much broader issue: Which system is better for economic development? On the one hand the branch banking system had greater lending capacity than did the unit, or restrictive, banking system. But one could then argue – as Richard Sylla suggests in Chapter 11, this volume – that the United States substituted for this deficiency by developing more open and deep capital markets. Capital markets in the United States are broader and deeper than those in almost any other country. So perhaps U.S. citizens received something in exchange. In addition, both the Canadian system and the U.S. system have advantages and disadvantages compared with the European universal banking system (see Chapter 7, this volume). Each banking system represents a different mix of market-based and institution-based financial systems. Which model is superior is an open question.

REFERENCES

Beckhart, Benjamin Haggott. 1929. "The Banking System of Canada." In H. Parker Willis and B. H. Beckhart, eds., *Foreign Banking Systems*. London: Isaac Pitman, & Sons, Ltd. pp. 120–82.

Bordo, Michael D., Angela Redish, and Hugh Rockoff. 1994. "The U.S. Banking System from a Northern Exposure: Stability versus Efficiency." *Journal of Economic History* 54:325–41.

1995. "A Comparison of the United States and Canadian Banking Systems in the

Twentieth Century: Stability versus Efficiency." In Michael D. Bordo and Richard Sylla, eds; *Anglo-American Financial Systems: Institutions and Markets in the Twentieth Century.* Chicago: Irwin, pp. 11–40.

1996. "A Comparison of the Stability and Efficiency of the Canadian and American Banking Systems, 1870–1925." *Financial History Review* 3 (pt. I, April): 49–68.

Bordo, Michael D., Peter Rappoport, and Anna J. Schwartz. 1992. "Money versus Credit Rationing: Evidence for the National Banking Era, 1880–1914." In Claudia Goldin and Hugh Rockoff, eds., *Strategic Factors in Nineteenth Century American Economic History: A Volume to Honor Robert W. Fogel.* Chicago: University of Chicago Press for the NBER, pp. 189–223.

Breckenridge, R. M. 1910. *The History of Banking in Canada.* Washington, D.C: U.S. National Monetary Commision.

Capie, Forrest. 1995. "Prudent and Stable (but Inefficient?): Commercial Banks in Britain." In Michael D. Bordo and Richard Sylla, eds., *Anglo-American Financial Systems: Institutions and Markets in the Twentieth Century.* Chicago: Irwin, pp. 41–64.

Carr, Jack L., G. Frank Mathewson, and Neil C. Quigley. 1994. *Ensuring Failure: Financial System Stability and Deposit Insurance in Canada.* C. D. Howe Institute, Observation no. 36. Ottawa: Renouf.

Curtis, C. A. 1931. "Banking Statistics in Canada." In *Statistical Contributions to Canadian Economic History.* Toronto: Macmillan, vol. 7, pp. 138–62.

Hannah, Leslie. 1995. "Effects of Banking Cartels." In Michael D. Bordo and Richard Sylla, eds., *Anglo-American Financial Systems: Institutions and Markets in the Twentieth Century.* Chicago: Irwin, pp. 51–64.

U.S. Comptroller of the Currency. Various years. *Annual Report.* Washington, D.C.: U.S. Government Printing Office.

U.S. Federal Deposit Insurance Corporation. 1940. *Annual Report.* Washington, D.C.: U.S. Government Printing Office.

DISCUSSION

Question: You use the rate of return on assets and on equity to measure the efficiency of the portfolio for Canada and the United States. Are you sure that you are not also measuring a cartel effect?

Prof. Bordo: We thought of this – this issue has been raised before. If you look at the balance sheet breakdown, you'll see another factor called X, which captures everything else. We tried to measure X and we tried to devise measures of the different costs of banking in the two countries. This job was fairly difficult if costs were broken down a little bit. We couldn't come up with a clear answer. It's a good criticism. I don't know what the answer would be.

Prof. Calomiris: As you know, Professor Bordo, I agree with the story you are telling, but I don't want to simply agree with you. There is a note of caution that should be taken regarding the interpretation that you are giving to the difference between the early Canadian and the late Canadian experience. I think that you are trying to get the data to do too much for you. I also think that economic theory actually points you in a different direction from where you are headed.

When you look at the stability measures in Canada, you find that the deposit loss rates (between the United States and Canada) are roughly comparable but slightly better in Canada early on and much better later on. This difference is mainly attributable to a few events. You interpret these events as the growing pains of Canadian banking. Another interpretation is that you have a small sample – just a few events. I like this interpretation better because the results on the loan ratios and the capital ratios, which I also had dwelled on in my paper, reveal that it must be a small-sample problem.

Think about a depositor who has a risk tolerance. So you pay 3 percent interest on deposits, and there's a certain amount of risk of loss that I'm willing to bear. That can be shown as an indifference curve; if your bank holds higher assets to capital, then you are going to have to have lower liabilities to capital. You must keep either your leverage low or your risk low by holding more reserves. This is a deposit-risk isoquant. Canada is at one point along the isoquant and the United States is at another. These are the comparisons that you made in Table 4.4 and I made in my research, so we agree there.

I think Canadian banking is more efficient than you do – depositor losses weren't that much lower in the nineteenth century. But what does this result tell us? It tells us that if the depositors are similar – if they have similar risk aversion and are earning the same rate of interest – then any differences in ex post losses to depositors must be caused by a small sample. If U.S. and Canadian depositors are bearing the same rate of interest and have the same risk aversion, then on average, over a long period of time, the loss rates to depositors in the two countries should be identical.

So the efficiency of the Canadian banking system was shown in that it could satisfy a given amount of depositors' risk aversion with a higher loan–asset ratio and a higher asset–capital ratio. It could satisfy the same amount of depositor risk aversion by having less reserves and greater leverage.

Prof. Bordo: But it's not a small period. We're talking about fifty years of data!

Prof. Calomiris: Yes, but the differences in the pre–World War I period are driven by a few events that took place in a few years.

Prof. Bordo: It was more than just a few events – not just one or two failures, but seven, eight, or nine.

J. Caprio: But taking your comments to the extreme, Professor Calomiris, you could be interpreted as saying that regulation doesn't matter.

Prof. Calomiris: No. It matters a lot. If you regulate these banks as unit banks they still have to satisfy customers. To satisfy them, they have to hold more reserves and more capital, which is costly to society. So regulation matters, but it won't necessarily show up in deposit loss rates. Since it does, I'm suspicious that it's a small-sample problem.

J. Caprio: But it is still plausible that they didn't insulate themselves from other disturbances enough to offset the disadvantages of being a unit bank.

Prof. Calomiris: All I'm saying is that over a sufficiently long period of time under the assumptions of rationality, these will all average out.

J. Caprio: Let me turn it around, though, because the international parallel – the point that I would have taken from Professor Bordo's paper – is not just to promote branching. Because many of our economies are very small, they are in a sense equivalent to unit banking systems. They have capital controls that force the banks to be very concentrated – they have to hold domestic assets, so they're like unit banks in the United States. Therefore, we should be pushing for lower capital controls fairly early on, rather than abiding by the conventional wisdom, which calls for these as the last step to financial reform.

Question: I have two questions. First, if you look at international experience with the consolidation process, are countries more likely to end up like Britain, with an oligopoly of five banks, or like Canada, with a dozen banks and competition? Second, what is the influence of central banking practices on the development of the systems?

Prof. Bordo: I know from the U.K. case that the government's posture was part of the story. It encouraged this cartelization because it enabled the Bank of England to control the economy. In a sense the cartel was cemented in the interwar period and then again after World War II, and it fit into the package of controls that developed after the collapse of the gold standard. The Bank of England used the other banks to control the capital markets. This wasn't the case in Canada, again we posit because of its very close proximity to the U.S. financial system. If the United States had gone the route of capital controls and excessive intervention, Canada would have too. I think it's more an accident of history that the Bank of Canada did not operate with a heavy hand.

Stories are told in Canada about an implicit cartel, the fact that the Bank of Canada during the early postwar period would use moral suasion to convince Canadian banks to change their lending practices. They didn't exert monetary control directly through the normal channels, but they did use the banking system in a way similar to the British. Charles Goodhart would describe Canada as being closer to the United Kingdom than I might. Still, I can't give you a clear prediction of the number of banks that will arise in equilibrium.

Question: How many countries ended up with cartelized systems as opposed to reasonably competitive systems?

Prof. Bordo: I think most countries ended up with cartelized systems. Canada might have been one of the more competitive countries. I don't know if I could compare it to some of the Western European countries or to Australia. I think Japan moved much closer to a cartelized system than Canada did. I think the policy message that emerges is that you don't want to create a banking cartel. Small countries want to have the advantages of diversification in nationwide branching or even intercountry branching, but not through a cartel. A cartel will generate its own inefficiencies.

Comment: In essence you end up with a dilemma because if you choose nationwide branching, you're likely to end up with a cartel.

Prof. Bordo: To form a cartel, government support is needed because in an open world economy there will always be a bank that will compete with that cartel and undercut it. In a sense the British cartel was successful because it had exchange controls and capital controls – all kinds of regulation in the financial system.

J. Caprio: It could have licensed more foreign banks. If insufficient competition became a problem, Canada could have admitted other banks as well.

Prof. Bordo: Right. And that's what Canada eventually did. The pressure came in from the other side to admit banks and to let the near banks – the trust companies – become banks (they are called Class Two banks). In a sense they opened up the system.

Prof. Williamson: When I lived in Vancouver twenty years ago, I thought it peculiar that I was banking at the Bank of Montreal. But it didn't seem to bother anyone else there. The story of nineteenth-century U.S. farmers was that "they farmed the land, and the banker farmed the farmer." There was a great suspicion of bankers, and state legislatures were strongly opposed to branch banking. Today, what is the opinion of branch banking compared with supporting the local bank? Do you think the political climate in nineteenth-century Canada was that much different than that in the United States?

Prof. Bordo: I think the political climate was a lot different. I don't think Canada was as democratic a country as the United States. The Canadian banks were chartered banks. They started off in the early nineteenth century by getting royal charters. They were part of the power establishment in Canada, which has always been more concentrated than that in the United States. And it has been less open to competition in just about every respect. Only in the twentieth century did the populist movement in the West generate pressure to set up a central bank. The Canadian banks were opposed to establishing a central bank. They thought that they ran the system well themselves. One of the main political arguments for establishing a bank in Canada was western dissent and fear of monopoly power. So I think there is a big difference between the two countries. In a sense Canada was following the European tradition more than the United States. The United States was reacting to the European tradition.

Comment: When establishing any system of regulations, a lobby to build support and to reinforce it almost always forms. I think that a lot of U.S. history is in some sense misinterpreted because of the work of these lobbies. There was a popular dislike of banks, but it was also true that much of this dislike was organized, orchestrated, and promoted by the unit banks. I looked at a referendum in Illinois in the 1920s that decided whether or not to have branch banking or unit banking. The unit bankers put in an enormous lobbying effort. The results are counter to the populist argument. We find that the weakest support for unit banking comes from the area where we would think populism would be strongest – in the southern states.

Prof. Calomiris: Returning to what Professor Bordo said about concentration, one of the key things that the U.S. Supreme Court did early in the nineteenth century was to rule that the Commerce Clause did not prevent the states from restricting entry in banking. That decision was crucial because it meant that the struggle over branch versus unit banking was going to be fought at the state level. And at the state level the possibility of having a critical mass of politicians bought off by focus groups was much greater – they probably never would have won at the national level. But unit banking was established in many states, and that difference is also very important. If New York and San Francisco had been lobbying for a national bill on whether we were going to have unit banking, we might not have gotten it, but they weren't. Nebraska decided by itself.

J. Caprio: This session is really important because it focuses on two recommendations: first, that more competition is better, and second, that limits on capital mobility are acceptable. However, for small countries, this advice essentially endorses a system akin to unit banking. The Canadian–U.S. comparison suggests that less competition – merely keeping the market contestable – and highly diversified branching is the way to go. Many developing country authorities do not want to encourage their banks to lend abroad, and encourage or legislate the opposite. Yet when a domestic shock hits – such as the recent Mexican crisis – one has to wonder how much sounder the banking system would have been and thus how much faster the recovery if the banking system had a large part of its portfolio invested overseas. Small countries might be better off encouraging greater diversification, rather than limiting it.

CHAPTER 5

Deposit insurance

Eugene White

Despite its imperfections, the U.S. financial system remains a very attractive model for architects of financial systems in developing countries and transition economies. The U.S. system efficiently transfers and redistributes funds from one sector to another with a high degree of safety and soundness. Of all the U.S. financial system's components, the banking sector is perhaps the weakest. And yet even this part of the system may look good to developing countries and policy makers.

The U.S. banking sector includes all the institutions that take deposits and make loans, including commercial banks, savings and loans, savings banks, and credit unions. To examine the development of deposit insurance and its role in the performance of the U.S. banking sector, it is important to focus on the big picture: the banking sector in the United States has become less important over time. Relative to other parts of the financial system, the banking sector has undergone a very slow and almost steady contraction throughout the twentieth century. For example, in 1900 commercial banks held approximately two-thirds of the assets of all financial intermediaries. This ratio has fallen steadily, and today commercial banks hold less than one-third of these assets. Although several factors underlie this decline and the movement of much activity off balance sheet, the leading factor has been regulation. Regulation has come from both the federal government and state governments. It has constrained the expansion of banks and contributed to the widespread failure of individual institutions.

This chapter analyzes the role of deposit insurance in depository institutions, focusing on commercial banks. Commercial banks are still, by far, the largest group of depository institutions and their experience is representative. Severe geographic and product line constraints are the central problems of banks in the twentieth-century United States. These constraints have prevented them from meeting the changing needs of their household and business customers and weakened their ability to withstand external shocks. Over the course of the twentieth century customer demand for long-term credit has increased. Households have wanted to purchase houses, plan for retirement, and pay for their children's education. Businesses have wanted to increase their capital stock and expand their plant and equipment. Yet the character of U.S. commercial banks was defined in the nineteenth century, during which they were essentially institutions that provided short-term credit. This focus was the result of the prevailing nineteenth-century banking doctrine, the real bills doctrine, which held that banks would only be considered sound if they offered loans to finance the production and distribution of goods. Thus, banks were prohibited from holding equity and restricted in their holding of debt with long-term maturities. Complicating this picture was the general prohibition on branch banking. In most states banks were forced to operate out of a single office. This constraint produced a highly fragmented industry – at its largest, there were 30,000 commercial banks in the United States.

As a result of this evolution banks could not grow in size or sophistication and thus could not meet the needs of their growing business customers as the economy entered the era of the modern corporation. Branching restrictions forced U.S. banks to remain small relative to the emerging industrial enterprises. Furthermore, restricting banks to one geographic area created small banks that found it difficult to diversify their deposit base and their loan portfolio. Consequently, they were prone to suffer or even fail when they were hit by external economic shocks. When commercial banks were formed in the middle of the nineteenth century, their design was appropriate for an economy of small firms and local markets. But by the beginning of the twentieth century it was clearly inappropriate.

Indeed, the history of U.S. banking in the twentieth century can be partly read as an attempt to escape regulation. To avoid geographic constraints, banks used legal loopholes to acquire other banks, changed the law if they could, and when they failed, created surrogate forms – bank holding companies and chain banks. Although larger institutions were built, particularly in California and New York, the industry remained fragmented by any European standard. On the side of product line restraints, banks moved into a variety of new activities where the law permitted, including trust activities and financial advice.

The most important diversification in the twentieth century came in investment banking and the brokerage business. Blocked by laws that prevented them from holding equity, commercial banks responded in the 1920s by setting up wholly owned securities affiliates that could enter investment banking and brokerage without restrictions. The larger banks had an advantage because they recognized that they had lost their biggest business customers to investment banks. Profiting from the restrictions on commercial banks, investment banks had created the huge U.S. market for equities and long-term debt to meet nineteenth-century industry's need for long-term financing. The commercial banks' securities affiliates gave them a new vehicle for competing with investment banks. Now commercial banks could handle firms' short-term credit needs through their ordinary operations and their long-term credit needs through securities affiliates. In fact these two activities were complementary in information gathering, servicing customers, and diversifying their portfolios to insulate banks from business cycle fluctuations. Securities affiliates were very successful after a short time, and they took over about half of the investment banking business. They thus represented a real threat to the independent investment banks.

Given time, commercial banks might have slowly whittled down the major product line and geographic barriers, but this process was halted abruptly during the Great Depression (1929–33). The regulations imposed after 1933, which were collectively part of the New Deal reforms, not only halted the trend toward greater product and geographic diversity, they turned the clock back. The banking sector became a loosely organized cartel into which entry was difficult and pricing by interest rates was limited. Competition between different financial intermediaries was sharply reduced, and investment and commercial banking were separated. Indeed, a very narrow definition of a commercial bank, in terms of geography and products, prevailed after this period.

Although many new forms of control were added to the banking system, the most prominent of these was deposit insurance, which was first offered to commercial banks, then to savings and loans and mutual savings banks, and finally to credit unions. In fact, deposit insurance is probably the most important monument of the New Deal reforms. Although many other regulations have disappeared, deposit insurance remains in place. Interest rate controls, which had a long and tortured history, were finally consigned to the dust bin of history in the period 1980–86, and barriers to branching – especially interstate branching – have weakened and partly disappeared in the past ten years. Limitations on products are much more resilient, and deposit insurance remains universally acclaimed. Furthermore, its coverage has grown over time and there is little political will in the United States to alter deposit insurance substantially.

Behind this attitude stands the firm conviction of policy makers and many economists that deposit insurance was adopted purely out of public interest to guarantee the stability of the banking system. But this chapter will show that deposit insurance was adopted because of the success of a very narrow group of special interests that wanted to tilt the structure of the financial system in their favor. Deposit insurance was a U.S. invention arising from the politics of the U.S. banking system in the depression years. It is an invention that does not merit international imitation.

The history of deposit insurance

The adoption of federal deposit insurance in the Banking Act of 1933 represented a remarkable change in public opinion. Until the 1930s there was very little support for nationwide deposit insurance. Even after the banking crisis of 1933, strong opposition remained. One authority on U.S. banking and its history, Carter Golembe, noted that "deposit insurance was not a novel idea. It was not untried. Protection of the small depositor, while important, was not its primary purpose. And finally, it was the only important piece of legislation during the New Deal's famous 100 Days, which was neither requested nor supported by the administration" (1960, pp. 181–2).

How did deposit insurance emerge in the United States? The congressional debate – deposit insurance was passed in 1933 amid a vigorous discussion – makes very interesting reading. Economists often consider congresspeople as being relatively ill-informed of the merits of any piece of legislation. But in the debate over deposit insurance, they discussed moral hazard, adverse selection, and incentive compatibility. They were well aware of these issues, given the previous experience with deposit insurance at the state level.

Six states before the Civil War and eight states after the Civil War had adopted deposit insurance (Table 5.1). The motivation behind all of these insurance schemes was to maintain the stability of small unit banks and insulate them from recurrent economic disruptions and bank failures. All fourteen states that enacted deposit insurance between 1829 and 1917 were unit banking states that were trying to find ways to stabilize the banking system. In a sense, we can think of these states as small and diversified economies, trying to find a way to protect their banking systems. The other states chose to follow the Canadian or Scottish system of branch banking, and they did not show much interest in deposit insurance.

Experimenting with deposit insurance

Among the pre–Civil War systems there were three successes and three failures. Their performance can be related to the ways in which incentives for deposit insurance were set up. The three successes were the systems in Indiana, Iowa, and Ohio. But these systems included a very small number of banks, which had strong incentives to police one another. They were mutual guarantee systems – if one bank failed the other banks were obliged to repay its creditors in full. This approach created a very effective cartel, which was good for maintaining bank safety but not efficiency.

The unsuccessful pre–Civil War experiments – Michigan, New York, and Vermont – were much more like later deposit insurance systems, including the federal system. The industry was not cartelized, assessments were fixed, and supervision provided by the states was very weak. These three systems produced very large bank failures, sufficiently large to bankrupt the insurance fund, and noteholders and deposit holders suffered losses.

A second round of experimentation with guarantee systems was stimulated by the panic of 1907 (Table 5.1). As was the case with the pre–Civil War deposit insurance systems, these systems were established in unit banking states. The eight states adopted the design features of the failed antebellum

Table 5.1. *Pre-Federal Deposit Insurance Corporation (FDIC) insurance systems*

New York 1829–66	Safety fund with upper bound on assessments, limited regulatory authority
Vermont 1831–58	Safety fund with upper bound on assessments, limited regulatory authority
Michigan 1836–42	Safety fund with upper bound on assessments, limited regulatory authority
Indiana 1834–65	Cartelized industry, mutual guarantee without limit, strict supervision and enforcement
Ohio 1845–66	Restricted membership, mutual guarantee without limit, strict supervision and enforcement
Iowa 1858–66	Cartelized industry, mutual guarantee without limit, strict supervision and enforcement
Oklahoma 1907–09 1909–23	Limited regulatory authority, unlimited special assessments, and upper bound on annual assessments
Texas 1909–25	Safety fund with upper bound on assessments, weak regulatory authority
Kansas 1909–29	Safety fund with upper bound on assessments, weak regulatory authority
Nebraska 1909–30	Safety fund with upper bound on assessments, weak regulatory authority
South Dakota 1909–31	Safety fund with upper bound on assessments, weak regulatory authority
Mississippi 1914–30	Safety fund with upper bound on assessments, weak regulatory authority
North Dakota 1917–29	Safety fund with upper bound on assessments, weak regulatory authority
Washington 1917–29	Safety fund with upper bound on assessments, weak regulatory authority

Sources: Calomiris (1989), White (1983).

systems. Their systems suffered very large losses and went bankrupt in the 1920s because of poor incentive mechanisms. These insured banking systems suffered the problems of moral hazard and adverse selection, and there was a large increase in the number of banks that failed in the agricultural decline of 1920s.

By the 1920s unit banking in the United States came under very strong economic pressure because of the post–World War I recession and the decline in agricultural prices. Banks failed at historically high rates even as the rest of the economy continued to thrive. The surviving banks faced tougher competition, and the failure of small banks in the 1920s began to erode the barriers to branching. In this environment smaller unit banks found it harder to compete, and they turned to the political arena to secure protection.

The protection they were most eager to secure was federal deposit insurance. Federal deposit insurance was an old remedy, first proposed in Congress in 1886. Between 1886 and 1933, 150 bills for different types of deposit insurance schemes were introduced in Congress. Although these proposals differed in their particulars, they shared the fundamental features of the eight post-1907 systems – fixed assessments and modest regulations. Such schemes involved cross-subsidization of risk across states: states with higher risks of failure would gain at the expense of states with lower risks of failure. One would thus expect the bankers in vulnerable states, and hence the members of Congress from those states, to favor a national insurance scheme. But one important problem arose. Compared with state insurance schemes, federal deposit insurance was very attractive to those states that had high-risk banking systems because of these undiversified unit banks. But at the same time, it was less likely to pass because the branching states – those with larger, urban, diversified banks – also had very powerful voices in Congress. These two groups were evenly balanced for a long time, preventing legislation from making headway before 1933.

Batting for deposit insurance

It is striking that federal deposit insurance was adopted in 1933, because the weakening position of smaller, particularly rural unit banks should have made them less effective as a special interest group. Their decline should have led to a reduction in the likelihood of federal deposit insurance schemes. But by 1932 the reverse occurred: there was a nationwide call for deposit insurance. And surprisingly, even members of Congress from states in which branch banking was strong pushed for some form of deposit insurance. This change occurred largely because of the extreme, unrelenting, and mistaken monetary contraction engineered by the Federal Reserve beginning in 1929. This contraction provoked large-scale bank failures and gave the political entrepreneurs in Washington the opportunity to press for their own special interest remedies.

The key to the success of deposit insurance in this new environment was the chairman of the House Banking Committee, Representative Henry Steagall (D, Ala.). He assumed the office in 1930 and was a very strong advocate of state deposit insurance. He held that deposit insurance was necessary for the survival of the unit banking system, and he had a strong aversion to any form of branching within states or across state boundaries. The House Committee thus had a chairman whose position on deposit insurance was unyielding and who would use the power of his office to secure it.

Deposit insurance had equally powerful opponents in Congress, the most important of which was Senator Carter Glass (D, Va.), who held sway over the Senate Banking Committee. He pushed his own panacea, which was to separate commercial and investment banking. According to this throwback to the real bills doctrine, separating commercial and investment banking activities made the banking system safe again. Steagall would not accept any banking bill that did not include deposit insurance and Glass would not consent to any bill that included it. Thus, very little moved in the way of banking reform in 1931 or 1932.

Looking back as far as the elections of 1932, there is little reason to think that deposit insurance had much of a chance. The Democratic Party, which was confident of victory given that the Republicans had been blamed for the depression, did not mention deposit insurance in their party platform. Senator Glass had Roosevelt's ear, ensuring the separation of commercial banking but not the passage of federal deposit insurance. The key to the success of deposit insurance was the absence of any change in the Federal Reserve's deflationary monetary policy. As more banks failed, the crisis in the payment system intensified. States that were afraid that their banking systems would collapse declared bank holidays – a nice name for shutting down the banking system. They decided that it was better to shut down the banking system and prevent anyone from withdrawing money rather than to let banks fail en masse.

Nevada began the practice, declaring a holiday in October 1932, and the process slowly built up speed. By March 3, 1933, thirty-six states had some form of banking holiday. When Roosevelt took office, there was some talk of a possible devaluation. Fear of a run on the dollar encouraged the Federal Reserve to raise the discount rate, worsening banking problems. Thus, on March 6, 1933, Roosevelt ordered a national bank holiday, shutting down the entire banking system to halt this crisis. On March 11 a partial opening of the banking system began, but only strong banks were allowed to open. When the banking holiday ended, only 12,000 banks opened with $23 billion worth of deposits, and another 5,000 banks remained unlicensed. Unopened banks held more than $3 billion. These figures stand in contrast to the end of December 1932, when about 18,000 banks were open, holding $28 billion in deposits. In this environment Congress began to debate what to do.

Explaining Congress's response

To put this dramatic banking collapse in perspective it is useful to compare it with today's savings and loan problems. Between 1930 and 1933, 9,000 banks were suspended, incurring losses of $2.5 billion, half of which was borne by depositors and half by shareholders and other creditors. How do these losses compare with the costs of today's savings and loan problems? At most, the price level has risen about tenfold, making these losses about $25 billion. Since the savings and loan crisis cost about $200 billion, the

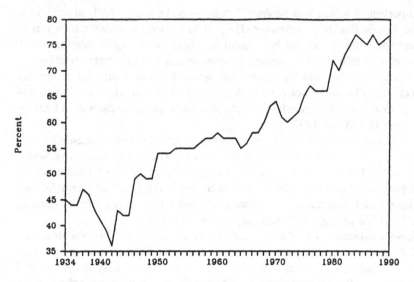

Figure 5.1. Percentage of total deposits insured, 1934–1990.

Great Depression losses seem small by comparison. The political economy of how losses are shared explains why we had a major banking reform in the 1930s but relatively little changed in the 1980s, even though the crisis involved larger sums.

What happened in Congress in 1933 is very interesting because Congress decided not to bail out the depositors at this time. There were petitions to do so, and a few members of Congress suggested the idea, but Congress did not aid injured depositors. Instead, it adopted a system of deposit insurance that protected the existing safe banks, and hence their depositors in the future. The political change that led to the adoption of deposit insurance was the result of widespread losses suffered by depositors. Although there were years of high losses before the Great Depression, the period 1930–33 was a watershed (Figure 5.1). The president, the secretary of the Treasury, the head of the Senate Banking Committee, and the American Bankers Association were all opposed to deposit insurance. Even the Federal Reserve, which was not allowed to speak on the issue, was quietly opposed to it. This coalition was formidable opposition, and it offered all the arguments good economists today give against deposit insurance. But they were overcome by the unit banking lobbying, bolstered by the public's fear over the safety of its deposits.

The public's trust in banks changed radically during the Great Depression, partially because bankers were portrayed as perpetrators rather than victims of the Depression in the media and in congressional hearings. In cartoons bankers were caricatured as gangsters wearing top hats and playing craps with their depositors' funds. The media thus helped Steagall, who was an astute political entrepreneur. He responded to the deadlock with Glass in Congress by wooing the public. At the same time Steagall was careful to argue in Congress that he was designing a system that would avoid moral hazard and adverse selection problems.

Until the 1920s, even though depositors made losses, very few people outside of unit bankers were interested in or talked about a deposit insurance system because losses were modest and limited. But when the failure of the 1930s occurred, everyone, even if they hadn't suffered a loss, felt threatened because they knew people who had lost money. In this kind of environment the public was willing to listen to a credible panacea. And this change gave Steagall enough power to block all other banking legislation and secure Glass's acquiescence and the president's signature.

The Banking Act of 1933 set up a temporary insurance fund, and a permanent insurance fund was established in 1935. The temporary insurance fund was very limited, reflecting the initial compromise. It insured only $2,500 worth of deposits per account. The Banking Act of 1935 raised this amount to $5,000. Insured banks were charged a premium of one-twelfth of 1 percent of their deposits. This legislation represented a clear victory for the small rural banks and lower-income people with small accounts. The losers were the large city banks and wealthy depositors, who, in effect, were being taxed to pay the premium for insuring small accounts. Depositors in failed banks also lost because they were not bailed out. Innovating activity that built larger, stronger banks was thus brought to a halt, and the system was frozen.

The political economy of deposit insurance reforms

The passage of deposit insurance legislation in the United States is an informative episode about the political economy of financial regulation. Unit banks would never have been able to, by their own lobbying effort, overcome the opposition of the stronger urban branching banks had the Great Depression not occurred and mobilized the public, who took comfort in the idea of deposit insurance regardless of its long-term consequences. Once protected, the public ignored the issue of deposit insurance and again lost interest in the political debate. The politics of banking regulation returned to the smoke-filled rooms of Congress, where special interests vied with one another for influence over legislation.

The next bill on deposit insurance was the Deposit Insurance Act of 1950. Small banks pressed for an increase in coverage to $10,000 (Table 5.2). Wartime inflation had reduced the real value of the $5,000 maximum (in 1980 dollars) from $30,000 to about $17,000. Small banks were also finding it harder to compete with large banks. Large banks opposed the increase in insurance coverage. But they were induced to compromise by the offer of a

Table 5.2. *FDIC and Federal Savings and Loan Insurance Corporation (FSLIC) deposit insurance, 1934-1989*

Years	Maximum insured deposit amount	Maximum insured deposit amount adjusted for inflation (1980 dollars)
1934–49	$5,000	$30,800–17,300
1950–65	$10,000	$34,200–26,150
1966–68	$15,000	$38,150–35,500
1969–73	$20,000	$45,800–37,100
1974–79	$40,000	$66,850–45,400
1980–89	$100,000	$100,000–66,450

Source: White (1991).

prorated rebate of assessments. The insurance fund was growing in the absence of major failures. But this compromise was a devil's pact because insurance coverage was increased in real terms while the growth of the fund was retarded by rebating. But given the insurance, the public was not alarmed by this deal.

Looking at the trend in deposit insurance over the course of the century, there is an almost inexorable expansion of protection, moving farther and farther away from limited coverage and a mutual guarantee of bank funds. This movement is driven by special interests, who, once they had their foot in the door, began to push for more. There was a steady upward climb of the percentage insured, driven partly by increasing limits, but also by an increasingly informed public creating multiple accounts (Figure 5.2). Thus, insured deposits increased from 45 percent to nearly 80 percent. With higher coverage, less monitoring took place as more and more deposits were insured. This higher coverage combined with the "too big to fail" doctrine made coverage nearly universal.

Turning to the moral hazard consequences of deposit insurance, some explanation must be given for why it took so long for moral hazard to manifest itself in the banking system. Following the establishment of deposit insurance, banks were very safe, and it took them a long time to change. They were safe because the Great Depression profoundly altered bank portfolios. It shrank bank deposits and bank loans. It is only a slight exaggeration to say that banks got out of the business of lending. During World War II banks and savings and loans stuffed their portfolios with government bonds. Hence, by 1950 these were very safe institutions, given the dual shocks of the Great Depression and World War II. They also faced tight regulations. It took banks a long time to unwind from this position. Eventually, competition stimulated them to take more risk, and it was only in the 1970s that increased risk taking was first noticed. The disasters of commercial banking and savings and loans after the 1970s were the result of allowing insured banks to enter

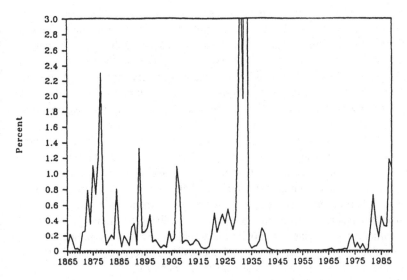

Figure 5.2. Failed bank deposits to total deposits, 1865–1989.

more risky areas of activity, while limiting examinations, supervision, and discipline.

What to do? Should deposit insurance be recommended? The short answer is no. The historical record teaches three lessons. First, deposit insurance was not adopted primarily to protect the depositor. There were many ways to increase the soundness of the banking system, and the problems of deposit insurance were well known from the state experiments that preceded the FDIC. The leading alternative, with which contemporaries had experience, was to allow branching and the diversification of institutions by geography and product line. But monetary contraction and the politics of the banking crisis empowered the small unit banks. Second, the historical record of federal and state insurance plans shows that it is all but impossible to escape the moral hazard and other problems inherent in deposit insurance. This was also true for Canada, which adopted deposit insurance in 1967 and soon began to experience similar kinds of problems. Third, in setting up banking regulations, including deposit insurance, a banking lobby will be created that will campaign in the future to protect the industry as it stands, and the industry will be pushed on a course that will be difficult to alter. The state experiences also contain one lesson: if the government is willing to reduce competition, allow tight cartelization, and impose tight supervision and control, deposit insurance can work for at least twenty years.

Although history does not recommend deposit insurance, it does show that the public is greatly concerned about the safety of its deposits. U.S. financial history is littered with all kinds of schemes to protect depositors or to protect noteholders. The designs of these systems were influenced by special interests, but they were also driven by the public's desire for protection. The key problem is one of information. For the vast banking public – that is, households and small businesses – it is very costly to monitor the performance of banks and decide which is the safest choice among all alternatives. If deposits of each bank are unequally safe, choosing is a difficult task, particularly when the economy is subject to economic fluctuations and there is a dispersion of performance by institution.

What plan could a policy maker offer that would not have all the perverse effects of deposit insurance? History provides at least one alternative: regulators could require each bank to offer deposit accounts that are segregated, treasury bill mutual funds. Banks could then advertise these funds as safe assets, perhaps guaranteed or backed by the government. This type of account is in effect insurance from the government, offering the same guarantee as government bonds. But it removes the wrong incentives for financial institutions that arise from insuring bank deposits. There is a strong historical precedent for this type of arrangement (see Chapter 4).

Between 1864 and 1914 the creation of currency was the task of national banks. These bank notes were backed by U.S. government bonds. They became completely safe assets regardless of which institution issued them. National banks did fail, but never because of note issuing, and no noteholder ever experienced a loss. The system allowed people to choose between safe national bank notes, which bore no interest, and deposits, which were not safe but carried interest. This system functioned very well. Other monetary and banking issues created problems, including the absence of a central bank until 1913, but the public was generally very satisfied with national bank notes.

To conclude, deposit insurance was the peculiar creation of the U.S. banking experience generated by some of the worst features of the system. It is inappropriate for developing or transition economies. Deposit insurance presents enormous incentive problems and requires additional regulations and close supervision to make it workable in the short run. These conditions may demand too much from bank regulators in developing countries, as it did for regulators in the United States. There are simpler, less costly alternatives that may achieve the same basic objective.

REFERENCES

Calomiris, Charles W. 1989. "Deposit Insurance: Lessons from the Record." *Economic Perspectives of the Federal Reserve Bank of Chicago* (May–June):10–30.

    1993. "Regulation, Industrial Structure, and Instability in U.S. Banking: An Historical Perspective." In Michael Klausner and Lawrence J. White, eds., *Structural Change in Banking*. Homewood: Business One-Irwin, pp. 19–116.

Deposit insurance 97

Golembe, Carter H. 1960. "The Deposit Insurance Legislation of 1933." *Political Science Quarterly* 75 (2) (June):181–95.
White, Eugene N. 1983. *The Regulation and Reform of the American Banking System, 1900–1929.* Princeton, N.J.: Princeton University Press.
1992. "The Effects of Bank Regulation on the Financing of American Business, 1860–1960." In Vera Zamagni, ed., *Finance and the Enterprise.* London: Academic Press, pp. 158–79.
White, Lawrence J. 1991. *The S&L Debacle: Public Policy Lessons for Bank and Thrift Regulation.* New York: Oxford University Press.

DISCUSSION

Question: Even if a comprehensive deposit insurance system is problematic because of the moral hazard problems you mentioned, what about encouraging a limited scheme to protect those with small savings?

Prof. White: The fact is that regulations, when they're initially adopted, can appear innocuous. But once they are established, a lobby is created, which may capture the legislature or a portion of the legislature, to push for further assistance. There is a tendency to expand over time. People say, "We can do something better. We can design a very narrow form of deposit insurance and it will work. It won't create problems." I doubt that very much. A limited system may work for a short time, but it's going to grow up. There is a clear danger that a system of deposit insurance will expand over time just as the U.S. system did.

J. Caprio: I have two questions. First, how can you "give up" deposit insurance, especially in an open economy? Might not depositors move funds offshore to insured accounts? Can governments credibly agree not to bail out deposits? Second, the proposal for narrow banking makes a lot of sense if you can again issue a credible promise that you're not going to bail out the institutions that you're calling "nonbanks," which will issue risky liabilities. This is a tough issue. In this country we had to bail out Chrysler. If narrow banks can hold only government bonds, those accounts are going to pay low interest rates. We've seen that when interest rates fall, people start looking further out along the risk spectrum. You can imagine a big shift of deposits from Citibank to American Express. If American Express gets into trouble, and it is now a lot bigger, is the government going to let it go under?

Prof. White: First, I really wasn't preaching for narrow banks, and I don't want to do so. I think that the case of the national banking system is instructive in some sense. The U.S. economy was a much simpler economy at that time, and it did devise a system that protected the currency. Some banks failed, but there was at least one safe asset. This asset reduced the public's demand for greater control. But the implicit guarantee of the whole banking system is really an aspect of the central bank's activities and thus depends much more on how the central bank behaves. But you don't want to create a special interest lobby. If there is no established lobby, government will find it easier to resist bailing out the failures.

Question: Is the problem that you are describing unique to financial guarantees? I don't think that you've done a very good job building the case that the deterioration of the system in the 1950s, 1960s, and 1970s was inevitable. What aspect in particular made it so?

Prof. White: If you look at the pattern of development of financial intermediaries in the United States throughout the twentieth century, the traditional intermediaries that were subject to the heaviest regulation experienced a broad decline, and they have all become subject to some kind of insurance – whether they are a savings and loan, a mutual credit union, or an insurance company – administered at the state level, not at the federal level. It is very difficult to give them any kind of insurance that is not based on risk. Even schemes that are devised to have risk-based premiums are very crude efforts. It is very difficult to devise appropriate incentive-compatible deposit insurance for an institution that needs to be flexible. Some worked, but those that worked had other undesirable characteristics.

H. Baer: Is it clear that the undesirable aspects of a mutual guarantee system would persist in a unit bank regime?

Prof. White: It would be difficult. One of the kinks was that the monitoring was undertaken by all the banks, which would then be jointly liable, which is incompatible with free entry. In other types of institutional arrangements – such as clearing houses that substituted for central banks before the founding of the Federal Reserve – there was a real problem. They could help each other, but they also had to monitor one another. They maintained a club and tended to exclude banks, thus creating a danger of lack of coverage. Hence, they weren't quite as successful as private central banks. They might be successful at protecting one another, but excluding banks that didn't meet the standards they set could allow a crisis to spill over into their system.

Prof. Calomiris: I don't think the cartel aspect is really necessary. I think you can generate competition among mutually reinforcing groups. The historical case is that of the German savings groups. They had mutual insurance clearing houses, and often more than one competed in the same city. They protected people against collusion. I want to come back to Jerry Caprio's point, which I think is the showstopper. I don't know the answer to it. Regardless of how good a system you design, not just for banks but for any corporation, to the extent that governments in the twentieth century have decided that there can't be ex post losers on a large scale, how do we solve that problem? I know of only one attempt by a government to try to do this – the Chilean banking legislation of 1983, in which the government explicitly said, "We saw disaster happen because we couldn't tie our hands." Banks realized that being big meant that they were more likely to be bailed out, so they merged as the copper market was failing. And they did get bailed out. We see moral hazard disasters that we want to try to fix by setting up a very complicated arrangement to tie our hands. I don't know whether such an arrangement is going to work. I suggest that anyone who is advising countries with such hazards look at the example of Chile.

Prof. White: Have these banks managed to be successful for ten years?

Prof. Calomiris: So far so good. But I don't know what's happened to the price of copper in the last ten years.

Comment: Wasn't there a case in New Zealand, which doesn't have deposit insurance? In the 1980s when they went through liberalization, a bank failed, and the government allowed it to fail, although it bailed out the depositors.

Prof. Calomiris: The book on the East Asian miracle that the World Bank just published has about six pages of tables that list all of the countries in which there has been a major bank bailout in the past twenty years. I was teaching a large group of students from all over the world and each was from a country on that list.

Prof. White: I think the Chilean method is the correct way to go. The government has to be very explicit – it can't say just before the bank fails that all depositors are going to get a "haircut." They have to say it far enough in advance and make a lot of very threatening sounds. Otherwise, people will become politically active and force a bailout. One of the interesting features in the U.S. case is that people didn't get bailed out in 1933. People were aware that they could get burned and thus may have stayed away. The lobby of people promoting a bailout was really relatively small compared with the number of people who would have had to pay for that bailout.

J. Caprio: Indeed, that is the essence of the change. If we had the same set of tables that Professor Calomiris was just talking about and we looked at where depositors actually incurred losses, then I don't think we would have needed half a page to explain, let alone six. People's basic understanding of what they are exposed to has changed in the past sixty or seventy years. The question is similar, then, to an individual country where there has been a sequence of bailouts – can government enter with a credible threat that there won't be a bailout? In some countries they may let some small institutions go under, but it is really difficult to find a situation where a big institution has been threatened and its depositors have lost.

D. Vittas: An important factor for this change of attitude is that now many more low-income people are customers of banks, whereas sixty years ago this was not the case.

J. Caprio: That's why I'm surprised that no one has mentioned the argument that depositors can't see through the veil of the bank. Several studies show that at least in the United States, stockholders and even some bank insiders couldn't see through to understand the position of the banks. They bought in just before banks were downgraded. If depositors really can't monitor banks, maybe legislation should be passed to protect those with small deposits. But the game plan is to try to make sure that the bank doesn't grow any further.

Prof. White: There must be another way to ensure safety rather than the traditional deposit insurance scheme. In fact, people in the United States have an alternative: money market mutual funds. In the 1970s and 1980s people put their money in rapidly growing money market mutual funds. This behavior is very interesting because those funds were essentially uninsured banks, and big banks at that. People received regular statements, with certified public accountants saying that these uninsured banks had all assets listed. The assets are very short-term, and the uninsured banks look a little bit like a very traditional nineteenth-century bank with lots of liquidity and very safe assets. People were thus willing to deposit funds with them even if they didn't have the imprimatur of the FDIC or the FSLIC. So, maybe in the end there is some hope that people will select safe intermediaries, given the opportunity.

CHAPTER 6

Contingent liability in banking: Useful policy for developing countries?

Anthony Saunders and Berry Wilson

Bank owner contingent liability has been an important component in the developmental history of many industrial countries. For example, Scotland imposed unlimited liability on bank owners until 1862, when banks were allowed to adopt a limited liability designation. As a result, Scotland was relatively free of the banking and monetary upheavals that occurred in Britain and the United States. In addition, the United States conducted a long regulatory experiment with double liability, which started with the "free banking" movement in the early 1900s and was phased out as part of the post-depression reforms of the 1930s.

Thus, some form of contingent liability has been seen in the development of many industrial countries, suggesting that contingent liability systems might play an important policy role for many developing countries. This chapter traces the history of contingent liability in banking, with particular emphasis on Scotland and the United States. We discuss the potential advantages of contingent liability in a developing country context, as well as theoretical weaknesses and possible solutions.

We also argue that double liability and deposit insurance are not incompatible regulatory policies, even though federal deposit insurance was legislated in 1933 to replace double liability. In fact, they coexisted prior to 1933 – national bank notes carried a federal guarantee against loss at redemption. Further, in 1991 the Federal Deposit Insurance Corporation Improvement Act (FDICIA) legislated an early closure rule that was meant to impose greater regulatory discipline by enforcing postclosure losses on bank stockholders, much as with double liability.

Unlimited liability and free banking in Scotland

White (1984) provides an extensive analysis of the history of unlimited liability in Scotland in the eighteenth and early nineteenth centuries. During this period Scottish banking featured a free banking approach with unregulated entry and a universal right to issue bank notes. In addition, unlimited liability to bank creditors was imposed on bank stockholders. Also during this period Scotland lacked a central bank, a national monetary policy, and formal bank supervision. Nonetheless, the economy developed from being largely agrarian to industrial without suffering the monetary upheavals and bank panics that characterized other developing countries at the time, such as Britain and the United States.

Unlimited liability of bank owners was an important element in the success of Scottish banking (White 1984:142–4). The unlimited liability rule lasted until 1862, when banks were allowed to adopt limited liability. Throughout the first half of this history bank notes were the predominant form of bank liability, with deposit banking gaining in importance only as disposable income grew.

The unlimited liability provision effectively minimized the losses suffered by bank noteholders and other creditors. White (1984:41) reports that actual losses from Scottish bank failures were well below those suffered by bank creditors in England. In addition, Scottish banks were not prone to the bank runs and contagion effects that characterized British and U.S. banks at the time. Apparently, Scottish noteholders had little incentive to "run" because of the effective coverage provided by unlimited liability. Scottish banks further reduced potential postclosure losses through branch banking and clearinghouse arrangements, as well as through the lack of reserve pyramiding that minimized spillover effects. The low incidence of spillover effects fostered competition among banks for the business of failed banks. Therefore, the recycling of failed bank liabilities (i.e., bank notes) was efficient, and the impact on the national money supply was minimized.

Three key factors were vital to the success of unlimited liability in Scotland. First, the identities of bank owners were publicly available, and their level of wealth could be verified. Therefore the degree of noteholder protection from unlimited liability could be assessed by aggregating individual owner wealth. Second, under Scottish bankruptcy law bank owner liability extended to both personal and inheritable wealth. This intergenerational extension of liability expanded the safety net available to bank creditors.

Finally, the transfer of ownership claims in private and provincial banks required that ownership first be dissolved before a new bank could be formed. This provision allowed the transfer of control to be monitored, minimizing adverse selection problems that might arise if ownership was transferred to people that held less personal wealth.

Finally, despite the elimination of unlimited liability in 1862, banks could still create reserve liability through the unpaid capital of a stock issue. A portion of unpaid capital was callable at a future date to supply additional bank capital. The remaining unpaid-capital portion was a reserve liability that was callable to satisfy liability claims only if the bank failed. The level of unpaid and reserve liability was set at the discretion of the issuing bank.

Double liability in the United States

Under double liability bank stockholders could lose twice on their bank investment. First, contributed capital was lost if the bank failed. Second, after a bank failure stockholders could be assessed up to the par value of their shares to satisfy creditor claims. The par value of extended liability was the "double" liability that bank stockholders faced. Initially double liability was thought to provide adequate protection for bank creditors to cover most of their potential losses. Double liability became increasingly common in many states after 1837.

Bank chartering

Bank chartering in the new U.S. confederation began with the Bank of North America in Philadelphia, which was granted a perpetual charter in 1782 by the Continental Congress. The bank also issued the confederacy's first paper convertible into specie (Klebaner 1990:4). Chartered banking subsequently developed rapidly, with charters granted to the Massachusetts Bank (Boston) in 1784, the Bank of New York (New York City) in 1784, and the Bank of Maryland (Baltimore) in 1790.

During this early period in U.S. history, banks were chartered by special legislative grants from individual states and the federal Congress. Charters were granted in limited supply and only by the chartering authority. This policy restricted access to banking in comparison to the free banking policies of Scotland. Bank charters were effectively grants of monopoly rights, which bank owners often protected by attempting to preclude the establishment of new banks in their area. Consequently, bank chartering became highly politicized and in turn motivated the free banking movement in the early 1830s.

Valuable charters allowed banks to generate profits without excessive risk taking, which gave banks an incentive to keep capital and reserve levels high to prevent the regulatory loss of their charter. Saunders and Wilson (1995) term the resulting positive relationship between bank capital and charter value the "charter value hypothesis." Keeley (1990) provides evidence linking declining capital ratios to declining U.S. bank charter values since the 1960s, which, in turn, were further linked to the deregulation of interstate banking restrictions. The conservative banking style induced by positive charter values also protected bank noteholders and other creditors from potential loss, much as unlimited liability did in Scotland at this time.

Free banking

Free banking in the United States originated in Michigan in 1837 and New York in 1838. One goal of this movement was to depoliticize the bank chartering process by allowing relatively free entry into banking. With free entry came a large increase in the number of banks and greater competition among banks, allowing profits from banking to be shared more widely.

The increase in competition and erosion of charter values lowered incentives for banks to conservatively manage risk. "Wild cat" banking practices developed where poorly capitalized banks issued large amounts of bank notes. Thus, it is not surprising that double liability had its roots in the free banking period. Double liability offered bank creditors greater protection from loss and gave bank owners incentives to control risk taking.

Several important features distinguished double liability from unlimited liability used in Scotland. First, under double liability bank stock was, for the most part, freely traded by auction and by dealers in the United States, although many states required stockholders to be state residents (Klebaner 1990:14).

Second, stockholder liability was generally pro rata, implying that individual stockholders were not liable for the assessment shortfalls of other stockholders and were released from liability once their double liability was satisfied. This provision protected bank owners from each other, but lessened the incentives for bank owners to monitor other owners' wealth. The pro rata provision also made ownership claims more freely transferable, which created potential adverse selection problems.

National banking

Double liability was adopted for national banks when the National Banking Act of 1863 created a national banking system. The double liability provision was modeled on state statutes, and its adoption for national banks spurred further adoption by individual states. By 1930 only ten states had not adopted some variation of double liability. Colorado had adopted triple liability, and California banks were subject to unlimited liability.

During this period double liability coexisted with a federal guarantee of national bank notes. Bank notes were the predominant liability of national banks, much as in Scotland. Issuing banks were required to hold eligible treasury bonds with the comptroller of the currency holding collateral against their note issue. If the bank failed and was closed, the comptroller would then pay off bank notes at par value, using the bonds held from that bank to satisfy claims. In addition, double liability assessments would be made against bank stockholders to defray any residual claims. Therefore, double liability and a federal guarantee of bank notes were used jointly to satisfy creditors. (In Scotland unlimited liability alone generally provided sufficient protection for bank liability holders.)

Although bank notes were the predominant form of bank liability during earlier U.S. history (Klebaner 1990:27), deposit banking grew in importance, particularly as federal reserve notes replaced circulating bank notes after the creation of the Federal Reserve System in 1913. But depositors did not have the federal guarantee extended to bank noteholders and, therefore, were covered by double liability protection only if the bank failed. As a final note, banks did hold collateral in the form of bonds against government deposits, which effectively made government deposit claims senior to those of general depositors (O'Connor 1938:74).

The end of double liability

The early 1930s witnessed the most severe banking and economic crisis in U.S. history. By 1933 most regulators realized that double liability had failed to protect depositors and foster a stable banking system. The federal guarantee afforded national bank notes had not been extended to depositors, despite several attempts to legislate federal deposit insurance since the Federal Reserve Act of 1913.

Accordingly, double liability was phased out and replaced by federal deposit insurance of bank deposits. The Banking Act of 1933 repealed double liability for all new common stock issues of national banks. The Banking Act of 1935 repealed double liability on existing shares of national bank stock, as long as depositors were given six months' notice. States followed suit in repealing their own double liability statutes.

Double liability was abandoned for several reasons. First, it had failed to prevent bank runs and spillover effects and thus provide banking stability, particularly during the 1930s. Second, double liability made recapitalization difficult during the 1930s. Previous panics were shorter and economic recovery occurred sooner, making recapitalization easier. The length of the recession in the 1930s and the nationwide scope of the banking crisis made bank stock that carried double liability difficult to issue. Therefore, double liability relief made sense at least temporarily, to allow banks to recapitalize. Finally, the double coverage of both federal deposit insurance and double liability was thought unnecessary, even though double coverage had existed earlier (with double liability as residual).

Advantages of contingent liability systems

A contingent liability system has three advantages over limited liability. First, because double liability imposes postclosure losses on bank stockholders, it increases incentives for banks to hold capital and decreases moral hazard incentives, such as a "go for broke" strategy. Second, a contingent liability system can ameliorate asymmetric information problems between bank creditors and bank owners. Third, contingent liability can lead to more efficient capital formation if potential capital sources are predominately in the form of fixed wealth, as is the case in many developing countries.

Amelioration of moral hazard incentives

Banking systems operating under limited liability can be plagued by moral hazard problems and "go for broke" incentives, as shown by the large losses associated with the thrift crisis during the early 1980s. In contrast, the post-closure losses imposed under a contingent liability system (such as double liability) gave banks, particularly financially distressed banks, incentives to hold greater capital and to control risk taking,.

There is some evidence that double liability fostered a more conservative banking system. Macey and Miller (1992) argue that voluntary liquidation by banks was more common during the double liability period and minimized depositor and stockholder losses. In contrast, the current U.S. system of limited liability and fixed-rate deposit insurance gives bank stockholders fewer incentives to liquidate voluntarily, and the FDIC has become the major vehicle for recycling failed bank assets.

For example, between 1863 and 1912 there were 525 national bank closures and 2,357 national bank voluntary liquidations, indicating a high rate of asset recycling before bank failure occurred. Between 1913 and 1928 there were 125 failures and 2,072 voluntary liquidations. Finally, from 1929 to 1933 there were 1,280 failures and 1,343 voluntary liquidations. These numbers suggest that bank failures might have been more prevalent during the Great Depression without double liability.

Losses to national bank depositors during the double liability period averaged only 44 cents per thousand dollars of deposits (Macey and Miller 1992). In contrast, FDIC losses in 1985 equaled approximately $1.20 per thousand dollars of bank deposits. Therefore, losses during the double liability period were fairly conservative.

Sources of bank management discipline

As argued earlier, double and unlimited liability increased regulatory discipline on banks by imposing postfailure losses on bank stockholders. In addition, bank depositors and other creditors exerted discipline on bank management by requiring risk-based premiums for deposits and through the ominous bank run threat. But because liquidation of bank assets to quell a bank run was potentially costly, bank runs could even threaten the solvency of solvent banks.

Both depositors and stockholders were sources of management discipline, but an asymmetric information problem could arise between these groups. Typically, most bank depositors were thought to be uninformed about the true solvency of the bank. These uninformed depositors based withdrawal decisions on imperfect signals of bank solvency, such as long withdrawal lines. In contrast, informed depositors, such as large corporate depositors, could quickly withdraw funds if bank solvency was threatened. Because of this information asymmetry, double liability imposed the greatest threat of loss on those stakeholders most informed about the bank's condition, that is, the stockholders.

One goal of federal deposit insurance in 1933 was to protect uninformed depositors by limiting initial deposit insurance coverage to $5,000 per account. But because the rate charged to banks for deposit insurance coverage was fixed (non-risk-based), it introduced the well-known moral hazard problem of deposit insurance. Arguably, if double liability had been retained as a complement to federal deposit insurance, the regulatory discipline of double liability would have offset the moral hazard incentives introduced with deposit insurance. Indeed double liability had coexisted with the blanket federal guarantee of national bank notes, without the moral hazard problems that arose in the 1980s with deposit insurance.

Capital formation advantages

Contingent liability may allow more efficient capital formation in developing countries if capital is mostly fixed wealth. In this case contingent liability can be viewed as a form of off-balance-sheet capital (e.g., land and other fixed assets), available to creditors if the bank closes. Arguably, off-balance-sheet capital may be of equal or greater value to liability holders as on-balance-sheet capital for several reasons. First, book asset values may not accurately reflect market asset values, while off-balance-sheet capital may be easier to value. In addition, off-balance-sheet capital may be of higher quality than on-balance-sheet capital if its value is less volatile. Finally, off-balance-sheet capital may diversify the bank's asset portfolio and thereby reduce expected creditor losses.

Allowing part of a bank's capital to be held off balance sheet may have other advantages. Because wealth in many developing countries is locked up as fixed assets, capital formation may be difficult and costly, in that it requires costly liquidation of fixed assets, which would reduce available on-balance-sheet capital. Therefore, double liability enables a more efficient use of assets to form capital and attract depositors. Winton (1993) presents a formal proof of these assertions.

Free-rider and adverse selection problems

Despite the advantages discussed earlier, contingent liability systems are also prone to adverse selection and moral hazard problems. Stockholders' efforts to monitor management increase the equity value of the bank by increasing manager discipline. In addition, contingent liability increases the value of monitoring management performance. But because of decreasing returns to scale, monitoring incentives are greatest for the wealthiest stockholders. A free-rider problem thus arises in that less wealthy stockholders will rely on the monitoring efforts of wealthier stockholders, who then bear the monitoring expense.

An adverse selection problem also arises when ownership claims can be freely and anonymously traded. Ownership claims have greater value to investors with less personal wealth, because they have less to lose if the bank fails. In a free and anonymous exchange market, investors with less personal fixed wealth will outbid those with greater wealth, and consequently the value of double liability will erode through time. Eventually, the bank stock will be owned by investors with no fixed wealth, and double liability will collapse to limited liability.

Furthermore, bank creditors have incentives to monitor the erosion of double liability. As erosion occurs, creditors will demand higher premiums as compensation for bearing greater risk. Ultimately the erosion of double liability and the cost of higher premiums are borne by owners who do not sell their claims. A transfer of wealth is thus created from nonselling to selling owners, giving rise to incentives to regulate ownership transfer.

Transferring ownership claims in Scotland required that the entire partnership be dissolved and then reformed. Dissolving the partnership allowed new owners to be evaluated and either approved or disapproved. In addition, the unlimited liability did not fully transfer with the change in ownership. Owners who sold remained liable for a period after ownership transfer. These devices helped to prevent adverse selection problems and the erosion of unlimited liability protection.

In contrast, in the United States bank ownership shares could be freely and anonymously traded. But other devices were potentially useful for preventing erosion of the double liability claim. For example, bank stock during this period was relatively expensive compared with current bank stock prices, particularly when inflation-adjusted. Typical bank stock prices ranged from hundreds to thousands of dollars per share. In contrast, current U.S. bank stock prices range within roughly $20 to $40 per share. These high prices restricted bank ownership to wealthy individuals.

In addition, during this period bank stocks were thinly traded with large bid–ask spreads, implying that ownership claims were relatively expensive to trade. Bid–ask spreads in the range of 5 to 20 percent were common, implying that owners sold at, for example, a 20 percent discount relative to buyers, with the spread paying for inventory and transaction costs of the broker.

Because of high underwriting and other issue costs, most new stock issues took the form of subscription rights to current bank stockholders. Rights offers tended to further concentrate ownership with current stockholders. Finally, many banks served as their own transfer agents and maintained stockholder lists. Therefore, ownership information was readily available to bank insiders.

There were thus implicit restrictions on ownership transfer during the double liability period, in terms of high stock prices and high bid–ask spreads. Rights offers also tended to keep ownership concentrated. As a result, banks tended to be closely held, with bank managers also serving as major stockholders. The benefits of being closely held were seen in terms of reduced agency costs.

Empirical results

Saunders and Wilson (1995) examined two measures of bank performance,: first, the market–capital ratio – market equity value (price per share times the number of shares) divided by the market value of assets (market equity value plus book value of debt); second, bank charter value – the ratio of the market value of assets to the book value of assets, which reflects expected future monopoly rents (Table 6.1).

Capital ratios were approximately twice as high before 1933, when double liability was imposed, than after 1933. These high capital ratios reflected both the market discipline imposed by uninsured depositors and that imposed by stockholders under double liability. The reason for the decline in capital ratios after 1933 is somewhat ambiguous, since the reforms of the 1930s included both the repeal of double liability and the advent of deposit insurance, as well as a host of other reforms such as the Glass–Steagall Act.

Comparing the measures of peak charter value before and after deposit insurance, we see an overall decline. Therefore, the regulatory costs of double liability and the limitations faced by banks during this earlier period, such as high underwriting costs, did not adversely affect their estimated charter values.

Finally, Saunders and Wilson (1995) find that the decline in bank capital ratios after the 1930s was, for the most part, not linked to the decline in charter values during this period. The authors theorize that the change in incentives with the elimination of double liability and advent of federal deposit insurance had a larger impact on bank capital structure decisions.

Policy lessons

This chapter has discussed the importance of contingent liability systems in the development of many industrial countries. Fundamentally, contingent liability allows stockholders to bear more of the risk in contractual relations with bank managers and with bank liability holders. This may be particularly important in developing countries where information asymmetries are more important and the legal structure less developed. The advantage is that banking sector instability from bank runs and contagion effects may be reduced or eliminated.

The chapter also argues that contingent liability allows more efficient capital formation in countries where capital is mostly fixed wealth. Allowing

Table 6.1. *Comparison of capital and charter values before and after federal deposit insurance (1933) (percent of total assets)*

Period	Peak market–capital ratio	Peak charter value
Pre-1933	27.9 (1902)	1.16 (1902)
	27.7 (1929)	1.19 (1928)
Post-1933	13.4 (1961)	1.09 (1961)

land and other fixed assets to serve as off-balance-sheet capital may reduce valuation problems with on-balance-sheet capital and reduce risk through diversifying capital sources.

Finally, greater risk bearing by bank owners can also decrease moral hazard incentives, such as "go for broke" strategies. Developing countries are increasingly adopting deposit insurance schemes, where the moral hazard incentives are well established. We have argued that extended owner liability along with deposit insurance may help minimize these incentives.

REFERENCES

Keeley, M. 1990. "Deposit Insurance, Risk, and Market Power in Banking," *American Economic Review* 80:1183–200.
Klebaner, B. J. 1990. *American Commercial Banking: A History*. Boston, Mass.: Twayne.
Macey, J. R., and G. P. Miller. 1992. "Double Liability of Bank Shareholders: History and Implications." *Wake Forest Law Review* 27:31–62.
O'Connor, J. F. T. 1938. *The Banking Crisis and Recovery under the Roosevelt Administration*, Chicago: Callaghan.
Saunders, T., and B. Wilson. 1995. "Bank Capital Structure: An Analysis of the Charter Value Hypothesis." Working Paper. Salomon Center, New York University, New York.
White, L. H. 1984. *Free Banking in Britain: Theory, Experience and Debate, 1800 – 1845*. Cambridge University Press.
Winton, A. 1993. "Limitation of Liability and the Ownership Structure of the Firm." *Journal of Finance* 48:487–512.

DISCUSSION

Comment: One supportive comment is that around the turn of the century, 90 percent of national banks' capital was owned by people living in the same county as the bank, resulting in a very nondiversified bank holding structure. A second point is that double liability actually increased the "lemons problem" for insider trading – in which selling by insiders may signal bad news to outsider investors. Double liability actually increased the possibility that insiders were selling because of bad news. Therefore, the problem that adverse selection created was potentially offset by a lemons problem. Another point is that the informed depositors discussed earlier were likely other bankers, who quickly withdrew before the bank was in trouble.

Question: Presumably one concern with double liability is how much capital to require on-balance sheet and how much off-balance sheet. Was this requirement stable throughout the double liability period?

Prof. Wilson: Capital levels were relatively stable up to the 1930s, despite some large swings. Also, as stated in Macey and Miller (1992), the 51 percent collection rate on stockholder assessments was stable during this period, including the early 1930s. Therefore, capital levels both on and off balance sheet were stable.

Question: Were there restrictions on selling stock for less than par value during this period? For example, with a rights offer the stock might be sold at $50 when the par value was $100. Then, in effect, you would have triple liability; that is, you create $100 of off-balance-sheet liability for every $50 of capital contributed on-balance sheet. Second, are the capital ratios discussed above strictly on-balance sheet, and therefore do not reflect off-balance-sheet capital?

Prof. Wilson: Apparently, par value was limited to at least $100 per share, with adjustments made for stock splits.

Question: When you describe the advantages and drawbacks of double liability in terms of the difficulty in recapitalizing, it's as if we are describing small-scale rather than large-scale banking. Perhaps the transition from very small-scale to small-scale to large-scale banking in the United States affected the value of double versus limited liability. Our analysis has focused on bank capital structure decisions, particularly with the regime shift from double liability to deposit insurance. But you're right, we have not yet analyzed potential scale effects that may have been important during this period.

Question: If we compare your story with that of Canadian banks, I wonder how much trust there was in this off-balance-sheet capital. One test might be to look at today's finance companies, which have roughly the same level of capital without deposit insurance, perhaps indicating that uninsured institutions require 15 to 20 percent real capital. Also, it would be interesting to consider what's happening at Lloyds of London today. People are not happy when unlimited liability gets called. They may decide that they were defrauded by management. So its not always the case that you can easily get your hands on unlimited capital holders.

Prof. Wilson: That seems to have been part of the argument for phasing out double liability in 1933. Small-scale stockholders had been victimized by ''banksters.'' Also, contingent liability may work best in a developing country setting.

Question: You said before that double liability works better if wealth is verifiable, which gives the impression of a banking system by and for the rich. People talk a lot about convertible preferred stock and subordinated debt. How would they fit in?

Prof. Wilson: In the United States these instruments can supply only limited market discipline. Current regulation does not allow acceleration clauses. For example, if the instrument has a sinking fund and the bank misses a payment, the security holders have no recourse. The same is true for other types of restrictive covenants. The security holder cannot precipitate bankruptcy if a covenant is violated.

Question: Could you explain how unlimited liability is complimentary to double liability. Also, isn't this system primarily for very small banks, with double liability breaking down in a large banking system? Further, isn't there an efficiency cost with a system of a large number of small banks?

Prof. Wilson: In a hypothetical transition from unlimited liability to double liability to limited liability, it is still possible to maintain a level of contingent liability in terms of the closure rule enforced. For example, under the early closure rule mandated by FDICIA, banks could be closed at or below 2 percent book capital, implying that stockholders could suffer postclosure losses. Therefore, the level of contingent liability involves both the closure rule and the choice of how much liability can be on-balance sheet.

Question: One could possibly conclude that double liability performed better than the government-sponsored insurance system. But wouldn't you have to know how the role of banks has changed within capital markets to draw conclusions about double liability?

Prof. Wilson: Perhaps I can appeal at this point to the premise in finance that ownership decisions are independent of capital budgeting decisions.

CHAPTER 7

Universal banking and the financing of industrial development

Charles W. Calomiris

In this chapter I address three questions about universal banking. First, what is universal banking? Second, why might universal banking be an effective organizational structure for a banking system, particularly in a newly industrializing economy? Third, what is the evidence supporting or contradicting the view that universal banking reduces corporate financing costs for a newly industrializing economy?

I define *universal banking* as a banking system made up of large-scale banks that operate extensive networks of branches, provide many different services, hold several claims on firms (including equity and debt), and participate directly in the corporate governance of the firms that rely on the banks as sources of funding or as securities underwriters. That is an encompassing and therefore narrow definition of universal banking. But it suits my purposes. I will examine the pre–World War I universal banking system in Germany – which satisfies my narrow definition – and explore the synergies among the different elements in my definition.

To answer the question of whether universal banking reduces corporate financing costs, I will contrast the cost of financing industrialization in the United States and in Germany during the second industrial revolution (roughly 1870–1913). This period is important to examine for two reasons. First, the second industrial revolution involved large-scale production and distribution activities (emphasized by Chandler 1977), which brought a new challenge to financial markets – the rapid financing of very large minimum-efficient-scale industries. Because large-scale production is typical of modern industrial practice, I think that the lessons from the second industrial revolution are broadly applicable to contemporary developing countries.

Second, this industrial revolution involved many new products and new technologies, particularly in the machinery, electrical, and chemical industries. The novelty of these production processes posed severe information problems for external sources of finance. Firms producing electrical machinery, chemicals, and power plants were producing new goods in new ways on an unprecedented scale. The need for quick access to large quantities of external finance was accompanied by greater information and control costs because of the difficulty of evaluating proposed projects and controlling the use of funds.

I will argue that in the second industrial revolution, Germany enjoyed lower industrial finance costs than the United States. High finance costs in the United States reflected the absence of universal banking, prevented by regulatory limits placed on U.S. banks. These high costs retarded industrial growth in the United States relative to its potential and biased production processes away from fixed-capital-intensive industrialization toward a greater reliance on raw materials and labor (Calomiris 1995 contains a more detailed discussion).

Measuring the allocative efficiency of the financial system

I define the *allocative inefficiency* of capital markets as the shadow cost differential between firms' sources of internal funds (accumulated retained earnings) and firms' sources of external funds (loans from outsiders or stock flotations). That cost differential reflects information costs, as well as physical contracting costs, which make sources of external funds more costly than sources of internal funds. Calomiris and Himmelberg (1996) show that for constant marginal costs of external finance, this shadow cost appears as a linear "wedge" in the Euler condition relating the firm's marginal product of capital to the firm's cost of funds under full information.

This shadow cost is different from what is often termed the firm's "cost of capital," which is defined as the interest cost (for debt) or the sum of expected dividend payments and capital gains (for stock). Indeed, those costs (after adjusting for risk) must be equal to the firm's cost of internal funds – arbitrage ensures that (after controlling for differences in transaction costs, which permit markets to be segmented) expected rates of return are the same after controlling for market expectations of risk.

The shadow cost of external funds can be observed only when firms place securities in public markets. The sum of fees and expenses paid by the firm to place its securities relative to the net proceeds from the securities offering provides a measure of the shadow cost of external finance. Under the assumption of constant marginal cost, the shadow cost difference between internal and external funds will equal the ratio of the sum of the direct and indirect costs of the issue relative to the net proceeds of the issue (the gross proceeds less the direct and indirect costs). Direct costs refer to the fees and expenses paid by the firm to the underwriter and his or her agents. Indirect costs refer to other hidden costs (e.g., the predictable underpricing of an initial public offering or the adverse announcement effects of seasoned offerings on stock prices). Direct costs account for most of total issuing costs (for a more detailed discussion, see Calomiris and Himmelberg 1996).

Because underwriting costs provide a reasonable measure of the shadow cost difference between internal and external funds, and because that shadow

Table 7.1. *Investment banking costs in the United States before World War II (percentage of issue)*

	1925–29			1930s		
	Common	Preferred	Bonds	Common 1935–38	Preferred 1935–38	Bonds 1935–38
Issues < $5 million						
Total costs	Na.	8	6	18	10	5
Compensation	14–23	7	5	16	9	4
Other expenses	Na.	1	1	2	1	1
No. of issues	Na.	96	423	241	206	210
All to public, IBs[a]				*1938*	*1938*	*1940*
Total costs	Na.			22	12	
Compensation	9–23			20	11	2
Other expenses	Na.			2	1	1
No. of issues	Na.			68	37	76
All to public, IBs[a]						
Total cost, underw. issues				23 (16)	4 (9)	3 (31)
Total cost, best-efforts[b]				21 (52)	14 (28)	16 (1)

Note: Na. means not available.
[a] All issues of securities to the public transacted through investment bankers (IBs).
[b] Best-effort issues are placed by investment bankers without price guarantees.
Sources: Stock issue cost ranges for the 1920s are from Calomiris and Raff (1995: Table 4–9). All other data are from Calomiris (1995:296).

cost measures the difference between the actual marginal cost of investment and the full-information marginal cost of investment, underwriting costs are a useful measure of the allocational efficiency of capital markets. This measure is particularly useful in cross-country comparisons. Conventional measures of the firms' cost of capital – interest rates or expected returns to stockholders – can differ within or across countries because of geographic barriers or differences in risk or risk aversion, rather than because of differences in the allocative efficiency of financial systems. In contrast, the shadow cost differential between internal and external funds is a direct measure of capital market allocational efficiency across, as well as within, countries (once one has controlled for selectivity bias with respect to the sample of firms that choose to issue securities).

The main component of underwriting cost is the "spread" (or commission) earned by the investment bank. German equity underwriting costs were much lower than those in the United States during the second industrial revolution (Tables 7.1–7.3). These reported differences understate the true differences in the allocative efficiency of the two financial systems for two reasons. First, Calomiris and Raff (1995) argue that post–World War I costs in the United States were likely lower than pre–World War I costs, so the

Table 7.2. *Costs of flotation of primary common stock issues offered through dealers, post–World War II*

	Number of issues	Average cost (percentage of proceeds)
Issue < $5 million		
1935–38	241	18
1945–49	208	15
1951–55	178	15
1963–65	369	12
Issue > $5 million		
1940	11	12
1945–49	49	8
1951–55	52	6
1963–65	107	7

Source: Calomiris (1995:299).

measured differences between German and U.S. costs in Tables 7.1–7.3 are less than the differences measured during the pre–World War I period.

Second, selectivity bias also leads to understatement of the differences in the costs of bringing equity to market in the two countries. Firms in the United States were much less likely to issue common stock because most found the cost of issuance prohibitive. Thus, only well-seasoned firms (those with relatively low information and transaction costs) issued stock. From 1900 to 1913 the volume of net bond issues (net of retirements) in the United States was roughly the same as stock issues. During the same period in Germany gross bond issues (which are greater than net bond issues) were only half the volume of equity issues. Moreover, to the extent that equity was issued in the United States during this period, it was typically associated with corporate reorganization, rather than the financing of new capital investment. Looking at balance sheets of nonfinancial corporations in the two countries in 1912, bonds and notes accounted for more than half of the book value of corporate equity in the United States, but only 10 percent in Germany (Calomiris 1995: Table 5).

The data on commissions for common stock issues earned by German banks from 1893 to 1913 include all firms in the electrical industry (including manufacturers of electrical equipment and operating power plants) and a subset of firms in the metal manufacturing industry (Table 7.3). Both of these industries are important producers of new products, and both are central to the second industrial revolution.

The metal manufacturing industry includes many small firms, while the

Table 7.3. *Bankers' commissions (spreads) and total issuing costs for German common stock issues, 1893–1913 (percent)*

	Mean bank spread	25th Percentile bank spread (%)	75th Percentile bank spread (%)	Mean total cost (%)	25th Percentile total cost (%)	75th Percentile total cost (%)
All issues						
Electrical	3.67	2.57	4.55	5.08	3.61	7.00
No. of firms	13	—	—	12	—	—
No. of observations	21	—	—	20	—	—
Metal mfgr.	3.90	2.94	4.35	5.30	2.78	7.60
No. of firms	19	—	—	15	—	—
No. of observations	30	—	—	20	—	—
Issues < DM 1 mill.						
Electrical	3.94	3.49	4.26	5.24	4.00	6.72
No. of firms	4	—	—	3	—	—
No. of observations	7	—	—	3	—	—
Metal mfgr.	3.45	2.78	3.86	5.29	3.33	6.92
No. of firms	10	—	—	15	—	—
No. of observations	18	—	—	15	—	—
1913 capital < DM 2 mill.						
Metal mfgr.	4.11	3.57	4.80	5.93	3.33	8.80
No. of firms	3	—	—	5	—	—
No. of observations	6	—	—	5	—	—

Note: Dashes in the table mean not available. *Bankers' spreads* are defined as the difference between the amount paid for an issue by purchasers and the amount paid by the banker to the issuing firm divided by the total amount paid for the issue. Percent total costs are the net funds raised by the firm (net of all expenses, including taxes, printing costs, and commissions) divided by the amount paid for the issue. Data are for firms that reported such information in *Saling's Borsen Jahrbuch* (1913) in the electrical industry (electrical equipment producers and power plant operators) and the metal manufacturers industry.
The sample includes all reporting firms in the electrical industry and all reporting firms whose names begin with A through K for the metals manufacturing industry.
Source: Calomiris (1995:294).

electrical industry is dominated by large firms. Together these two industries can provide some evidence on the role of firm size and issue size in determining bankers' commissions. For both industries I report small issues (less than 1 million marks, which equals $220,000 in 1913 dollars). For metals I also report data for firms with small total capital in 1913 (less than 2 million marks). Bankers' commissions averaged 3.67 percent for the electrical industry and 3.90 percent for metal manufacturing. Commissions on small and large issues are essentially the same: although small manufacturers' issues show lower average costs, the difference is not statistically significant for this small sample. Metal manufacturing firms with low total capital had average commissions of 4.11 percent, compared with 3.90 percent for the industry as a whole. Again, this difference is small and not statistically significant.

These data support the view that German bank commissions on common stock were roughly 3 to 5 percent and that they did not vary much by industry, firm size, or size of issue. In sharp contrast to the United States, where small firms paid much higher commissions than large firms (Mendelson 1967; Hansen and Torregrossa 1992; Calomiris and Raff 1995), small German firms in high-growth, capital-intensive sectors were able to issue common stock at the same low cost as large issuers. Thus, German capital market efficiency may have been of particular benefit to small, rapidly growing firms in these sectors.

Explaining the United States–German cost difference

It is sometimes argued that the greater efficiency of U.S. securities markets compensated for the inefficiency of the U.S. banking system. The cost differences just described demonstrate the fallacy of that argument. Banks and securities markets rely on each other to operate efficiently in a universal banking system – like that of pre–World War I Germany.

In the German universal banking system, firms progressed through a "financial life cycle." They began their banking relationship by taking very short-term loans (often carried on the books of the bank as overdrafts) directly from banks. Once a firm's favorable prospects had become sufficiently clear to the bank, the bank would reduce the firm's reliance on debt and would underwrite stock issues. The bank would place those issues within the bank's network of trust customers. Subsequent offerings could be made frequently to those customers and typically took the form of rights offerings.

Bank underwriters retained control over the voting proxies associated with those stock issues in their role as trust account managers. The bank operated on both sides of the equity transactions – as underwriter, trust account purchaser, and proxy manager. Just as important, its involvement in the issuing firm predated and followed the underwriting transaction. That meant that the bank knew the firm's track record prior to floating its stock and remained actively involved in corporate governance by concentrating proxy voting power in the banker's hands.

In the United States this degree of continuity was lacking in firms' financial relationships. But the problem was deeper. Both commercial bank lending and investment bank underwriting were hampered by the fragmentation of the financial system, which made industrial lending and securities underwriting unnecessarily expensive.

Commercial banks were less involved in industrial lending in the United States than in Germany. The lack of involvement was a new development in the United States, particular to the second industrial revolution. Beginning in the 1870s, the money-center banks in the East that had been the main sources of industrial finance during the first wave of industrial growth (1800–50) changed their orientation toward financing commerce. As Lamoreaux (1994) documents, during the earlier industrialization New England bankers had allocated almost all of their funds to industrial firms owned and operated by bank "insiders" (managers and directors). By the end of the nineteenth century those banks had switched to financing the commercial needs of "outsiders" and had developed commercial lending departments and financial ratio analysis for evaluating these arm's-length loans.

Why did this change occur? Lamoreaux convincingly argues that the switch did not reflect, as is sometimes argued, ideological changes or new regulations associated with the "real bills doctrine." Rather, the change in bank orientation reflected the increasing mismatch between the needs of large, Chandlerian industrial firms and the resources of small, single-office ("unit") banks. As industrial firms in new industries developed into large-scale, nationwide producers and distributors, their loan demands rose, but bank regulations that restricted branching and consolidation kept banks small. Banks could not meet the needs of these industrial clients without imprudently concentrating their lending. Some banks tried to expand and lobbied for greater rights to merge and branch. Limited successes were met with large increases in bank profitability, but ultimately banks lost that regulatory battle.

Some scholars have suggested that the decline of bank involvement in industrial finance was not very costly because investment bankers and securities market financing filled the void left by commercial bankers. It is true that J. P. Morgan and his colleagues made important inroads in industrial finance – including the expansion and restructuring of whole industries – and were actively involved in corporate governance of the firms whose finances they arranged (often termed the "Morgan collar"). It is also true that secondary markets for equity transactions were well developed in the United States during this period.

Nevertheless, access to the new investment bankers' brand of "finance capitalism" and to securities markets was severely limited. Only the largest, most established firms (e.g., major railroads, utilities, and industrial trusts) participated in the new system, and they were typically limited to issuing investment-quality bonds or preferred stock. Common stock issuance to finance new industrial activity was virtually absent (Doyle 1991). As a result, even much later in U.S. history investment banking costs were extremely high compared with those in Germany.

Why was it so difficult for firms to gain access to the securities markets and to the equity market in particular? The cost of investment banking was itself largely determined by the structure of the unit banking system. By restricting the size and geographic network of individual banks, the United States not only limited the opportunities for banks to lend directly to industry, but also raised the cost of underwriting and placing securities.

Indeed, unit banking was the only substantial regulatory impediment to both investment banking and universal banking in the United States. Carrying out commercial bank operations and equity underwriting and investing within the same bank holding company was not prohibited in the United States until the Glass–Steagall restrictions of 1933 (which divorced commercial banking and underwriting) and the Bank Holding Company Act of 1956 (which prohibited bank holding companies from owning equity in nonfinancial firms). But long before these acts, universal banking was effectively prohibited by unit banking.

To understand how unit banking prevented the development of universal banking and raised the costs of investment banking, it is useful to review the operation of the German universal banking system and to consider the sources of synergy between nationwide branch banking and underwriting. Commercial banking and underwriting are less costly when done together. It follows that unit banking's restrictions on the geographic scope and size of bank operations also prevented the development of an efficient system of underwriting, placing, and managing equity issues.

The synergies between commercial banking and underwriting can be divided into three categories: economies of information and control, "brick and mortar" network cost savings, and diversification benefits that reduce intermediaries' costs of funds. In each of these categories limitations on bank branching and consolidation undermine the links between investment banking and commercial banking and lead to higher costs for both activities.

Economies of information and control refer to reductions in the costs of gathering information and controlling management that arise in a universal banking system. For example, a bank that acts as a stockholder of a firm (or as a junior "stakeholder" through its fiduciary capacity as a trust account manager of stock) may be able to lend to the firm at lower cost, either because it already knows a lot about the firm or because its powers as a stockholder permit it to protect its interests as a creditor. Furthermore, if the firm experiences financial distress, the fact that the banker controls the firm's stock can reduce potential conflicts of interest between stockholders and creditors in developing a reorganization plan.

Much of the research on the benefits of allowing banks to combine equity and debt finance has emphasized these advantages. Similar benefits from allowing banks to own or control shares appear in studies of contemporary Germany and Japan and before the Glass–Steagall Act in the United States. That research has shown that close multidimensional relationships between banks and firms can reduce the costs of obtaining funds for firms, improve firm performance, make investment decisions less dependent on retained earnings, and make it easier for firms to resolve financial distress. In their study of banking relationships before and after the Glass–Steagall Act, De Long and Ramirez (1995) found that the value of the banking relationship for the firm was substantially reduced when the relationship narrowed to lending alone.[1]

Information and control advantages may also occur in a dynamic context. During their financial life cycles, corporations often progress from reliance on bank loans to the public issuance of common stock. Under universal banking of the German type, the same intermediary can hold the debt of the firm in the early stage of the life cycle, later underwrite shares of the firm, and then control voting proxies for the purchasers of those shares. Empirical evidence suggests that there are information cost advantages to having the same intermediary guide the firm through its life cycle in this way (Slovin, Sushka, and Polonchek 1992; Petersen and Rajan 1994). If the firm's financial service needs change over time, it is economical to give intermediaries the flexibility to provide different services and hold various types of claims on the firm.

Brick and mortar network cost savings are those that arise if the same delivery network provides a variety of financial services. This form of savings was very important for reducing corporate finance costs historically. Restrictions on bank networks in the United States made it impossible for banks to operate effectively as universal banks. Using the same branches to provide trust services, place securities in portfolios, lend, and accept deposits allows brick and mortar costs to be spread across many activities. The cost of providing each service is lower when they are combined within the same intermediary.

A key element of universal banking in the German case – which enabled information cost savings and brick and mortar cost savings from marketing securities – was the bank's involvement on both sides of the securities transactions it oversaw. The bank was an underwriter, a broker, and a trustee of the securities it placed. The bank thus retained an "equity stake" in the corporations whose shares were placed, which gave the bank an incentive to price issues fairly and to use its voting power properly. The bank retained an equity stake in underwritten issues because if firms' shares fared badly, the bank could lose trust customers (and future underwriting business) to its competitors. The cost savings of German universal banking could not have been accomplished if the banks had been required to separate dealing, brokering, and trust activities on individual securities transactions.

Universal banking can promote bank diversification because the income from different financial services are not perfectly correlated. Diversification reduces banks' costs of funds, which thereby reduces the costs banks charge their lending and underwriting customers. White (1986) and Brewer (1989) have argued that the benefits of bank diversification can be substantial, based on evidence of limited universal banking in the United States (both histori-

---

[1] Additional studies in the same spirit include Hoshi, Kashyap, and Scharfstein (1990, 1991), Ramirez (1995), De Long (1991), and Gorton and Schmidt (1996).

Table 7.4. *Nonagricultural growth in Germany and the United States*

	Germany		United States	
	Nonag. NNP (mill. marks 1913 prices)	Nonag. labor (thousands)	Nonag. value added ($ mill., 1879 prices)	Nonag. net income ($ mill., 1869 prices)	Nonag. labor ($ thous.)
1849			670		
1850	5,052				
1869			1,550	5,325	6,193
1870	8,431				
1871		8,796			
1889				7,543	12,540
1890	15,857	12,807			
1910–13				16,519	20,871
1913	37,210	20,267			

Note: NNP – net national product.
Source: Calomiris (1995:279).

cally and currently). Universal banking promotes diversification because the incomes from the variety of services that banks offer are not highly correlated.

Effects of the high cost of external finance in the United States

Did the high cost of external finance affect U.S. industrialization? It affected industrialization in at least three areas: the mix of inputs chosen in production, the ability to reap scale economies, and the ability to expand quickly, particularly in international markets.

Recent work on the economics of financing constraints (Carpenter, Fazzari, and Petersen 1994; Calomiris, Himmelberg, and Wachtel 1995; Calomiris and Himmelberg 1996) has emphasized that high financing costs encourage firms to substitute material and labor inputs for fixed capital inefficiently. Industrial buildings and equipment are less desirable inputs than materials and accounts receivable for a financially constrained firm because they are less liquid.

Evidence on the composition of tangible capital in pre–World War I Germany and the United States is consistent with the idea that low costs of industrial finance are reflected in input choices. Compared with Germany, the United States relied more on labor and materials than on hard-to-finance equipment. U.S. nonagricultural growth was more labor-intensive and less fixed-capital-intensive than that of Germany (Table 7.4). During the late nineteenth century U.S. nonagricultural producers increased output and labor

Table 7.5. *Components of tangible reproducible assets (percent)*

	Germany (1913)	United States (1912)
Dwellings	25	24
Other structures	31	35
Equipment	26	13
Inventories	10	10
Livestock	5	5
Consumer durables	3	13

Source: Goldsmith (1985:111).

at the same rate, but in Germany nonagricultural output rose twice as fast as labor input. Also, the U.S. inventory–fixed-capital ratio was much higher than that of Germany during this period (Table 7.5).

The potential for expanding quickly and reaping economies of scale was greater in German industrialization. Particularly in the electrical industry, Germany expanded rapidly and took advantage of scale and network economies in constructing its electrical utility industry, while U.S. industry developed inefficiently, as a patchwork quilt (Carlson 1991). Germany exported electrical equipment and set up utilities abroad, while the United States lagged behind.

U.S. institutional progress after World War I

Progress in reducing the cost of industrial finance in the United States coincided with institutional changes that increased the concentration of financial market transactions. The first changes occurred in the 1920s. In the face of extreme bank distress, many states relaxed branching and consolidation restrictions, and an unprecedented bank consolidation wave ensued (Calomiris 1993). As the preceding discussion would lead one to expect, this consolidation saw banks taking an increased role in industrial lending – the origins of bank securities underwriting through affiliates – and the rapid growth of bank involvement in trust management. There was also an unprecedented increase in the number of U.S. firms participating in the market for new equity issues in the late 1920s. These progressive trends were halted by regulatory intervention during the Great Depression, based on the (now-discredited) view that speculative behavior by large banks, and particularly their involvement in securities markets, had precipitated the depression (Calomiris and White 1994).

Subsequent institutional innovations outside and inside the banking system helped to reduce corporate finance costs (Calomiris and Raff 1995). Beginning in the 1930s, life insurance companies became involved in financing corporations by purchasing privately placed debt (in essence a concentrated, nonpublic issue of a bond). Private placements accounted for roughly half of all securities issues during the 1940s and 1950s.

In the 1960s, as private pensions and mutual funds developed, they took on an important role as concentrated purchasers of new public offerings of stock. Mendelson (1967) and Calomiris and Raff (1995) argue that the involvement of these institutional investors substantially reduced the cost of bringing equities to market in the United States.

Beginning in the 1970s, regulations guiding bank holding companies were relaxed, and the laws governing pension fund investments were changed, enabling a new partnership to form between banks and institutional investors in the form of venture capital affiliates of commercial banks. Venture capital investments by bank affiliates financed themselves largely through institutional investors' equity stakes in the fund. Often, institutional investors are involved in holding stakes in venture capital investments in firms and then continue their involvement as purchasers of equity once firms go public.

In the 1980s, in response to severe banking distress throughout the country, federal and state laws restricting bank consolidation were relaxed, prompting a second wave of bank consolidation. In the late 1980s the Federal Reserve Board (acting out of concern for the competitive viability of U.S. banks and with the approval of the courts) began to relax restrictions on the underwriting of corporate debt and equity by bank holding company affiliates or subsidiaries. Currently, legislation is pending in Congress that would repeal the Glass–Steagall Act's separation between commercial and investment banking.

All of these institutional innovations have helped to concentrate corporate lending, stock ownership, and underwriting, thereby allowing the advantages of "relationship banking," the concentration of financial claims, and the synergies of universal banking to be realized. A combination of macroeconomic distress, international competitive pressure, and the creative invention of new intermediaries has helped the U.S. financial system to overcome the regulatory mandate of financial fragmentation in recent decades. The lesson for developing countries seeking to design their financial systems seems clear: avoid the lengthy and costly detour of U.S. financial fragmentation.

REFERENCES

Brewer, E. 1989. "Relationship between Bank Holding Company Risk and Nonbank Activity." *Journal of Economics and Business* 41 (November):337–53.
Calomiris, C. W. 1993. "Regulation, Industrial Structure, and Instability in U.S. Banking: An Historical Perspective." In M. Klausner and L. J. White, eds., *Structural Change in Banking*. New York: Business One-Irwin, pp. 19–115.
    1995. "The Costs of Rejecting Universal Banking: American Finance in the German Mirror, 1870–1914." In N. Lamoreaux and D. M. G. Raff, eds., *The*

Coordination of Activity within and between Firms. Chicago: University of Chicago Press, pp. 38–71.

Calomiris, C. W., and C. P. Himmelberg. 1996. "Investment Banking Spreads as a Measure of the Cost of Access to External Finance." Working Paper, Department of Finance, University of Illinois, Urbana.

Calomiris, C. W., C. P. Himmelberg, and P. Wachtel. 1995. "Commercial Paper, Corporate Finance, and the Business Cycle: A Microeconomic Perspective." Working Paper no. 4848, National Bureau of Economic Research, Cambridge, Mass.

Calomiris, C. W., and D. M. G. Raff. 1995. "The Evolution of Market Structure, Information, and Spreads in American Investment Banking." In M. Bordo and R. Sylla, eds., *Anglo-American Finance.* Cambridge University Press, pp. 103–60.

Calomiris, C. W., and E. N. White. 1994. "The Origins of Federal Deposit Insurance." In C. Goldin and G. Libecap, eds., *The Regulated Economy: A Historical Approach to Political Economy.* Chicago: University of Chicago Press, pp. 8–73.

Carlson, W. B. 1991. *Innovation as a Social Process: Elihu Thomson and the Rise of General Electric, 1870–1900.* Cambridge University Press.

Carpenter, R. E., S. M. Fazzari, and B. C. Petersen. 1994. "Inventory Investment, Internal-Finance Fluctuations, and the Business Cycle." *Brookings Papers on Economic Activity* 2:75–138.

Chandler, A. D. 1977. *The Visible Hand: The Managerial Revolution in American Business.* Cambridge, Mass.: Harvard University Press.

De Long, J. B. 1991. "Did J. P. Morgan's Men Add Value? An Economist's Perspective on Financial Capitalism." In P. Temin, ed., *Inside the Business Enterprise: Historical Perspectives on the Use of Information.* Chicago: University of Chicago Press, pp. 1–45.

De Long, J. B., and C. D. Ramirez. 1995. "Banker Influence and Business Economic Performance: Assessing the Impact of Depression-Era Financial Market Reforms." Working Paper, Department of Economics, George Mason University, Fairfax, Va.

Doyle, W. M. 1991. "The Evolution of Financial Practices and Financial Structures among American Manufacturers, 1875–1905: Case Studies of the Sugar Refining and Meat Packing Industries." Unpublished Ph.D. Dissertation, Department of Economics, University of Tennessee, Knoxville.

Goldsmith, R. W. 1985. *Comparative National Balance Sheets: A Study of Twenty Countries, 1688–1978.* Chicago: University of Chicago Press.

Gorton, G., and F. A. Schmidt. 1996. "Universal Banking and the Performance of German Firms." Working Paper, University of Pennsylvania, Philadelphia.

Hansen, R. S., and P. Torregrossa. 1992. "Underwriter Compensation and Corporate Monitoring." *Journal of Finance* 47 (September):1537–55.

Hoshi, T., A. Kashyap, and D. Scharfstein. 1990. "The Role of Banks in Reducing the Costs of Financial Distress." *Journal of Financial Economics* 27 (September):67–88.

1991. "Corporate Structure, Liquidity, and Investment: Evidence from Japanese Industrial Groups." *Quarterly Journal of Economics* 106:33–60.

Lamoreaux, N. 1994. *Insider Lending: Banks, Personal Connections, and Economic Development in Industrial New England, 1784–1912.* Cambridge University Press.

Mendelson, M. 1967. "Underwriting Compensation." In I. Friend, J. R. Longstreet, M. Mendelson, E. Miller, and A. P. Hess, Jr., eds., *Investment Banking and the New Issues Market.* New York: World Publishing, pp. 198–227.

126   Charles W. Calomiris

Petersen, M., and R. Rajan. 1994. "The Benefits of Lending Relationships: Evidence from Small Business Data." *Journal of Finance* 49 (March):3–37.

Ramirez, C. D. 1995. "Did J. P. Morgan's Men Add Liquidity? Cash Flow, Corporate Finance and Investment at the Turn of the Twentieth Century." *Journal of Finance* 50 (2):661–78.

Slovin, M. B., M. E. Sushka, and J. A. Polonchek. 1992. "The Value of Bank Durability: Borrowers as Bank Stakeholders." *Journal of Finance* 48 (March): 247–66.

White, E. N. 1986. "Before the Glass–Steagall Act: An Analysis of the Investment Banking Activities of National Banks." *Explorations in Economic History* 23 (January):33–55.

DISCUSSION

Question: One issue that has come up a lot is the problem of unit banking in the United States. Has any other country made the same mistake, or is it a unique problem?

Prof. Calomiris: The answer is pretty much no. But from what I've heard recently, some of the emerging capitalist economies are stuck with a fragmented banking system. Japan is something of an exception. Japan imported U.S. banking theory but then rapidly realized its mistake and switched its model.

Question: When you compare the United States and Germany, two variables change at once. Conceptually, it would be nice to first vary the unit banking regulations and then vary all of the universal banking regulations. In relaxing the unit banking restrictions, two obvious candidates for comparison with the United States are Canada and the United Kingdom. Would we see a dramatic difference in financing patterns or in the efficiency of securities markets?

Prof. Calomiris: You noticed that I completely avoided any discussion of the United Kingdom. Determining whether banks in the United Kingdom suffered from "entrepreneurial failure" has been contentious. I avoided the United Kingdom because I thought that the distinction between it and the United States was not as clean as that between the United States and Germany and because industrialization in the United Kingdom was not as rapid.

Question: But you could compare the United States with Canada, which had comparable economic growth though it may have been more resource oriented. Or you could have made comparisons within the United States. Your analysis would suggest, for example, that financial markets in California should be much more efficient that financial markets in Chicago because California – which was as large then as some European nations – had an internal financial market that was unrestricted. Do you have any ideas about this? Is more research needed?

Prof. Calomiris: That's a good question. California had achieved large-scale banking only in the 1920s; it was only four or five years ahead of the general merger and branching wave.

Comment: I thought California relaxed restrictions on branching in 1900.

Prof. Calomiris: Despite allowing branching by law, California left it to the discretion of the superintendent of banking to approve a bank's application to establish branches. The superintendent made that determination based on the recommendation of the banks in the area where the branch would be located. Prior to 1916, that meant that Bank of America could not branch outside of San Francisco. Only after an agricultural depression hit California did things change. The unit bankers who had blocked Giannini invited him in. That action set a precedent, which became difficult to stop elsewhere. Distress is the best news for branch banking.

Question: You claim that we should not advocate unit banking for developing countries. Does that mean we should be advocating the German universal model? Or given that these models seem to be converging, is there a hybrid that makes the most sense for developing countries?

Prof. Calomiris: The United States system is becoming, de facto, a universal banking system. If you talk to people in the business, they'll tell you that relationship banking requires combined powers and large-scale operation. For example, Continental wanted Bank of America's delivery network and Bank of America wanted Continental's customer relationships. That, in large part, explains the merger of those two banks.

Question: You have demonstrated the superiority of the universal banking system until the second industrial revolution, but the story does not necessarily extrapolate to modern times. Today, universal banks fund few new firms; they deal only with those that have been on the stock market. What changes in the system would you identify as being most important for ensuring that banks remain or become very dynamic forces?

Prof. Calomiris: I have thought about this question before. It is true, by the way, that German nonfinancial firms have been issuing very little equity in the post–World War II period. Does that mean that universal banking has lost its way and that it functions differently in an industrial economy than in a developing economy? I don't know.

CHAPTER 8

Before main banks: A selective historical overview of Japan's prewar financial system

Frank Packer

The postwar experience of the Japanese banking system and its relevance to developing and transition economies has been receiving considerable attention recently.[1] This research has been motivated in part by the fact that the conditions in the defeated Japan of 1945 were similar to those in transition economies today, conditions such as high inflation and the need to switch from military to civilian production.

At the same time many of the postwar conditions in Japan were different from those faced by transition economies today. Before World War II, Japan had spent more than sixty years experimenting with and developing modern financial institutions. This chapter relates some highlights of that history, concentrating on the banks that sprang up from the large industrial conglomerates – *zaibatsu*.

How did the *zaibatsu* banks, the predecessors of the main banks of the postwar era, perform? They performed very well relative to their competitors and much differently relative to their postwar successors. Looking at the prewar setting also permits an exploration of banking stability. While the postwar Japanese system was free of major bank failures until 1995, the prewar banking system experienced numerous banking panics and failures, even among *zaibatsu* banks.

The main bank system and important supplements

Theoretically, the main bank system refers to a network of bank–firm relationships in which most large firms have a main bank. The main bank can

The author wishes to thank participants of the conference, two anonymous reviewers, and the volume editors for many useful comments. The author is particularly indebted to Hugh Patrick's broad perspective on Japanese financial history, as well as comments concerning this chapter. The views expressed represent those of the author and not the Federal Reserve Bank of New York or the Federal Reserve System.

[1] On the Japanese main bank system, see, e.g., Aoki and Patrick (1994), in particular the chapters by Aoki, Patrick, and Sheard and by Patrick.

be identified by three principal qualities. Typically, it is the largest lender to a particular client, making between 15 and 25 percent of the loans to that client, possibly more to many small companies. It holds a substantial block of shares in the client company and is always the largest bank shareholder, although it is often not the largest client company shareholder (because of ceiling regulations of 5 or 10 percent). And bank officers are commonly represented in the management of its bank's clients, particularly during times of financial distress.

Proponents of the main bank system point to its strengths, such as the active role taken in disciplining management, reduced costs of reorganizing and restructuring firms in financial distress and thus reduced loan premiums, and lower agency costs of external finance (Aoki, Patrick, and Sheard 1994). Even the nonexclusivity features, some of which are guided by external regulations and can be motivated by managerial risk aversion, can be positive.[2] If firms borrow from several banks, they can discourage opportunism on the part of the main bank. Also, other banks become an integral part of the main bank system by monitoring the main bank.

Important additions to this theoretical construct have been made, some of which were needed for the system to function effectively. For example, the postwar Japanese development banks were critically important, especially if long-term-credit banks are considered to be development banks. Development banks provided a much larger percentage of long-term finance than did the former *zaibatsu* banks in postwar Japan, allowing the *zaibatsu* banks to lower their burden of maturity transformation. During the high-growth era, long-term credit banks provided more than 50 percent of the loans for plant and equipment investment in 1956 for many key industries. In 1966 they still provided 36 percent of all plant and equipment loans (Packer 1994b).[3] Development banks did not play as important a role in the prewar financial system of Japan.

The banks also had to be concentrated and profitable. Often in a main bank system a main bank takes over some of the bad loans of other banks, loans that can be modeled as part of a dynamic equilibrium. But if the sector is not profitable, in particular if a main bank is not profitable, then it is not likely to be able to fulfill this function for large quantities of nonperforming

---

[2] One common regulation among many financial systems limits the exposure that any one financial institution can have to one borrower. In the United States, according to the 1982 Banking Act, national banks can lend no more than 15 percent of their capital to any single borrower on unsecured (marketable securities) loans. In Japan, according to the thirteenth clause of the Revised Banking Act of 1980, city, trust, and long-term credit banks are allowed to lend no more than 20, 30, and 40 percent of their capital, respectively, to any one company.

[3] The literature on the role of development banks in Japan's postwar era is growing. Calomiris and Himmelberg (1995), Horiuchi and Sui (1993), and Vittas and Kawaura (1994) cover the role of the Japan Development Bank; Packer (1994b) covers the long-term-credit banks.

loans. This inability is what many notice around the edges of the Japanese main bank system today (see Packer 1994a).

The system must also be able to credibly threaten businesses that fail with penalties; otherwise it runs the risk of offering soft budget constraints. The incentives for Japanese firms to cooperate with their banks in times of distress are increased by the fact that, if they go bankrupt, the managers will be fired, and the shareholders will not be compensated.

Zaibatsu and *zaibatsu* banks

Morikawa (1992) has defined *zaibatsu* as "a group of diversified businesses owned exclusively by a single family or extended family" (p. xvii).[4] In the late nineteenth century, during the early stages of industrialization, the *zaibatsu* did not dominate leading growth areas such as electric power and cotton spinning. And although *zaibatsu* did reorganize as more loosely knit networks (*keiretsu*) after the dissolution of the holding companies (during the U.S. occupation), today they are very different institutions (Hadley 1970). Nonetheless, many of the names of the early *zaibatsu* are still familiar today. According to Morikawa (1992) most of the principal *zaibatsu* were originally political merchants – either financiers handling tax revenues or enterprises selling other goods to the government. In the preindustrial era, Mitsui, the second oldest of the major *zaibatsu*, collected tax revenues from the economic zone around Osaka for the government located in what is now Tokyo. Rather than transport the cash directly to the government, they purchased promissory notes that merchants in Tokyo had written for purchases of Osaka goods. They then took these notes to Tokyo, collected from local merchants, and reimbursed the government. Yasuda was also in the exchange business, although it is a *zaibatsu* that was founded much later. *Zaibatsu* that were originally political merchants sold other goods to the government, such as military goods. Mitsubishi, for example, provided shipping services for the government and was granted a monopoly. Other *zaibatsu* had their origins as mining companies, such as the oldest, Sumitomo.

Although some of the *zaibatsu* were established after the industrialization and modernization of the late nineteenth century, all of the banks were founded by the early Meiji era. The *zaibatsu* that had begun as financiers – Mitsui and Yasuda – were the first to start banks in 1876 and 1880, respectively. They were followed by Mitsubishi and Sumitomo in 1895. These four private banks served as the major *zaibatsu* banks through the World War II era. Although national banks (eliminated in 1899) were unique in their right of note issue, the most economically meaningful distinction in terms of ac-

---

[4] The following discussion of the role and evolution of *zaibatsu* banks draws heavily on Morikawa (1992), particularly chapter 4.

tivity is to be made between the large banks and small banks of the era (Patrick 1972).[5] Many *zaibatsu* failed, particularly if they fell out of favor with the early Meiji government. The successful *zaibatsu* were those that became less dependent on government patronage over time. Many made deliberate efforts to transfer out of the traditional businesses that depended on government patronage. Relatively early in the Meiji era, Mitsui closed its bank branches that accommodated the government and eliminated many bad debts that were actually kickbacks to the government. Mitsubishi, after making a fortune from its shipping monopoly, downsized this business substantially after the government began to intervene. Yasuda, like Mitsui, also reduced its government deposits. The success of the *zaibatsu* was not dependent on large-scale privatization efforts: several *zaibatsu* that bought government properties failed and several succeeded.

The four major *zaibatsu* banks grew very rapidly, mirroring the growth of the *zaibatsu*. A few important aspects of their evolution should be mentioned. At the turn of the century Mitsui underwent a transition from an industrial to a commercial bank. At first, Mitsui Bank had lent principally to companies of its own *zaibatsu*: more than 80 percent of its long-term loans were extended to Mitsui members. When a large proportion of these funds became uncollectible and this knowledge became public (in the late nineteenth century), deposits fell considerably. During a transition in leadership, a decision was made to greatly reduce the long-term loans disbursed to companies in their own group, and reported profits rose considerably.

In the four biggest banks, efforts were made to reduce loan–deposit ratios as well as dependence on Bank of Japan credits. By the turn of the century Mitsui and Sumitomo were borrowing virtually nothing from the Bank of Japan. In all four banks, profits grew considerably, while loans as a percentage of deposits declined.

Limiting lending to related customers came to be considered a natural, prudential policy. In 1890 the government passed a law limiting lending to related firms to 10 percent of capital. This law was repealed in 1895, principally because the banking industry protested vigorously. But at the same time the major *zaibatsu* banks developed their own lending policies much along the same lines.

Mitsui Bank was a prime example. It issued a representative public statement in 1904 to the effect that it was extremely unsound and improper for

---

[5] Late-nineteenth- and early-twentieth-century banking consisted mainly of small, unit banks, reaching a peak of more than 2,300 banks in 1901. Banking law did not set any minimum bank size and entry was easy. Many of these were known as "organ banks" since they lent to their industrialist owners. The share of the big *zaibatsu* was not extremely large – along with First National, they constituted 17 percent of bank loans and deposits in 1910 – but increased dramatically in the first half of the twentieth century (Patrick 1967, 1984; Teranishi 1977).

Mitsui to invest in its own enterprises' funds received on deposit from others. The bank increased investment in and loans to electric power companies, railways, and local government operations that were outside of its group. By the early 1920s it was lending to only two of the nine major affiliates of the Mitsui group. A very small percentage of the liabilities of Mitsui *zaibatsu* companies came from borrowing, and an even smaller percentage of these consisted of borrowing from the Mitsui Bank. In the Mitsubishi *zaibatsu* only Mitsubishi Trading Company borrowed from the bank, and corporate bonds were underwritten for only two of its subsidiaries. Sumitomo also set limits on internal lending.

Clearly, the major *zaibatsu* banks were making a deliberate effort not to be viewed as organ banks. Because this was an era where many banks failed, it was very important to develop the reputation for having a good set of internal prudential guidelines that governed lending behavior. In the late nineteenth century Mitsui had seen that a reputation for having nonperforming loans could lead to a decrease in deposits. Some of the troubled banks in Japan today may have wished that they had adopted in the 1980s some of the policies of the early twentieth century.

By 1932 loans were a fairly small percentage of large Japanese firms' finance. Most of the finance of the companies of the big *zaibatsu* was internal (Patrick 1979; Hoshi 1993, 1995). This low percentage was partly the result of the policy shifts undertaken by Japanese banks in the early twentieth century to limit the growth of internal loans from *zaibatsu* banks. Of course, during the war and then in the postwar era, things looked very different. But Japan's prewar banking experience may carry its own set of lessons for transition economies.

The "hard" Japanese bankruptcy system and its historical origins

The origins of the hard bankruptcy system can also be found during Japan's early industrialization. By "hard," we mean a system whereby bankruptcy court procedures offer relatively little protection to managers and shareholders when a firm becomes insolvent. This system would later influence the evolution of the main bank system. Active bank governance during times of financial distress is encouraged by a hard bankruptcy system.[6] The fewer alternatives the firm has (to its bank), the more likely it is to depend on its bank, and the greater latitude the bank has to impose its own solution to financial distress.

Application to bankruptcy court in postwar Japan is discouraged by the large up-front deposit payments required from the applicant. And even if the

---

[6] One recent approach to creating a hard budget constraint in Hungary has been the creation of a hard bankruptcy law (Caprio 1994).

debtor can come up with the money, judges refuse to hear a large majority of the cases that come before them. They often refuse the bankruptcy application and refuse to issue a stay of creditor claims. Further, management and shareholders are punished severely. Management is usually fired, and shareholders are not compensated (Packer and Ryser 1993).

Another distinguishing characteristic of the Japanese bankruptcy system is that more than 90 percent of bankruptcies fall under the category "suspension of bank transactions." If a clearinghouse twice issues a notice of bills unpaid within a six-month period, all banks must suspend loans and current account transactions with the guilty party for two years. Because Japanese companies are so dependent on promissory notes to conduct transactions, suspending loans and current account transactions is the equivalent of capital punishment for the firm – it cannot survive if bank transactions are suspended. For this reason it is considered to be a category of bankruptcy by Japan's mercantile credit rating agencies.

The suspension mechanism originated early in Japanese industrialization (Ryser 1993). The Tokyo clearinghouse was established in 1891 by eleven banks, and its purpose was to net bills and checks from companies across banks.[7] Generally, the bills and checks presented to the clearinghouse would represent claims on the firm, which could be drawn from a current account at its transaction bank about six months after issue. Even today, most small and medium-size Japanese companies are financed largely by trade credit through the issuance of promissory notes of this sort. It is not uncommon for Japanese companies to be receiving more than six months' credit on suppliers' goods and services.

After the establishment of the clearinghouse, banks could submit promissory notes to the clearinghouse, which would net the claims and debts, allowing each bank to settle from its account at the Bank of Japan.

The historical record shows that the punishment for dishonored bills – when a firm did not have enough money in its account at the transaction bank to cover the obligation – gradually increased during the Tokyo clearinghouse's first ten years. In 1894 if a dishonored note was reported to the clearinghouse, a firm was suspended until a single bank asked for its release. In 1898 the rule was changed to require a majority of the members of the clearinghouse to request the release. Two years later the clearinghouse began fining members that had extended a loan to or otherwise dealt with suspended parties.

What followed in 1901 appears, in retrospect, to have been the most important of the new rules – mandated public disclosure of the suspension. Disclosure helped to make suspension a harsh punishment: not only member banks, but all other creditors, including trade creditors that might otherwise

---

[7] Osaka established a similar sort of clearinghouse earlier – in 1879 – but reorganized it following the Tokyo model in 1896.

accept future promissory notes, would know about the deterioration of the firm's finances. In 1904 repeat offenders were forced to wait two years before being able to appeal the suspension.

Suspension and dishonor rates dropped dramatically in response to these changes in regime. Defaulted bills as a percentage of total bills cleared dropped from 0.3 to 0.1 percent following the decision to disclose suspension publicly and dropped to .05 percent in 1904. Meanwhile, the values of cleared bills multiplied, and the use of promissory notes as a means of payment in Japan took off. Mayer (1990) provides evidence for the traditionally high reliance of Japanese companies on trade credit relative to Europe and the United States.

The interwar banking system and financial stability

The interwar era was a time in which several natural and financial shocks hit the financial system. Most notably, the great Kanto earthquake struck in 1923, killing 140,000 people and causing property losses estimated to be 30 to 40 percent of GNP. The earthquake immediately created a class of debt that couldn't be paid back. This debt overhang destabilized the entire banking sector until drastic reform and consolidation measures were taken in the late 1920s. Although bank panics occurred throughout the early twentieth century, the frequency and severity increased with the 1920s and culminated in the grand banking panic of 1927, which helped to stimulate a new banking act. Finally, there was an ill-timed return to the gold standard in 1930, which was highly deflationary.

But even during this era of financial volatility, the stock of private financial assets as a proportion of GNP increased dramatically – from around 100 percent in 1918 to about 250 percent in 1933 (Teranishi 1990). Time deposits in particular increased. Achieving a similar level of financial deepening after the postwar hyperinflation took more than twenty-five years. Financial deepening amid instability was achieved because alternative safe havens were available: the established *zaibatsu* banks and the postal savings system.

Also during the interwar era, differences between the first- and second-tier *zaibatsu* became more apparent. The large *zaibatsu* were very conservative during the boom of World War I, and they benefited from their conservatism in the unstable 1920s (Morikawa 1992). While firms of the large *zaibatsu* increased their use of bond and equity markets and the established banks increased their underwriting activities, many of the newer *zaibatsu* formed banks and achieved high wartime growth. But this growth was highly leveraged by loans from their related banks. The *zaibatsu* of Furukawa, Kawasaki, and Suzuki all ran into trouble in the 1920s because of their over-leveraged position; some of the banks of the newer *zaibatsu*, such as Asano and Fujita, failed.

The established *zaibatsu* banks increased their market share of deposits, as these banks were perceived to be secure. Their loan–deposit ratios were lower and capital–deposit ratios higher than those of most other banks, and they expanded their underwriting and securities business. They increased their corporate bond holdings more rapidly than their loans. The conservatism of *zaibatsu* banks was shown by the striking increase in bond issues and the transformation of the capital structure of large corporations (Hoshi 1993).

The 1927 banking crisis led to substantial reform. Although there had been many banking panics before 1927, in most of these the Bank of Japan had stepped in and provided emergency funding.[8] This funding was extensive during the panic of 1920. Further, the Bank of Japan had provided a large amount of special loans to banks in the wake of the great Kanto earthquake. Teranishi (1990) claims that providing rescue credits greatly increased the Bank of Japan's risk taking before the 1927 crisis, thus increasing the ultimate bill. The cost of rescuing or handling the failed banks in 1927 is estimated to have been 5 percent of GNP.

Which banks failed during the 1927 crisis? Part of the folklore of the 1927 banking crisis held that it was triggered by irrational runs that had little to do with the underlying solvency of the financial institutions. Amid a debate about bad earthquake bills, the minister of finance set off a run on one Tokyo bank early in 1927 when he testified before the Diet that the bank had failed. But the bank was still honoring bills. Runs on eleven other banks followed shortly thereafter. A few months later another crisis was triggered by a Diet debate on the same topic – twenty-one banks failed.[9] But Yabushita and Inoue (1993) have shown that the occurrence of bank runs was hardly random: proxies of solvency – such as dependence on the call market, the capital–deposit ratio, or the profit–capital ratio – were all negatively related to the probability of closing. Further, Teranishi (1990) showed that most of the banks that failed in 1927 had high debt exposure to related firms.

Banking reform, which had been in the works for awhile, was greatly accelerated by the 1927 banking crisis. A new banking law was passed soon after and came into effect in January 1928. The minimum capital requirement was increased from 1 to 2 million yen for ordinary banks in Osaka and Tokyo. Banks were also required to become joint-stock companies. Under these new requirements at least half of all banks were no longer eligible to function (Yabushita and Inoue 1993). There was also a move toward tougher collateral requirements in money markets.

[8] Yabushita and Inoue (1993) identify eighteen banking crises between the 1890s and 1927. At least eight appear to meet the Calomiris and Gorton (1991) definition of a "bank panic" – they involved a large number of banks in a brief period and resulted in the suspension of convertibility, government relief measures, or both.

[9] The Bank of Taiwan, tied to the Suzuki *zaibatsu*, failed when large city banks cut off loans to it in the call market.

After the 1927 reform, the number of banks decreased dramatically – from about 1,400 at the end of 1927, to 600 in 1933, and 357 in 1940.[10] The trend toward concentrating the Japanese banking system – a central feature of the postwar Japanese banking system – started well before Japan's war economy. To the extent that the banking law passed in 1927 played a role, it may be worth examination by today's transition economies.

Teranishi (1977) documents that during the era of financial instability and rapid consolidation, the postal savings system grew dramatically as local banks went out of business. About 65 percent of the time savings deposits that left the local banking sector went into the postal savings system. While the *zaibatsu* banks gradually increased their share of deposits through the twentieth century, this event was largely independent of the consolidation of the banking sector and the fall in the number of banks. *Zaibatsu* banks "found it the best policy not to involve themselves in the structural change among local banks" (p. 464). Rather, postal savings served as the principal safe haven for risk-averse depositors, particularly when consolidation accelerated after 1927. Likewise, the official financial system (treasury investments and loans), the principal outlet for postal savings funds during this era, handled the provision of funds owned by the failed local banks.

Lessons of the prewar experience for transition economies

Although policy makers in transition countries can learn a great deal from the experiences of the postwar financial system in Japan, they should keep in mind that Japan also experienced extraordinary industrial growth and financial institution building in the late nineteenth and early twentieth centuries. Keeping this caveat in mind, at least seven stylized facts are worthy of note.

First, business conglomerates that did not continue to depend on government patronage were more successful than others in making the transition to a modern industrial economy. Second, banks that made a conscious effort to lower their dependence on central bank credit were more successful than those that did not. Third, the establishment of procedures for punishing defaulting borrowers had a beneficial impact on the development of the payments system. Fourth, limits on the amounts of lending to related parties appear to have contributed to financial stability (and could have contributed more if the newer *zaibatsu* had been as prudent as the older *zaibatsu*). Fifth, bank bailouts without accompanying reforms, such as those undertaken by the Bank of Japan in 1920 and 1922, probably increased the likelihood of a more serious crisis, such as that of 1927. Sixth, capital standards – the minimum capital requirements established in the 1927 law – were a viable means

---

[10] The greatest number of banks was 1,867, reached in 1901. The government took several measures to promote consolidation in the early twentieth century (Yabushita and Inoue 1993).

of encouraging bank consolidation and more prudent lending. Finally, the public financial system served as a buffer when the banking sector was downsized.

REFERENCES

Aoki, Masahiko, and Hugh Patrick, eds. 1994. *The Japanese Main Bank System: Its Relevance for Developing and Transforming Economies*. New York: Oxford University Press.
Aoki, Masahiko, Hugh Patrick, and Paul Sheard. 1994. "The Japanese Main Bank System: An Introductory Overview." In Masahiko Aoki and Hugh Patrick, eds., *The Japanese Main Bank System: Its Relevance for Developing and Transforming Economies*. New York: Oxford University Press. pp. 30–49.
Calomiris, Charles W., and Gary Gorton. 1991. "The Origins of Banking Panics: Models, Facts, and Bank Regulation." In R. Glenn Hubbard, ed., *Financial Markets and Financial Crises*. Chicago: University of Chicago Press, pp. 109–73.
Calomiris, Charles W., and Charles Himmelberg. 1995. "Government Credit Policy and Industrial Performance: Japanese Machine Tool Producers, 1963–1991." Policy Research Working Paper no. 1434, World Bank, Washington, D.C., September.
Caprio, Gerard. 1994. "The Role of Financial Intermediaries in Transitional Economies." Paper presented at the Carnegie–Rochester Public Policy Conference, April 22–3. Rochester, N.Y.
Hadley, Eleanor. 1970. *Antitrust in Japan*. Princeton, N.J.: Princeton University Press.
Horiuchi, Akiyoshi, and Qing-Yuan Sui. 1993. "Influence of the Japan Development Bank on Corporate Investment Behavior." *Journal of the Japanese and International Economies* 7 (4):441–65.
Hoshi, Takeo. 1993. "Evolution of the Main Bank System in Japan." Mimeo, University of California, San Diego, September.
　1995. "Back to the Future: Universal Banking in Japan." Paper presented at the Conference on Universal Banking, Salomon Center, New York University, New York, February 23–4.
Mayer, Colin. 1990. "Financial Systems, Corporate Finance, and Economic Development." In R. G. Hubbard, ed., *Asymmetric Information, Corporate Finance, and Investment*. Chicago: University of Chicago Press, pp. 21–48.
Morikawa, Hidemasa. 1992. *Zaibatsu: The Rise and Fall of Family Enterprise Groups in Japan*. Tokyo: University of Tokyo Press.
Packer, Frank. 1994a. "The Disposal of Bad Loans in Japan: A Review of Recent Policy Initiatives." Paper presented at the conference Current Developments in Japanese Financial Markets. Center for International Business Education and Research, University of Southern California, Los Angeles, June 9–10.
　1994b. "The Role of Long-Term Credit Banks within the Main Bank System." In Masahiko Aoki and Hugh Patrick, eds., *The Japanese Main Bank System: Its Relevance for Developing and Transforming Economies*. New York: Oxford University Press, pp. 142–87.
Packer, Frank, and Marc Ryser. 1993. "The Governance of Failure: An Anatomy of Corporate Bankruptcy in Japan." In Allan Bird, ed., *Best Paper Proceedings*. New York: Association of Japanese Business Studies.
Patrick, Hugh. 1967. "Japan: 1868–1914." In Rondo Cameron, ed., *Banking and Economic Development*. New York: Oxford University Press, pp. 239–89.

138   **Frank Packer**

1979. "The Evolution of the Japanese Financial System during the Inter-War Period." Economic Center Discussion Paper, Yale University, New Haven, Conn.
1984. "Japanese Financial Development in Historical Perspective, 1868–1980." In Gustav Ranis, ed., *Comparative Development Perspectives*. Boulder: Westview, pp. 37–86.
1994. "The Relevance of Japanese Finance and Its Main Bank System." In Masahiko Aoki and Hugh Patrick, eds., *The Japanese Main Bank System: Its Relevance for Developing and Transforming Economies*. New York: Oxford University Press, pp. 353–408.
Ryser, Marc. 1993. "Sanctions without Law: The Japanese Financial Clearinghouse Guillotine and Its Impact on Default Rates." Mimeo, St. Gallen School of Economics, St. Gallen, Switzerland.
Teranishi, Juro. 1977. "Availability of Safe Assets and the Process of Bank Concentration in Japan." *Economic Development and Cultural Change* 25 (3):447–70.
1990. "Financial System and the Industrialization of Japan: 1900–1970." *Banca Nazionale del Lavoro Quarterly Review* (September):309–41.
Vittas, Dimitri, and Akihiko Kawaura. 1994. "Policy-Based Finance and Financial Sector Development in Japan." Washington, D.C.: World Bank, September.
Yabushita, Shiro, and Yabushita Inoue. 1993. "The Stability of the Japanese Banking System: A Historical Perspective." *Journal of the Japanese and International Economies* 7 (4):387–407.

DISCUSSION

Question: In the 1920s a large amount of bonds was financed outside the system. Given what happened on the deposit and lending side in the 1920s, it appears that the *zaibatsu* lost grasp of what was going on in the banking sector.

F. Packer: I agree with Teranishi's view that the 1920s was an era of great financial instability in which depositors lost confidence in certain segments of the banking sector. But the safe havens of the postal savings system remained, as did the major *zaibatsu* banks to a lesser degree. If certain banks or a postal savings system are in fact safe havens and are also capable of picking up the slack in lending, the impact of downsizing one part of the banking sector's availability of credit can be ameliorated.

Concerning bond issuance, because Japan had universal banking at that time and a large portion of issuance was underwritten by the *zaibatsu* banks (in cooperation with the Industrial Bank of Japan), the increase in issuance was not necessarily a sign that *zaibatsu* banks were losing business. This contrasts with the postwar period, during which, given the legal separation of banking and securities businesses, the banks have used their considerable political influence to repress the bond market.

Question: Isn't it ironic that from serving as a government safety net, the postal savings system evolved into an intermediary supporting heavier government management in the postwar era?

F. Packer: The war economy experience is relevant here. Postal savings continued to increase through the late 1930s and early 1940s, and government institutions evolved to channel those funds for the war buildup.

Question: Prior to the new banking law of 1927, did you say that there was mostly free banking?

F. Packer: By *free banking* I mean that one could found a bank with minimal capital requirements, and there were few restrictions on the rates charged or given on loans and deposits.

Comment: People here might like a tough bankruptcy law in the countries that they work on, but they will meet with resistance from local officials for different reasons. It also might cause a phenomenal jump in unemployment.

F. Packer: Particularly in postwar Japan, main banks were often pressured by both peers and the government to rescue the firm. The tough bankruptcy system put the banks in a strong position to throw out the management.

Comment: Many corporate organizations of the Far East are especially unified in that they are family-owned, have their own bank and related investors, and so on. We see now this system in some developing countries as well. Coming from a Western mindset, my inclination is to make rules forbidding related transactions and tied lending. But it almost sounds like operations in Japan were successful.

F. Packer: Recall that in the banking sector there were both government and endogenous movements to limit lending to other *zaibatsu* companies. Particularly when the limits were repealed, smaller or newer *zaibatsu* were less inhibited in this respect, which at times hurt the solvency of their lending institutions.

Comment: In some countries a small number of institutions have a substantial involvement with the old economy. When you tell the officials there to limit the size and percentage of loans made to a single lender, they tell you it won't work.

F. Packer: In Japan they passed a law that was later repealed in 1895 because many of the *zaibatsu* refused to accept it. But paradoxically, many *zaibatsu* banks later established their own internal lending limits to develop their reputation for solvency.

Question: In the 1920s how did the Bank of Japan bail out depositors? Was the Bank of Japan just liquefying, and were depositors still incurring losses?

F. Packer: My impression is that for the most part the Bank of Japan bailed out depositors completely and shut down the banks, absorbing the losses itself.

Question: Did self-imposed restraints start to weaken as precedents were established for the bailout solution?

F. Packer: Not in the large *zaibatsu*. During the boom of World War I they realized that boom conditions weren't going to last forever and that the growth of lending must be restrained. I'm sure a number of large Japanese banks today wish they had been as prudent during the boom of the 1980s.

Question: In addition to making depositors feel secure, there could have been other reasons that *zaibatsu* maintained a tough-line policy of limited lending to related parties. The *zaibatsu* themselves were very profitable, and they may have been able to finance everything they wanted to internally. It appeared as if *zaibatsu* companies were not borrowing that much from banks. Another related possibility is that although starting a bank may have been intended originally to create a captive source of funds, banking itself might have proved so profitable that the decision was made to make it a profit rather a cost center. Any comments?

F. Packer: I agree that both of those factors could have been reasons. These families were extremely wealthy and their first line of defense was substantial internal reserves. Furthermore, companies were expected not to be too dependent on outside borrowing.

Question: It appears that in the German case it was good to get closer to your client, but not in the early Japanese case. Do you have any feel for which type of bank worked better and whether it depended on the period? For example, in the period of instability were there banks that performed poorly even though only 15 percent of their total loans were made to related firms?

F. Packer: Of the banks that failed in 1927, one or two had 15 percent or less exposure to related firms, but most of them had considerably higher exposure. Other anecdotal evidence is that Mitsui improved its profitability considerably after changing its policy. Unfortunately, I don't have a consistent series of panel data that looks at the relation of bank or *zaibatsu* performance to related-firm lending.

Comment: There is no magic number determining how much lending can be made to related firms. It depends on the regime. In New England, perhaps the most successful example of industrial financing in world history, there was rapid accumulation of capital and increased productivity in the textile industry in the first thirty years of the nineteenth century. Ninety percent of lending by commercial banks during this period was to insiders, but those banks were also being monitored by savings banks, which acted as corporate watchdogs guarding over their pool of stock. In addition, the insiders were monitoring each other because they didn't want anyone to kill the golden goose (the bank).

CHAPTER 9

Thrift deposit institutions in Europe and the United States

Dimitri Vittas

The financial systems in most developing countries today have many features in common with the financial systems of the eighteenth and nineteenth centuries. Whether they had unlimited liability (as in Scotland in the eighteenth century), double liability (as in the United States in the late nineteenth century), or limited liability and special charters, commercial banks were the dominant institutions in the financial systems of European countries and the United States. Moreover, they were typically established by wealthy people and oriented toward businesses and other wealthy people – they effectively represented "banking for the rich by the rich." Insurance companies were underdeveloped and pension and mutual funds did not yet exist. As a result middle- and low-income people had limited access to formal financial services and relied on informal arrangements for borrowing. Meanwhile, their financial savings were unproductively hoarded under the mattress.

This gap in the provision of financial services can be explained by the low level and unequal distribution of income and wealth, high information and transaction costs, and weak enforcement mechanisms – features that are found in most developing countries today. But over time, different types of institutions, including savings banks, credit cooperatives, building societies, and credit unions, emerged in the United States and Europe to overcome these problems and fill this market gap. This chapter gives a brief historical review of the emergence and evolution of thrift deposit institutions in Europe and the United States and draws lessons for today's developing countries.[1]

The origin of thrift deposit institutions

Several types of thrift deposit institutions developed, and their ownership, functions, and orientation differed substantially across countries and across

---

[1] The term *thrift deposit institution* is used to distinguish these banklike institutions from the mutual insurance companies that have also encouraged thrift and played a large part in the evolution of financial systems. The achievements and shortcomings of mutual insurance companies have mirrored those of thrift deposit institutions.

types of institutions. Some institutions were established as publicly owned units, others were mutually owned by their members, and others were set up as foundations. Some institutions focused on mobilizing deposits from low- and middle-income groups and holding them in government debt. This pattern was followed by postal savings banks in all countries and by ordinary savings banks in countries (such as the United Kingdom and France) where government regulation required them to invest all their deposit funds in government debt. In still other countries, such as Germany, Italy, the Netherlands, Sweden, Switzerland, and the United States, savings banks were allowed to lend to firms and households (although in the United States regulations differed from state to state). Credit cooperatives were set up by farmers in rural areas and by artisans and small traders in urban areas. Their main purpose was to mobilize resources for lending to their members. Finally, building societies, savings and loan associations, and credit unions specialized in raising deposits from households and then lending the funds back to them for housing finance and consumer credit needs.

Internationally comparable data on the relative size of thrift deposit institutions are not readily available. A study conducted in the late 1970s (Vittas, Hindle, Frazer, and Brown 1978) on the deposits and other liabilities with the nonfinancial sector showed that thrift deposit institutions accounted for between one-third and one-half of total liabilities with the nonfinancial sector in Germany, France, Italy, and Japan – all countries in which insurance companies and pension funds played a very small part in the financial system (at the time). But even in the Netherlands, Sweden, Switzerland, the United Kingdom, and the United States, where institutional investors were more developed, thrift deposit institutions accounted for between one-fifth and one-third of all financial sector liabilities (Table 9.1). Also, the share of large commercial banks was not very large, even in countries such as the Netherlands and Sweden, where banking concentration was very high.

In the United Kingdom and the United States, building societies and savings and loan associations played an important role, but credit cooperatives did not emerge, and savings banks accounted for a small share of all resources mobilized (Table 9.1). In contrast, savings banks were very large in Germany and Switzerland and only slightly smaller in Italy, Sweden, and France. Credit cooperatives were large in Japan, France, and the Netherlands and to a lesser extent in Germany and Italy. Postal savings banks, including postal giros, were more important in France than in Japan, but they were also very large in Italy and the Netherlands. Finally, credit unions were large, at least as formal institutions, only in the United States.[2] The mid-1970s was the heyday of thrift deposit institutions. The growth of pension funds and mutual funds

---

[2] The data in Table 9.1 are based on published statistics in different countries. If the institutions were very small, statistics were not collected or published. Such was probably the case for credit unions in the United Kingdom and building societies in France.

Table 9.1. *Institutional shares in deposits and other liabilities with the nonfinancial sector, 1975*

	France	Germany	Italy	Japan	Netherlands	Sweden	Switzerland	U.K.	U.S.
Central bank	8.3	5.4	8.1	4.3	6.6	7.0	7.3	3.9	4.2
Large comm. banks	18.1	7.8	17.4	20.5	15.2	24.4	16.5	17.0	15.2
Other comm. banks	11.5	7.5	12.8	12.9	3.8	3.6	4.9	11.7	20.3
Savings banks	14.2	29.0	18.6	6.1	5.0	14.5	27.1	3.1	5.6
Postal savings	10.9	2.0	8.7	9.4	7.4	2.2	—	1.7	—
Credit co-ops	16.0	9.4	8.4	19.8	12.2	2.9	2.5	—	—
Building soc.	—	5.8	—	—	—	—	—	17.9	14.5
Credit unions	—	—	—	—	—	—	—	—	1.7
All thrifts	41.1	46.2	35.7	35.3	24.6	19.6	29.6	22.7	21.8
Long-term CIs	8.2	12.8	9.1	11.0	5.0	2.8	1.3	4.9	5.5
Insurance cos.	8.8	11.9	3.1	8.2	12.8	15.7	12.1	21.9	14.6
Pension funds	—	—	—	7.8	26.6	25.5	23.1	11.1	12.9
Mutual funds	2.5	1.4	0.3	—	2.4	—	4.8	6.5	2.3
Other insts.	0.5	7.0	3.5	—	3.0	—	0.4	0.2	3.2

Source: Vittas et al. (1978).

in the 1980s and a growing wave of conversions and demutualizations have caused a significant decline in their relative importance in most countries.

Why did thrift deposit institutions emerge in most European countries and the United States and how were they able to grow and acquire such importance in the financial systems of so many countries? What was their contribution to financial sector development and most broadly to economic development? And what is their relevance for the financial systems of developing countries, many of which have encouraged the development of similar institutions but with far less satisfactory results? These questions are examined after a description of the development of thrift deposit institutions in different countries.

Ordinary savings banks

Ordinary savings banks, so named to distinguish them from postal savings banks, came in two forms: banks that were required to invest all of their funds in government debt and banks that enjoyed greater freedom in their investment policies through expanded lending powers. The first category included savings banks in the United Kingdom and France, and the second savings banks in the United States (at least in some states), Germany, Switzerland, and other European countries.

Savings banks were largely created in response to the orientation of commercial banks toward industry and commerce and the wealthier segments of society. They encouraged thrift by providing safe and convenient outlets for the savings of wage earners and other low-income groups. But the motivation for creating savings banks was not purely altruistic. There was also concern about the impact of relief given to the poor on government and municipal funds. It was felt that if the poor could be encouraged to save, they would put less of a burden on wealthier segments of society. But although they were established to provide safe deposit facilities for the poor, and indeed initially put upper limits on the size of deposit accounts, savings banks in most countries deviated from this orientation early on and sought deposits from wealthier people.

Savings banks met with considerable success in most countries, largely because of their low transaction costs. Transaction costs were lower because of the simpler and more limited range of services provided and the reliance on unpaid staff. For example, in their early years savings banks were open only a few hours on one or more days a week, did not encourage withdrawals, and did not operate through full branches. In New England (and also in Australia) savings banks shared the same facilities as commercial banks and represented little more than special windows that were open a few days a week. Over time, savings banks became more business-like, were run by professional staff and managers, and developed their own branch networks. Although their relative efficiency in terms of transaction costs declined, savings banks were favored by a preferential fiscal regime, both with regard to the deposit facilities offered to their customers and with regard to the taxes they had to pay on their operations and profits.

Savings banks in Germany

The first German savings bank was founded in 1768 in Brunswick followed by the establishment of one in Hamburg in 1778 (Cahill 1913:75). From there they spread quickly to several other German cities, as well as to Swiss cities such as Bern and Zurich. Most German savings banks were public institutions, established by municipal and other local authorities and operated under their tutelage and guarantee, although their charters were approved by their respective state authorities. However, a few savings banks were established by private associations.

Savings banks were founded to prevent the poorer classes from falling into absolute poverty, by providing a place for the safe deposit of small sums of money. The first such banks were established in connection with efforts to reform the poor laws. Because they catered to the needs of low-income groups, most savings banks initially placed upper limits on deposit balances. In addition, they provided no credit facilities for depositors, as this service would have contradicted their stated purpose. Moreover, savings banks were required to invest in safe securities, and lending to poor workers was not considered safe.

About 280 savings banks had been established in Germany by 1836, and their number grew to 1,200 by 1850. The number of deposits held in savings banks increased steeply with the acceleration of industrialization after 1860. By 1913 deposits in some 3,133 German savings banks amounted to nearly 20 billion marks. By comparison, the eight big joint-stock banks held only 5 billion marks (Born 1983:107). In order to facilitate deposits and withdrawals, the savings banks established large branch networks and collecting agencies. These totaled well over 7,500 units in 1910, which, including head offices, created a total network of more than 10,000 outlets (Cahill 1913:77).

The creation of savings banks in Germany was motivated not only by the desire to provide savings outlets for low-income groups, but also by the pragmatic consideration that municipal funds for poor relief would be less strained if the poor accumulated savings. But the establishment of health insurance in 1883 and old age and disability insurance in 1889 eroded part of the original rationale for creating savings banks, and they increasingly became the banks for middle-class depositors. Unlike their counterparts in the United Kingdom and France, German savings banks were not required to deposit their funds with the state treasury or to invest in government bonds, and they began to give credit to small-scale manufacturers and artisans even in the early phase of their development. In 1911 about 60 percent of their deposits were invested in mortgage loans, secured on urban (40 percent) and rural property (20 percent). Slightly less than 25 percent of funds were invested in securities, and a very small proportion was invested in personal loans (Cahill 1913:75).

The maximum amount of deposits was set by each bank and its guaranteeing authority. As banks increased these limits over time in order to attract deposits from wealthier people, they introduced notice requirements – two-week, four-week, three-month, and six-month – that put limits on the amounts that could be withdrawn. These limits were not always upheld, but they provided a useful weapon of defense in times of monetary pressure. Given that they were funded from short-term deposits, savings banks were granting short- to medium-term mortgages that were effectively interest-only loans with a recall option. They were also able to vary the rate of interest on the loans in response to changes in market rates.

At the turn of the century the banks were under pressure to develop mortgages with annual sinking-fund payments. These were different from modern, annuity-type mortgages, in which capital is reduced on a monthly basis. Instead, sinking-fund mortgages accumulated a fund in an interest-bearing deposit account. But sinking funds created problems with respect to their rate of interest and their availability to borrowers. In some cases sinking funds earned interest at the same rate as mortgage loans, in others at the rate of savings deposits, and in still others at an intermediate rate. Sinking funds were not supposed to be available to borrowers and were often used to reduce the loan balance once a certain round sum was accumulated. But if borrowers were allowed to use the sinking funds for other purposes, any interest credited to them was adjusted to the rate paid on ordinary savings deposits.

Savings banks made mortgage loans for up to 50 percent of the value of urban properties and 66 percent of the value of rural land. Valuations were based either on appraisals prepared by specialized mortgage credit banks and insurance companies or, in the case of farm land, on approved multiples of the net yield declared for tax purposes. There were no laws or regulations restricting mortgage loans within their respective districts. But the multiples allowed were generally greater for properties located in the same district as the bank than for properties in other districts. Also, the loan–value ratios were higher for properties in the same district than for those in other districts. In order to encourage the creation of smallholdings, savings banks were prepared to use higher loan–value ratios (up to 75 or even 85 percent) for smallholdings and allotments in their own district, provided that at least 0.5 percent of the principal amount of the loan was repaid annually.

An important feature of German savings banks was their three-tier structure. Savings banks operated in local areas delineated by their guaranteeing authority but were supported by regional central giro institutions, which were in turn linked to a national giro institution. The three-tier structure emerged after 1908, when the savings banks were given the right to negotiate checks and proceeded to establish local giro associations for cashless payment transactions. A giro association was formed in every Prussian province and federal state by the municipal authorities. These associations founded central giro institutions as clearing centers for their affiliated banks. The central giro institutions also managed the liquidity reserves of individual banks and provided a mechanism for transferring funds from savings banks with surplus resources to those with excess demand for funds. The first central giro institution was created in Saxony in 1909. In 1918 a national giro institution was founded as the center point for all giro institutions. Thus, the savings banks were united through this large nationwide giro network and also gained access to money and capital markets.

Despite their public ownership, German savings banks operated very effectively. They were hit by the hyperinflation of the 1920s, but were able to survive because of their local authority guarantees. Following the currency reform, their savings deposits, mortgage loans, and mortgage bonds were all reduced to 25 percent of their book value, and the savings banks were able to resume their expansion. In 1930, 70 percent of their assets were long-term loans in the form of mortgages and public sector debt, including loans made to local authorities. But they also maintained substantial liquid funds with their giro institutions and provided short-term credits. In conjunction with the central giro institutions, the savings banks became universal banks that competed with commercial banks, particularly for the business of medium-size enterprises and middle-income households.

Savings banks have always funded their long-term loans and bonds with short-term deposits. This practice has exposed them to interest rate risk, a problem from which they continue to suffer. But because of their state guarantees and their strong liquidity positions, they have been able to survive, albeit suffering from periods of poor profitability. Today, German savings banks are under pressure because they are publicly owned and because they need external capital to finance expansion. There are calls for their privatization and eventual absorption into the commercial banking sector, but it is not clear if and when any privatization will take place.

Savings banks in the United Kingdom

Unlike in Germany and other European countries, where savings banks were founded with the explicit support of local authorities, the initiatives to form savings banks in the United Kingdom came from private individuals, mainly clergymen and wealthy philanthropists. The first U.K. savings bank was established by the Reverend Henry Duncan in Ruthwell, Scotland, in 1810. Reverend Duncan played a central role in advocating savings banks for lower-income groups. But the Ruthwell Savings Bank was predated by an earlier initiative in London. In 1804 the Tottenham Benefit Bank was established to enable poor people in Tottenham to safely deposit their savings in an institution that was guaranteed by "a few respectable persons of property." According to Born (1983), this institution paid 5 percent interest per year, but in its first years did not invest its funds, and the interest was paid out of the pockets of the "respectable persons" who managed its business (Born 1983:108).

The number of savings banks in the United Kingdom grew to 26 by 1815, 78 by 1816, and 465 by the end of 1818 (Olmstead 1976:6). They were established as private institutions, but were bound by law to deposit their funds with the department of national savings, which invested these funds in government bonds. The rate of interest paid to savings banks was often higher than the coupon rate on government bonds, although bond holdings suffered losses when interest rates rose. During the Crimean War the value of bonds held on behalf of the savings banks had a shortfall of £4 million against total savings deposits of £9 million. But the savings banks were insulated from these losses. By 1861 their number had increased to 638, although following the creation of the Post Office Savings Bank in that year, many savings banks closed down. Their number fell to 483 by 1873 (Born 1983:109).

Attempts to expand the lending and investment powers of savings banks were frustrated – not least because of opposition from the established commercial banks – until the mid-1970s, when the trustee savings banks were reorganized and their powers expanded. They were subsequently merged into one group that culminated in the 1987 flotation of the TSB Group as a full-fledged, stock-owned universal financial institution. Despite the restrictions on the utilization of their deposit funds, the trustee savings banks were able to expand in number and through branch networks and to diversify into many ancillary services, including both mutual fund management and insurance services.

Savings banks in France

The first French savings bank was the Caisse d'Epargne de Paris, which was founded in 1818 by the directors and shareholders of an insurance company. More than 350 savings banks were established by 1845, mainly by private groups or municipal authorities. French savings banks were required to place their deposits with the Caisse des Depots et Consignations, a state institution founded in 1816 and accountable to the French Parliament.

When an individual's deposit reached Fr 50, it had to be converted into a perpetual state annuity in the holder's name. Thus, savings banks funds were used to finance the public debt, partly in the form of floating debt and partly in the form of perpetual annuities. But perpetual annuities created liquidity problems and losses for the banks if they had to be sold in times of crisis and at low values.

Despite these recurring problems, the savings banks appealed not only to low-income groups but also to wealthier segments of the population. To maintain the low-income orientation of savings banks, the government imposed upper limits on deposit accounts. Over time, the French savings banks, like their counterparts in the United Kingdom, developed extensive branch networks and diversified into ancillary services. Benefiting from low transaction costs, fiscal incentives, and the controls on interest rates on retail deposits, they continued to account for a large share of household deposits, although in the past decade they have suffered from the emergence of money market mutual funds and the growing popularity of mutual funds and life insurance policies.

Savings banks in the United States

Savings banks in the United States appeared a few years after those in the United Kingdom and at more or less the same time as those in France. The first institutions to begin operating were the Philadelphia Saving Fund Society and the Provident Institution for Savings in Boston, both of which opened in 1816. The Savings Bank of Baltimore was organized in 1818 and the Bank for Savings in the City of New York in 1819 (Payne and Davis 1956:12–18).

These institutions were strongly influenced by the success and rapid expansion of savings banks in the United Kingdom. They were established by men who were active entrepreneurs not only in insurance and commercial banking, but also in industry and commerce. Yet despite their backing by prominent personalities in the business world, the first application to obtain a charter for a savings bank in New York was rejected "in consequence of the principles not being distinctly comprehended and the preponderant objection against the incorporation of any more banks" (Krooss and Blyn 1971: 61). The petition was rejected because it aroused the opposition of the antibank group, and for this reason the supporters of savings institutions in Philadelphia and Boston avoided using the word *bank* in their titles.

The number of savings banks increased quickly as this institutional innovation spread to other eastern and mid-Atlantic states. By 1820 there were ten savings banks with more than $1 million in deposits. Their number rose to fifteen by 1825 and to fifty-two by 1835, with more than $10 million in deposits. But their business was very unevenly distributed. More than half of the deposits were made with New York savings banks, while about three-quarters of New York savings deposits were held with the Bank for Savings.

As in other countries the U.S. savings banks were at first founded to ameliorate the condition of the poorer classes. In line with their primary objective to provide deposit facilities for the poor, some savings banks restricted the size of deposits and some paid declining graduated interest rates (a lower rate for balances above a certain limit). Savings banks in New York and most other states were subject to investment constraints that forced them to invest in federal government debt or in local state and city bonds. The Bank for Savings in New York played a crucial part in financing the construction of the Erie Canal. In 1821 it held 30 percent of the canal's stock, which was tantamount to a public bond (Olmstead 1972:824). Banks in Massachusetts and Maryland were not required to invest in public sector bonds, although they were prohibited from investing in bonds of other states or from lending to corporations or people residing in other states. But even these banks initially placed their deposits in safe investments, mostly local state and city bonds. Savings banks also deposited their funds with commercial banks.

Gradually, but very early in their history, the restrictions on deposits and investments of savings banks were dismantled. Thus, Pennsylvania repealed the restriction on the size of deposits in 1824, and New York permitted mortgage loans in 1830. Savings banks, especially those more concerned with safety than growth, began to reorient themselves toward wealthier groups. They expanded their business hours and began to move out of public sector bonds and into loans secured by mortgages or securities and even into loans based on personal security. By 1825 the Baltimore Savings Bank had put three-quarters of its assets in secured loans. These loans were concentrated among a small group of merchants. In Massachusetts loans on personal security accounted for about one-quarter of assets in 1835 (Krooss and Blyn 1971:62).

The Massachusetts Hospital Life Insurance Company was created in 1823 as a life insurance company but operated more like a savings bank or a trust. It was founded by prominent Bostonian financiers and industrialists to provide income for the Massachusetts General Hospital and to offer savings bank services for the rich and middle classes. Contrary to early savings bank practice, this institution did not take deposits of less than $500 for less than five years, and it discouraged the business of those who could take care of their own affairs. The Massachusetts Hospital Life Insurance conducted very little life insurance business, but became known as the "Great Savings Bank." It became the largest financial institution of its day and was the most important source of medium-term finance for New England industry, especially the textile industry (Davis 1960:8). The first president of the Massachusetts Hospital Life Insurance was William Phillips, who was also president of the Massachusetts Bank and the Provident Institution for Savings. Ebenezer Francis, who was the driving force behind its creation, was a director of the Boston Bank and later the first president of the Suffolk Bank (Krooss and Blyn 1971:58–9).

Savings banks were the fastest-growing financial institutions in the United States by the middle of the nineteenth century. Their deposits grew from $10 million in 1835 to $150 million in 1860. Although they continued to attract deposits from low-income groups, their customers also included wealthy people. In addition to federal, state, and city bonds, savings banks were investing in corporate securities and making business and mortgage loans. In the mid-

1850s, well over 50 percent of New York savings bank assets were in government securities and more than 40 percent were in mortgages. In Massachusetts loans on personal security and mortgages accounted for 60 percent of assets. But the savings banks suffered from liquidity problems during the crisis of 1857, and they were forced to build up their liquid assets, shifting their focus to government bonds.

Nevertheless, savings banks continued to expand until the crisis of 1873. After 1873 many savings banks suspended their operations, and although total losses were small, there was a sharp swing toward conservatism. In New York, regulations were imposed, limiting investments to government bonds and mortgage loans for less than 50 percent of appraised value. In other states savings banks faced increasing competition from commercial banks, which started to attract depositors with interest-bearing time deposits, and from building and loan associations.

The relative importance of mutual savings banks declined after 1890, mainly because they failed to take root in the fast-growing West. Between 1860 and 1890 their assets grew from $150 million to $1.7 billion. But after 1890 their growth decelerated sharply, and by 1922 their assets amounted to only $6.6 billion. In comparison, savings and loan associations held $2.8 billion and commercial banks $47 billion. During this period savings banks operated in sixteen states but played an important role only in New England and the mid-Atlantic states.

Unlike the public savings banks in Germany and other central European countries, which were promoted by forward-looking public officials, and the savings banks in the United Kingdom and France, which were fostered by clergymen and wealthy philanthropists, savings banks in the United States were mostly championed by men of industry and finance. As a result there were extensive interlocking directorships among the management of savings banks and that of commercial banks, insurance companies, and industrial and commercial enterprises. Over time, these interlocking positions gave rise to close links between savings banks and the financial and industrial establishment. And as a result savings banks provided considerable funds for financing industrial and commercial firms.

The most telling examples were the savings banks in New England, which were the most important suppliers of long-term finance to the textile industry. Savings banks provided 40 percent of all new long-term loans during the period 1840–60 to the eight leading textile mills. Trust companies provided 29 percent of the total, commercial banks only 4 percent, and individuals 22 percent (Davis 1960:6). Moreover, the savings banks charged lower interest rates on these long-term loans than the rates prevailing in the shorter-term markets, and they always observed the usury ceilings on interest rates. Savings banks also held corporate stock, and they were major stockholders of New England commercial banks. The close links between commercial and savings banks were evident from the sharing of branch facilities: savings banks were little more than special windows of commercial banks that were open a few days a week. Savings bank depositors benefited from this arrangement because of lower transaction costs.

Davis (1960) notes that banks in the United Kingdom and in the western United States tended to withdraw from affected markets when faced with binding usury ceilings, forcing firms to borrow from unregulated sources. Usury ceilings thus had the unintended effect of raising the effective cost of funds for industrial and commercial firms. Davis also notes that in the face of binding usury ceilings, nonprice rationing must have played an important role in finance. As a result firms that had good connections with savings banks through interlocking directorships obtained finance on more favorable terms than firms with no such connections. In particular, new industries "may well have found loan finance almost impossible to obtain through traditional channels in times of credit stringency" (Davis 1960:4).

One explanation for the behavior of savings banks is that they were provincial in their lending policies, preferring to keep their investments where they could be closely watched rather than seeking higher returns in out-of-state operations (Payne and Davis 1956:110–13). This pattern was seen among savings banks in all states and also reflected the pattern observed in Germany. The provincialism in investment policy and the geographic concentration of assets were a manifestation of the immobility of long-term capital in the United States until the last part of the nineteenth century (Davis and Payne 1958:404). This immobility could be attributed to the information problems that affected lending to or investing in companies located in other states.

But another explanation holds that the directors who managed the affairs of savings banks did not attempt to maximize the returns on their investments, but were quite happy to lend these funds to their own textile companies at below-market rates (Vatter 1961:216–21; Olmstead 1974:816 Davis 1961: 225). This explanation challenges the purely altruistic motivation of the founding men, who claimed to want to establish and manage savings banks for the sole benefit of the poorer classes (Payne and Davis 1956:20–1). Instead it suggests that these institutions became as useful to the founders and managers as to the people for whom they were ostensibly established. Olmstead (1974:816) raised the question of whether their objectives changed over time as they grew in importance. Their reorientation toward wealthier depositors lends some support to this view.

Lamoreaux (1994) argues that the insider lending that was pervasive in New England in the first half of the nineteenth century contributed to economic development. Ordinary investors who bought bank stock knew they were investing in the diversified enterprises of bank directors. Abuses were restrained by the importance of safeguarding the good reputation of the bank and its directors. Directors carefully monitored each other's borrowing to prevent excesses that might affect a bank's profitability and standing. But insider lending was facilitated by the low leverage of commercial banks and their small reliance on deposits. The low leverage was in turn built and sustained on the fact "that many large purchases of bank stock were made by insurance companies, savings banks, and other institutions whose investment decisions were controlled by the same groups of men who dominated the banks" (Lamoreaux 1994:71). On a group basis, the capital ratios were not as high as reported, though they were probably higher than bank capital ratios today. Insider lending declined substantially after 1870. First, successful families generated surplus capital and started gradually to transform the operations of their banks from financing vehicles for their industrial and commercial enterprises to autonomous profit centers. Second, banks suffered severe losses after the panic of 1873, while, as already noted, several savings banks collapsed. Third, bank profitability declined after 1870 and banks were forced to expand leverage by attracting deposits. This required a reduction in insider lending and greater reliance on objective assessments of creditworthiness. Did savings banks benefit or suffer from their promotion by men of industry and commerce and from the pervasive practice of insider lending? The evidence seems to indicate that they benefited during the period of expansion and prosperity, but that they probably suffered a heavy blow after the panic of 1873.

Even the Savings Bank of New York, which was not allowed to invest in nongovernment securities, was affected by the close links between the promoters and directors of the bank and the promoters of the projects that the bank financed (Olmstead 1976). Several of the directors helped to plan projects that the bank financed, while in other cases they actively prodded government planners to proceed with social overhead investments by assuring officials that finance from the bank would be forthcoming (Olmstead 1972:810). The directors stood to gain large nonpecuniary (and possibly indirect pecuniary) benefits from the success of the projects they so actively sponsored. Nevertheless, Olmstead (1974:834) concluded that the trustees of the New York Savings Bank were attempting to maximize the real rate of return on their portfolios, given legal constraints. Their primary objective was to pursue their depositors' interests, despite the many conflict-of-interest situations that arose. Olmstead also noted that state governments reaped substantial benefits from the investment constraints imposed on mutual savings banks in the form of lower interest payments on their entire debt. Moreover, the early constraints were instrumental not only in channeling savings bank assets into the financing of the Erie Canal, but also in indirectly helping to attract funds from other investors, who entered the market only after the canal was partially opened and was not nearly so risky a venture. The initial success of New York State in financing its public works encouraged other states to embark on similar projects (Olmstead 1972:838).

Postal savings banks

Although savings banks were initially established to provide safe deposit facilities for low-income groups, their reorientation toward high- and middle-income groups early in their development and their lack of extensive branch networks prevented them from filling the gap in savings facilities. To meet this need postal savings banks were established, the first in the United Kingdom in 1861. It was followed by ones in Japan in 1875, France in 1881, Austria in 1883, and the United States in 1910 (Born 1983:337).

Postal savings banks were created in order to encourage saving by low-income groups. Although they paid a modest interest rate (in the United Kingdom the rate was lower than that paid by the trustee savings banks), their main attractions were safety, since they had the explicit backing of the state, and convenience, as they operated through nationwide networks of post offices. The services offered by postal savings banks were often complemented by postal giros, which offered money transfer services through the post offices. Postal giros took the lead in many European countries in the late 1950s in automating payment services and offering more efficient clearing services.

Unlike postal giros, which are found mostly in central and northern European countries, postal savings banks were created in almost all countries. Their record in mobilizing resources has varied from modest to impressive, and their relative success can be attributed to a number of factors. For example, they have done better in countries where commercial banks and other competing institutions had small branch networks (such as in Japan) or in countries where they have enjoyed fiscal advantages that were denied their competitors (such as in France). In Japan commercial bank networks have been subject to strict official regulation; in France only deposits with the postal and ordinary savings banks have benefited from fiscal incentives. The relative importance of postal savings banks has been greatest in the former communist countries, where they had the monopoly on collecting household deposits. Despite establishing the first postal savings bank, postal savings in the United Kingdom did not grow very large relative to the domestic financial system, mainly because commercial banks, building societies, and trustee savings banks were able to develop large branch networks and to offer more attractive deposit facilities.

The most successful postal savings bank has been that in Japan, which, on the basis of resources mobilized, is by far the largest financial institution in the world. Its total deposits amount to nearly $1.5 trillion at current rates of exchange – more than three times larger than the assets of the largest banks. The success of the postal savings bank in Japan is often attributed to the fiscal advantages conferred on deposits of up to 3 million yen. But this explanation is not correct because the fiscal incentives applied for all small deposits, not just those made with the postal savings bank. The success of the postal savings bank came mainly from the convenience of its vast branch network (only in the 1980s did the branch networks of all other deposit institutions match that of the post office) and, to a lesser extent, from the safety of explicit government backing. Safety was more important in the past, when bank runs afflicted the Japanese financial system. But it has clearly been less important in the past fifty years as official Japanese policy sought to prevent the failure of any bank. The importance of the safety factor was shown during the banking crisis of April 1927, when thirty-seven banks were unable to meet demands for deposit withdrawals. As a result, deposits at the five biggest banks increased by about 30 percent within a year of the crisis and by about 28 percent at ordinary savings banks, which were not affected by the crisis. But the deposits of the postal savings bank almost doubled in the same period (Born 1983:253).

Until recently, postal savings banks were required to place their deposit funds in government debt. This requirement converted such deposits into a captive source for financing government budgets, and in many countries the returns offered to depositors were highly negative in real terms. But in recent years there has been a trend to expand the lending powers of postal savings banks and in some cases to merge them with existing commercial banks or to convert them into full-fledged commercial banks.[3]

Credit cooperatives

Credit cooperatives, in particular the Raiffeisen banks, were hailed as the most wonderful institutions in the world by a report of a U.S. commission that studied European agriculture in the first decade of the twentieth century (Metcalf and Black 1915). Positive views were also expressed in a U.K. report on German agriculture (Cahill 1913). This favorable assessment was not affected by the disputes and divisions that afflicted the movement in Germany. It reflected the success of credit cooperatives in mobilizing resources and offering credit services to German farmers, artisans, and small traders and in avoiding failures. As in the case of savings banks, these institutional innovations generated considerable interest in other countries and they quickly spread to several neighboring countries.

Credit cooperatives were created to meet the credit needs of small farmers in rural areas and those of artisans and small traders in urban areas, thus protecting them from the high rates charged by moneylenders. Like savings banks, credit cooperatives benefited from low transaction costs, as they often

---

[3] For example, in Sweden the post office savings bank was merged with a previously state-owned commercial bank to form the PK Bank in 1974. More recently, the PK Bank was merged into the Nordbanken. In the Netherlands the postal savings bank was first merged with the postal giro to form the Postal Bank in the late 1970s. The new bank was later taken over by another commercial bank, which itself was subsequently taken over by the ING group, a financial conglomerate with interests in both banking and insurance.

operated out of the kitchen of a farmer and relied on unpaid managers and staff. In addition, because of their reliance on local knowledge and peer monitoring, their loan losses were unusually low.

Credit cooperatives used the joint and several unlimited liability of members to raise funds from nonmembers and to make loans on the security of the character, moral worth, industry, sobriety, and thrift of their members, reinforced by peer pressure and mutual oversight. Thrift was motivated by the principle of unlimited liability, which also contributed to a high loan-repayment record. Effective peer monitoring was facilitated by the small size and small area of operation of most credit cooperatives.

Credit cooperatives were championed by men of high integrity and social standing, such as clergymen, wealthy philanthropists, and public officials. The protagonists emphasized self-help and developed a three-tier structure. Regional units facilitated the flow of funds across individual cooperatives and also provided valuable audit and control services, while national units represented the joint interests of credit cooperatives and provided a link to national money and capital markets. Urban credit cooperatives, whose areas of operation were large, abandoned the concept of unlimited liability very early in their development. But all types of credit cooperatives emphasized the need to accumulate reserve funds to be used during times of difficulty.

Despite the clear advantages enjoyed by credit cooperatives in terms of lower transaction and information costs and lower loan losses, Guinnane (1993:1) notes that their critics in Germany and elsewhere argued that their success was not attributable to their higher efficiency, but rather to their reliance on local boosterism in the form of unpaid managerial labor. In addition, critics accused credit cooperatives of being patronage devices through which local elites controlled both poor people's access to credit and, with it, their own customers, laborers, and so on. But the great success of these institutions in the ensuing 100 years strongly suggests that these criticisms overly exaggerated any underlying tendencies of patronage and control.

Credit cooperatives in Germany

Credit cooperatives were first established in Germany in the 1840s. The first cooperatives were urban credit cooperatives that were founded by Hermann Schulze-Delitzsch and catered to the needs of artisans and small traders. The first rural credit cooperatives were established in the 1860s by Friedrich Wilhelm Raiffeisen and Wilhelm Haas. These institutions were oriented toward farmers and other people living in small villages. Both types of cooperatives initially had unlimited liability. After passage of the law on credit cooperatives in 1889, most urban cooperatives gradually adopted limited liability, but rural cooperatives continued to rely on unlimited liability. Both types of credit cooperatives experienced rapid growth.

By the mid-1860s, 80 urban credit cooperatives were operating with nearly

20,000 members. A general association of trading and economic cooperatives was created in 1864 to represent their joint interests, while a central cooperative bank was also established in the same year in Berlin as a partnership limited by shares. Although the purpose of the central cooperative bank was to act as a clearinghouse for credit cooperatives – accepting their deposits and granting them credits on current accounts – credit cooperatives made little use of its services, and the central cooperative bank engaged in ordinary commercial and investment banking. But it suffered substantial losses in this business and was merged with the expanding Dresdner Bank in 1904. Despite the problems of their central cooperative bank, urban credit cooperatives continued to expand. Their number rose to 740 with more than 300,000 members by 1870 and to 1,500 with more than 800,000 members by 1913. More than 1.5 billion marks in credit was provided in 1913 (Born 1983:111–12).

The number of rural credit cooperatives also increased very rapidly. There were 30 such cooperatives by 1866 and about 100 by 1872, when Raiffeisen created the first central cooperative bank for rural credit cooperatives at Neuwied. Two more central banks were founded by Raiffeisen in quick succession, and all three were united to form the German Agricultural General Bank in 1874, which was a registered society with unlimited liability. But Schulze-Delitzsch objected to the creation of a central bank without share capital and took the matter to the courts. As a result, the central bank for rural cooperatives was dissolved and reconstituted in 1876 as a joint-stock company called the German Agricultural Central Loan Bank (also referred to as the Central Raiffeisen Bank). It was owned by societies that participated in the Federation of Raiffeisen banks.

The rural credit cooperatives were further divided in 1877 between those founded by Raiffeisen, who favored the creation of a three-tier structure with considerable central control in order to level out the differences between poor and rich cooperatives, and those founded by Haas, who defended the independence and autonomy of individual cooperatives and wanted to limit the role of central bodies to the representation of common interests, counseling, and cash audits. Despite this division, the number of rural credit cooperatives continued to expand, reaching more than 1,700 by 1890 and nearly 17,000 by 1913, when they had a total membership of 1.5 million (Cahill 1913:98). Their total assets amounted to 3 billion marks, representing about 5 percent of the total assets of German banks (Guinnane 1994b:43). By 1913 fifty-two regional central banks were operating in addition to two national ones: the Central Raiffeisen Bank and the Prussian Central Cooperative Bank, a state bank that was established in 1895. The total assets of all credit cooperatives accounted for 8 percent of all banking assets in 1913.

The creation of central banks intensified the ''system dispute'' between Schulze-Delitzsch and Raiffeisen. Opposition to a central bank with unlimited liability was based on the argument that individual societies should not assume double unlimited liability – their own and that of other societies. But another source of system dispute had to do with the use of share capital and entrance fees. Although both Schulze-Delitzsch and Raiffeisen favored unlimited liability and the accumulation of reserves to strengthen the solvency of credit cooperatives over time, urban cooperatives introduced share capital, which, together with accumulated reserves, would provide a first buffer, while the joint unlimited liability of members would provide a second line of defense. Raiffeisen was opposed to levying entrance fees and the institution of share capital, as they would have prevented poorer farmers from joining.

In the early days of credit cooperatives, three types of liability structure were discussed: unlimited liability, unlimited contributory liability, and limited liability. Unlimited liability implied that members were individually and collectively responsible for the debts of the cooperative. In case of insolvency the cooperatives would first apply a per capita levy on all members. But if the cooperative still had unsettled debts after three months, creditors could sue individual members for the full amount of the remaining debt. Although members had a right of restitution from the cooperative, if other members were much poorer, the likelihood of recovery would be very small. For this reason joint and several unlimited liability made more sense in communities where all members were small farmers and had more or less equal financial means.

The concept of unlimited contributory liability was introduced by the law of 1889. Under this arrangement per capita levies could be imposed on members, but creditors could not start proceedings against individual members. Contributions not recovered from individual members, owing to their insolvency, could be divided equally among remaining members. Thus, members' liability continued to be unlimited, but the process of debt recovery would be subject to a long and tedious procedure that undermined the ability of cooperatives to raise debt from nonmembers. This form of liability was adopted by only a small number of cooperatives.

Limited liability involved both the purchase of a share in the cooperative and the agreement to pay an additional predetermined fixed sum of money in case of insolvency (this was similar to the concept of double liability that prevailed in commercial banks in the United States in the second half of the nineteenth century). In Saxony and Pomerania, where most rural credit cooperatives with limited liability were found, the additional liability was between forty and fifty times the nominal value of each share. In these two provinces landowning members had suffered from the collapse of some urban credit cooperatives with unlimited liability rules. When limited liability was legalized by the act of 1889, it was adopted by rural credit cooperatives to counter the mistrust of landowners (Cahill 1913:114–20).

Because of their different orientation, urban and rural credit cooperatives developed different operating characteristics. The urban cooperatives focused on short-term lending, operated in bigger areas, and had larger membership. After the adoption of limited liability, which was probably made necessary by the wide area of operations, large membership, and, therefore, the inability of members to monitor each other, some urban credit cooperatives were faced with solvency problems from bad loans. In contrast, most rural credit cooperatives had a small membership and operated in a narrow and well-defined area. This setup facilitated peer monitoring and supported the maintenance of unlimited liability. From the outset, rural cooperatives were able to make loans for five to ten years, repayable in installments. The security was based on the character of the borrower, the purpose of the loan, and two other members standing as sureties. Between 1895 and 1910 only 19 rural credit cooperatives out of 10,000 were involved in bankruptcy proceedings. During the same period there were 69 cases of insolvency among the more than 1,000 urban credit cooperatives, and a total of 386 bankruptcies among 6,000 ordinary commercial banking and credit undertakings (Cahill 1913:118).

The concept of unlimited liability was supplemented by the creation of a three-tier structure to ensure the good performance and stability of rural credit cooperatives (Guinnane 1994b). The three-tier structure enabled rural cooperatives to overcome their funding exposure, which arose because they made long-term loans from short-term deposits. Credit cooperatives were also vulnerable to liquidity problems that could be caused by a shock affecting all members in a local area. The regional cooperatives provided liquidity management, funding, and auditing services, all of which increased the general creditworthiness of credit cooperatives. They also forced discipline on individual cooperatives and kept fraud and mismanagement under control.

This impressive record inspired the authors of the report of the U.S. commission from the state of Washington to describe the Raiffeisen system as the most wonderful system in the world, "capable of creating capital out of nothing" and to assert that "moral character, industry, sobriety, and thrift were better security than property!" The enthusiasm with which the Raiffeisen banks were greeted in Europe is exemplified by several statements from the sponsors of credit cooperatives in Italy. The first statement was made by Luigi Luzzatti, who established the first urban credit cooperative in Milan in 1865:

> The rural bank, which arose without capital, rich only in its invisible treasure of mutual trust and human solidarity, is the fruit of the modest, unrecognized virtues of the country folk, bound together by bonds of mutual affection, who assist and watch over each other with the subtle vigilance of neighbors. And, lo and behold, these humble folk, void of economic lore, have accomplished a miracle, due to the fact that a moral and not a material impulse guided their work, the miracle of creating capital out of nothing. (Metcalf and Black 1915:114)

Luzzatti also declared: "The security of a cooperative bank is the moral character of its members. To make these banks secure, we have to make the lazy man industrious, the drunkard sober, the improvident thrifty, and even the illiterate educated'' (Metcalf and Black 1915:115). A third statement was made by Leone Wollemborg, who founded the first Italian rural credit co-operative in Loreggia in 1883:

> Suppose you have 100 small working farmers, all possessing honesty, industry and labor capacity; this is their only capital. A capitalist might with safety make them a loan of fifty francs each; but some of these men will certainly be afflicted with sickness, death or lack of employment. It is impossible to say which will thus be unable to pay, but it is certain that it will only be a certain proportion. Experience has shown that 98 will pay. In order to meet the liability, the group must undertake to become responsible for the other two who are likely to be unable to pay. There will be 98 men to repay the loan made to 100. They will thus be able to assume responsibility for a loan of 49 each instead of 50, for they will have to assume responsibility for the two unable to pay and by making themselves collectively responsible for the loan, they will be able to make it for 49 multiplied by 100. It is thus seen that the mathematical formula on which these banks are able to secure their capital is nothing more than an application of the same principle which governs insurance. Therefore unlimited liability is the first principle. The other principle is limitation of the area of operations, restricting it to certain localities, and this limitation of area also constitutes the justification of the principle of unlimited liability. It would not be fair to expect a man to make himself responsible for a loan, the use of which was beyond his control. But when the loans are strictly limited to people residing in the same locality, all can become vigilant and act as inspectors for their own protection. And you will find that inspection thus exercised is far superior to any government inspection, since each man has been rendered personally liable and is acting as inspector in his own interest. As one of the farmers said: ''We are 100, all acting as spies on the others to see that nobody does anything wrong.'' (Metcalf and Black 1915:68)

Credit cooperatives in other European countries

The preceding observations were based on the German experience, as Luzzatti was a student of Schulze-Delitzsch and Wollemborg a student of Raiffeisen. Despite extolling its virtues, Italian credit cooperatives did not adopt unlimited liability because peasants were ignorant of the workings of organized credit, and men owning property were unwilling to become liable for poor neighbors without property. Nevertheless, credit cooperatives made considerable progress in Italy. The growth of rural cooperatives was stimulated by the cooperation and support provided by savings banks and by urban credit cooperatives, known in Italy as ''people's banks.'' Credit cooperatives spread in several other European countries, such as Austria, Belgium, France, the Netherlands, Switzerland, Hungary, Poland and other Eastern European countries. Credit cooperatives were also well developed in Canada, although they eventually evolved into credit unions.

As in the case of savings banks, credit cooperatives were promoted in most countries by clergymen, wealthy philanthropists, or, as in the case of Schulze-Delitzsch and Raiffeisen, local officials and politicians. In general, the promoters emphasized self-help and opposed relying on government financial assistance, except for publicity and education. France was the one exception – the "crédit agricole" was supported by a substantial loan from the Bank of France. This condition was imposed by the government on the Bank of France as a condition for renewing its charter in 1897.

There was an intriguing contrast in authorities' attitudes in Germany and in France. When the cooperative movement was founded in Germany, the authorities were at first opposed to it. The king of Saxony forbade the first convention of cooperative societies called by Schulze-Delitzsch at Dresden in 1859. Moreover, both William of Prussia and Bismarck were hostile, seeing cooperation as an insidious form of socialism intending to undermine government. But later on, in view of the success of the cooperatives and their contribution to the prosperity of the rural population, the attitude of the authorities became very favorable and supportive (Metcalf and Black 1915:22).

In France the creation of credit cooperatives was promoted by Louis Durand, who studied the Raiffeisen system and began to establish in 1893 what were known as the "caisses Durand." But the republican government of the time perceived the caisses Durand to be a ploy of reactionary forces associated with the Catholic Church. To preempt their initiative, the government enacted a law that promoted the creation of both local and regional agricultural banks that were effectively established along departmental lines and thus subject to political control (Bonin 1992:29–32). The regional banks played a key part in rediscounting the bills of local banks and distributing central bank credit to local banks established in accordance with the provisions of the republican law. The availability of state credit and perhaps also the fact that the credit cooperative system was developed from the top down generated a low level of deposits, as farmers preferred to deposit their money with the savings banks (Metcalf and Black 1915:230–5).

After World War I the French authorities passed legislation that encouraged the creation of "banques populaires" by merchants, craftsmen, and professionals in order to increase the supply of credit to the middle class. The Caisse Centrale des Banques Populaires was founded in 1921, followed by the Chambre Syndicale des Banques Populaires, which intended to strengthen the control and supervision of individual banks, which had suffered many failures. In addition, measures were taken to consolidate and expand the operations of agricultural credit cooperatives, of which there were already more than 4,000 by World War I. The Caisse Nationale de Credit Agricole was created in 1920, and it helped expand the number of rural credit cooperatives to about 10,000, of which about two-thirds belonged to the favored public network and the rest consisted of "caisses libres" (Born 1983: 240–1).[4]

Credit cooperatives did not meet with much success in the United Kingdom and Ireland. Several reasons were advanced for the failure of credit cooperatives in the United Kingdom. First, the large branch networks established by joint-stock banks made credit facilities available to a larger number of farmers than in other countries, implying that fewer farmers relied on loans from moneylenders at high rates. Second, farmers had access to trade credit from suppliers. Third, unlimited liability was unpopular in the United Kingdom, where limited liability by share capital was widespread. Fourth, average farmers and smallholders were allegedly unwilling to disclose their financial condition to their neighbors and were also allegedly reluctant to borrow in cash (as distinct from trade credit, given in kind) (Metcalf and Black 1915: 258). Another possible factor was the greater concentration of land ownership and larger size of farms in the United Kingdom, implying that there were fewer smallholders than in other countries.

In Ireland, although Irish bankers argued that credit cooperatives failed simply because there was no need for them, other observers maintained that credit was expensive for smallholders and credit cooperatives could have been a solution to the problem. The failure of credit cooperatives in Ireland has been attributed to several factors (Guinnane 1994a). First, because most cooperatives were established with unlimited liability, they didn't attract the more prosperous locals whose burden in case of insolvency would have been unequal with respect to poorer members. However, the absence of prosperous locals deprived the credit cooperatives in Ireland of the monitoring and expertise that was a crucial factor for the success in Germany. Second, Irish cooperatives failed to develop the central banks that were a feature of the German system. Although credit facilities were obtained from the state and from joint-stock banks, the failure to develop strong central auditing federations deprived Irish cooperatives of the discipline and good record keeping found in Germany.

Third, Irish farmers were reluctant to force their neighbors to repay their loans or face adverse consequences. Thus, a major rationale for the creation of credit cooperatives, the discipline exerted by peer monitoring, was absent in Ireland. Fourth, Irish farmers were reluctant to borrow from credit cooperatives and thus disclose their financial position to the entire community. In contrast, German farmers were reportedly happier borrowing from their local credit cooperatives than from banks. Irish farmers were even reluctant to place deposits with credit cooperatives and thus expose themselves to pres-

---

[4] The Caisse Nationale de Credit Agricole played a central role in the distribution of subsidized credits to French farmers after the end of World War II. Today, the French Credit Agricole, like the Dutch Rabobank, is among the largest universal banks in Europe.

sures to extend personal loans or to act as cosigners for loans. Because the Post Office Savings Bank was established in the United Kingdom and Ireland before credit cooperatives, the need to provide deposit and savings facilities in rural areas that were not well served by commercial or savings banks – one of the rationales for the emergence of credit cooperatives in Germany – was not pressing. Another important factor may have been the purchase of land by tenant farmers that was made possible through government mortgages. Although mortgage payments were probably lower than land rents, the assumption of large debt sharply reduced the ability of farmers to borrow from other sources.

The experience of Irish credit cooperatives supports the arguments explaining credit cooperatives' lack of progress in the United Kingdom. The failure of credit cooperatives in Ireland also underscores the importance of cultural and educational factors, the importance of sequencing institutional innovations, and the difficulties of transplanting institutions and practices from one country to another.

Building societies and savings and loan associations

In several continental European countries savings banks and credit cooperatives, as well as mortgage credit banks, were able to expand into mortgage banking and housing finance. They thus filled the gap in the provision of housing finance to middle-income people that was created by the orientation of commercial banks toward industrial and commercial companies and wealthy individuals. But in the United Kingdom and the United States (as well as several other Anglo-American countries, such as Australia, New Zealand, South Africa, and, to a lesser degree, Canada), where savings banks and credit cooperatives were either not successful or not allowed to engage in lending, building societies and savings and loan associations emerged to fill this gap. These institutions specialized in the provision of housing finance but funded their operations from short-term deposits rather than long-term bonds.

Building societies and savings and loan associations (initially known as building and loan associations) had common roots and followed fairly similar paths of development, at least until the Great Depression (Vittas 1992). They originated in the early terminating societies that appeared in the United Kingdom in the second half of the eighteenth century and in the United States in the first half of the nineteenth century. The early terminating institutions were followed in both countries by serial institutions and then by permanent institutions. In both countries they suffered from fraud and mismanagement, and the instruments used were very similar.

Early building societies in the United Kingdom and building and loan associations in the United States were created as cooperative ventures, established by relatively wealthy merchants, craftsmen, and professionals to enable cooperative members to buy homes. As terminating institutions, they wound up their operations once all members achieved their goal. Each member agreed to make regular subscriptions until a relatively large sum of money was collected. This rule implied that these institutions were established for relatively long periods (usually slightly less than twelve years, but ranging between ten and fourteen years) and that members were able and willing to undertake long-term commitments.

An apt description of how terminating institutions operated is given by the rules of the Oxford Provident Building Association, which was the first U.S. building society, founded in 1831 in Frankford, Pennsylvania (Bodfish and Theobald 1938:30–9). This association also underscored the common roots of thrift institutions in the two countries, since the Oxford Provident was established by two English-born manufacturers and an English-born doctor in association with a lawyer and a school teacher, who was also a surveyor and conveyancer. The rules of the Oxford Provident stipulated that members had to subscribe for between one and five shares, each having a par value of $500. They were required to pay an initial $5 for each share subscribed and then $3 a month on each share. A member was entitled to borrow $500 for each share held. Whenever $500 was accumulated in the treasury of the association, a loan of that amount was offered to the member who bid the highest premium. Loans were not made for building houses more than five miles from the market house in Frankford or outside of Philadelphia County, and no member in arrears on his contributions or fines was allowed to bid for a loan. Borrowers were charged a flat fee of $3 to cover the costs of examining title papers and making disbursements in accordance with progress in the construction of the house being financed. Borrowers were required to pay $2.50 a month for the loan, equivalent to an annual rate of interest of 6 percent, in addition to their $3 monthly contribution. A fine of 25 cents was imposed on members who failed to pay their contribution and an additional 25 cents on borrowers who failed to pay their monthly interest.[5]

Despite the problems they faced, the number of building societies increased quite rapidly, although early records were far from comprehensive (Cleary 1965). Between 1780 and 1820, 69 societies were founded, and in the ensuing fifty years more than 3,000 societies were created. But because

---

[5] When it was organized, the Oxford Provident had thirty-six members who subscribed for a total of forty shares (four members subscribed for two shares each and the others for one). The highest premium bid for the first loan was $10, but the first borrower, who was a lamplighter, was unable to keep up with his payments, and his membership, property, and obligations to the association were transferred to another person. The Oxford Provident was terminated in 1841, more or less as originally planned. A second Oxford Provident was almost immediately established with seventy-nine members and shares with a reduced par value of $200 and monthly contributions of $1. The second Oxford Provident was terminated in 1851 and was followed by a third one set up in 1852, which evolved into a serial association.

most societies were of the terminating type, only about 1,500 societies were operating in 1869. In the United States, building and loan associations grew slowly at first, but they took off after the 1870s, becoming the main type of thrift institution in most states outside of New England. They experienced very rapid growth in the late 1880s, their number increasing from around 2,000 in 1888 to more than 5,000 in 1893.

The great strengths of early societies were their mutual character and the high degree of mutual trust among their members. Every member was equally involved in the affairs of the society as lender, borrower, and officeholder (members took turns holding office). Monthly meetings were held at inns and were considered social events as well as business meetings. But early building societies faced many problems, such as ensuring that members paid their dues, permitting withdrawals, accommodating new members, supplementing their funds with borrowing in order to accelerate the granting of mortgage loans, and utilizing surplus funds. Serial terminating institutions provided a partial answer to these problems, but it was the advent of permanent building societies (and permanent building and loan associations) that enabled the separation of borrowers and investors and allowed these institutions to extend loans for fixed terms, as well as to raise funds through shares and deposits on different terms and conditions.

But these innovations weakened the institutions' mutual character and gave rise to imprudent and fraudulent behavior. The history of building societies in the nineteenth century is replete with episodes of such behavior and of changes in legislation that sought to establish more prudent standards. With the growth in the number of permanent societies, loans started to be made on security other than houses, with some societies providing advances against more speculative properties, such as factories. Advances to speculative builders were also made, exposing societies to considerable losses when builders went bankrupt. Many societies borrowed excessive amounts to finance their operations. Few of them had an adequate capital structure or held enough of their assets in liquid form. Because funds could be withdrawn on demand, severe problems were created when a society failed and depositors made a run on other societies. Competition led to even more generous advances and less careful selection of securities. Geographic diversification involved lending in distant locations, where a lack of knowledge of local conditions created problems with the evaluation of properties and assessment of borrowers' creditworthiness.

Accounting practices also left much to be desired. In particular, the treatment of discounts on advances created difficulties. Many societies gave advances to borrowers who accepted the largest discount on the nominal amount of the advance. These discounts were then treated as realized profit available for distribution to members instead of being amortized over the life of the advance. This practice had an adverse impact on the long-term performance of societies because the returns to members in later years were much lower and because borrowers with speculative and more risky ventures tended to offer the largest discounts.

Several societies experienced an increase in fraudulent activities both internally (by officers) and externally (by borrowers). Lack of adequate supervision allowed directors and officers to take out society funds for their personal use. In some cases borrowers defrauded societies, usually by overstating the value of properties, with the help of officials. Outsiders, such as builders and solicitors, engaged in fraudulent activities involving dummy purchasers and forged deeds.

The advent of permanent building societies and building and loan associations was also associated with a geographic expansion of operations that led to the emergence of "nationals," that is, institutions with operations in several regions or states. Unlike savings banks and credit cooperatives in continental Europe, building societies in the United Kingdom and savings and loan associations in the United States did not establish a three-tier structure that would have allowed geographic diversification of risk without loss of local knowledge and thus obviated the need for nationals. Nationals engaged in more aggressive competition and adopted sharper practices that in many cases involved outright fraud and mismanagement.

In the United Kingdom the most serious fraud involved the Liberator Society, a London-based society that had risen to become the largest in the movement. At the time of its failure in 1892, the Liberator was nearly twice the size of its nearest rival. In a situation reminiscent of the worst offenders in the savings and loan debacle of the 1980s, the Liberator had only 2 percent of its mortgages in ordinary advances when it failed; the vast majority were in second and third mortgages to companies controlled by its director. The collapse of the Liberator had an adverse impact on the growth of building societies for many years to come. Prudential controls were tightened further, but geographic expansion and diversification were not banned.

In the United States, nationals began to appear in the 1880s. Unlike most associations, which were small, local institutions, they sought to attract funds by establishing branches throughout the United States and by using aggressive advertising and selling techniques. Not all nationals were outright frauds, but typically they were promotional ventures for the benefit of their organizers. They used misleading advertisements and door-to-door selling and paid high commissions to agents. They charged stiff membership fees and various expense fees for insurance and other overhead costs. And they imposed heavy fines on late payers and profited from forfeiture of sums paid on lapsed shares. Because they made loans on extremely risky projects at very high interest rates and because they managed their assets poorly, nationals were among the first to fail when the 1893 depression hit.

The failure of the largest national, the Southern Building and Loan Association of Knoxville, Tennessee, in 1897 had an adverse impact on the whole movement. Responding to strong complaints by local associations, many states enacted regulations that required building and loan associations to confine their operations to local areas. This regulation was in line with the geographic limits imposed on commercial banks and reflected widespread populist concerns about out-of-state financial institutions. But at the same time these rules prevented savings and loan associations from geographically diversifying their loan portfolios.

After the turn of the century and until the onset of the Great Depression, both building societies and savings and loan associations expanded rapidly, especially during the boom years of the 1920s. Institutions in both countries refined their instruments in response to the volatility of interest rates caused by World War I and the growing competition on deposits from commercial and savings banks. During this period the use of variable-rate mortgage loans started to spread, while strong emphasis was placed on promoting home ownership and thrift.

At that time building societies and savings and loan associations were the only types of lenders that provided mortgage loans with maturities in excess of ten years, based on regular repayment, either through the share-accumulation, sinking-fund method or through reducing self-amortizing balance loans. Most other lenders (commercial banks, savings banks, and insurance companies) provided loans for shorter periods, say up to five years, with bullet repayment provisions and thus no regular amortization and often with the right of recall. This practice has been attributed to the information and enforcement costs that lenders faced (Snowden and Bu-Saba 1992). These costs were lower for building societies and savings and loan associations, in which members had some common bond. And thus these institutions were better able to increase the maturity of their loans.

Two additional factors explaining this difference include government regulations, especially important in the United States, where commercial banks were not at that time permitted to engage in longer-term mortgages, and the orientation and marketing philosophies of commercial banks, which emphasized short-term lending. Commercial banks had plenty of opportunities to expand their loan portfolios without needing to focus on long-term mortgages.

Practice in the United States changed after the measures taken during the Great Depression. These included government insurance and guarantees for twenty-year and then thirty-year loans at fixed rates, a practice that proved catastrophic for savings and loan associations in the 1970s and 1980s (Vittas 1992). In the United Kingdom the large commercial banks continued to abstain from mortgage lending up to the late 1970s. In large part this was caused by their reluctance to borrow short and lend long and their failure to appreciate that lending long at variable rates, a practice that building societies had perfected over time, avoided the interest rate exposures that concerned them most. Commercial banks changed their approach in the 1980s, aided in part by the abolition of lending controls and the declining opportunities for growth in corporate lending – a result of the advent of securitization and other institutional changes.

Credit unions

Credit unions were developed in North America in the early part of the twentieth century. They were designed as an extension of the credit cooperatives that thrived in Germany at the end of the nineteenth century. The term *credit union* is often used interchangeably with *credit cooperative*. For the purposes of this chapter, credit unions are oriented toward consumer credit (and more recently toward housing finance) and credit cooperatives toward small traders, artisans, and farmers.[6]

Credit unions were promoted in North America by Alphonse Desjardins, who founded these institutions in Quebec and other Canadian provinces and then established the first credit union in New Hampshire in 1909. Credit unions were created to provide more convenient and less expensive credit facilities to their members, who were mostly salaried employees and factory workers. They were formed on the basis of a common bond among their members, which lowered their monitoring costs. They also benefited from low transaction costs because they often operated from offices and factories, not needing to build extensive networks or engage in expensive advertising campaigns.[7]

Credit unions were promoted heavily in Canada and the United States by their proponents, and they too prospered because they provided small loans at reasonable interest rates and at the same time paid relatively high dividends (interest) on members' credit balances. There were more than 1,300 credit unions in the United States in 1930, holding less than $50 million in assets. But their number increased substantially after World War II. At one point there were more than 25,000 operating, although their number has declined in recent years. Today there are slightly more than 12,000.

In Canada there are nearly 1,100 credit unions. Credit unions are much

---

[6] But the distinction between credit cooperatives and credit unions, as well as that between credit cooperatives and savings banks, is difficult to establish in practice and may reflect differences in terminology rather than function.

[7] To the extent that credit unions specialize in consumer credit, they represent a formal extension of rotating savings and credit associations. These are found in most countries, especially countries in the early stages of financial development, and facilitate saving for relatively large consumer expenditures. Rotating savings and credit associations involve a small number of individuals, typically from six to forty, who pay a regular amount on a periodic basis into a common pool that is then made available to each member in rotation. Because of their small size, rotating savings and credit associations rely on a common bond among participants, often their place of employment or a neighborhood or membership of a local church or a club. Rotating savings and credit associations are often associated with social gatherings, similar in concept to the early, terminating building societies.

smaller in other Anglo-American countries such as Australia and Ireland, and particularly small in the United Kingdom and New Zealand, where they have been squeezed out by commercial banks (with large branch networks and a strong retail presence), savings banks, and building societies. Credit unions have not emerged as a distinct group in continental European countries, mainly because their activities have been subsumed by the credit cooperatives that also serve tradespeople, artisans, and farmers.

Evaluation and relevance for developing countries

Several factors shaped the emergence and growth of these institutions in different countries, including perceived gaps in financial markets, the institutions' rapid spread in neighboring and even distant countries, the role of leadership with integrity and vision in promoting their establishment, the change in orientation in the early stages of their development, and the operating efficiency and comparative advantage they enjoyed over other institutions.

Common influences

The general success and growth record of thrift deposit institutions in the eighteenth, nineteenth, and much of the twentieth centuries suggest that gaps in the market for financial services were real and that these institutions had the wherewithal to make a positive contribution to financial sector development. The perceived gaps in the supply of financial services emanated from the specialization of commercial banks in dealing with industrial and commercial companies and their reluctance to seek the business of middle- and low-income people or artisans, small traders, and farmers. Today, the unwillingness of commercial banks to provide financial services to these groups is attributed to the problems caused by high information and monitoring costs, as well as the weak enforcement mechanisms that characterized these segments of the market in earlier periods. The relative success of thrift deposit institutions is explained by their ability to overcome these problems.

But an additional and not necessarily exclusive explanation holds that commercial banks found it more profitable to deal with the business sector (and wealthy individuals) and did not have the organizational capacity and incentives to expand into small-firm, household, or rural banking. In other words, given their financial and human resources, commercial banks had more than enough to do in trade and working capital finance. They had little incentive to expand into more risky activities, such as term finance and mortgage banking, or into the mass banking business, which required a much bigger investment in infrastructure and would have swamped their facilities if it was pursued without expanding their branch networks.

What was remarkable about the institutional innovations seen in the different types of thrift deposit institutions was their rapid spread into neighboring and distant countries. Today, the spread of ideas is explained by the extensive communications links between different countries and the globalization of markets. Initiatives to create mutual funds and financial futures markets around the world, let alone pension funds based on individual retirement accounts, are examples of how fast and how far new ideas can travel these days. International acceptance of privatization and economic deregulation within less than fifteen years is another example. The work of institutions like the World Bank also contributes to the faster propagation of these ideas. In earlier periods news traveled at a much slower pace, and the rate of diffusion was measured in decades rather than years. But the spread was still quite remarkable given the mass communications technology that prevailed at the time.

Individuals that provided inspiration and leadership in first creating and then propagating the spread of different types of thrift deposit institutions were crucially important in most countries. These individuals were instrumental in establishing the fundamental principles of operation of different institutions and in ensuring their success at the initial stages of development. Of course, there were individual leaders who exploited these institutions for personal gain and who behaved imprudently and even fraudulently. But once these institutions were well established, their survival was secured as long as they continued to serve a useful purpose and there were enough managers with honesty and integrity to see the institutions through temporary crises and enable them to resume their growth. The experience of building societies in the United Kingdom is characteristic in this respect. Despite repeated crises and failures because of fraud and mismanagement, the good forces in the movement were able to prevail in the long run and led building societies to a very high level of achievement.

Another interesting feature that was common among thrift deposit institutions was their change of orientation at an early stage of development. Savings banks were created to encourage the poor to save, but in most countries they quickly reoriented their services to middle-income people and, if allowed, expanded into lending. In the United States, savings banks became major lenders to large industrial firms and had very close links and extensive interlocking directorships with commercial banks and insurance companies. In Germany, savings banks became the banks of the middle classes and developed close relations with the small and medium-size firms that are the backbone of German industry.

Building societies and savings and loan associations also changed their orientation from being formalized, money clubs helping their members to acquire a house into institutions that promoted thrift and home ownership. The formal change in orientation came with the advent of permanent institutions that permitted the separation of borrowers and investors. Credit cooperatives stayed closer to their original orientation – providing credit to their members – particularly for as long as members were subject to unlimited liability. But after the adoption of limited liability, credit cooperatives became more similar to other financial institutions, although still retaining a localized character, which was facilitated in Germany and some other countries by their three-tier structure.

Also common were the lower transaction and information costs of thrift deposit institutions compared with other financial institutions (commercial banks or insurance companies). Lower transaction costs resulted from the use of unpaid managers and other staff, particularly in their early years of operation, and the lack of a need to build expensive infrastructures or incur other operating costs such as advertising. Lower information costs stemmed from the local nature of their operations and the common links among their members, which allowed them to overcome the problems caused by information deficiencies and weak enforcement mechanisms. Lower information costs implied lower operating expenses in screening borrowers and lower loan losses from defaulting borrowers. Low information and transaction costs allowed much smaller spreads, making thrift deposit institutions more competitive than traditional moneylenders. Their comparative advantage over commercial banks and insurance companies depended more on their greater ability to make services (such as deposit facilities for low balances, long-term credits, and housing finance), available rather than on their lower spreads or lower loan charges. An additional competitive advantage was obtained from the fiscal incentives, particularly the exemption from income taxes, that thrift deposit institutions had long enjoyed in most countries.

Differences among thrift deposit institutions

Not all types of thrift deposit institutions thrived in all countries under review. But even if they took root, different institutions followed different development paths in different countries. Four main factors may account for these differences. The first was the structure of market gaps, which was itself the result of a dynamic interaction between functions and institutions. The second was related to the size and distribution of wealth. The third concerned cultural differences, including education and literacy. And the fourth concerned differences in organizational approach, especially the presence or absence of the three-tier structure.

The structure of market gaps and the interaction between functions and institutions probably explain why building societies and savings and loan associations thrived in the United Kingdom and the United States, but not in continental Europe. They also explain why, in contrast, credit cooperatives thrived in Europe but not in Anglo-American countries. Economists have argued that informational deficiencies and weak enforcement mechanisms explain why commercial banks were not more active in term finance and mortgage banking or in dealing with artisans, farmers, and poorer households.

But this analysis does not explain why commercial banks in Anglo-American countries did expand into some retail banking business in the nineteenth century, while those of continental Europe specialized almost exclusively in what could be called "corporate or wholesale banking."

Considering the organizational capacity of commercial banks in terms of their financial and human resources and their ability to respond to opportunities for profitable expansion provides another way to explain the structure of market gaps. Thus, commercial banks in Anglo-American countries, where large companies were able to obtain finance from nonbank sources, oriented themselves toward the retail market and built relatively larger branch networks that allowed them to develop relations with smaller firms. In central and northern European countries, in the absence of active securities markets and other sources of corporate finance, commercial banks maintained closer relations with larger companies and neglected households and small and medium-size firms.

As a result there was greater capacity for savings banks and credit cooperatives to emerge and grow in continental Europe. But once these institutions were established, there was less room for building societies to take root and grow, as savings banks and credit cooperatives were able to fill the gap in the provision of housing finance to relatively wealthy households.

In the United Kingdom the role of building societies was strengthened by the investment restrictions that were imposed on the trustee savings banks. In France, although savings banks were equally restricted, another type of institution – the mortgage credit bank – was created to fill the gap in mortgage banking. As a result, building societies have always played a very small part in the French financial system. Building societies have appeared in Germany, but despite benefiting from large fiscal incentives, their role has been secondary to that of mortgage credit banks and other thrift deposit institutions. Another example of the effect of the sequencing of institutional innovations is the creation of post office savings bank, in the United Kingdom and Ireland, which narrowed the scope for urban and rural credit cooperatives in these two countries.

The structure of market gaps and the interaction between functions and institutions may also explain why, despite perennial criticisms of commercial banks in many Anglo-American countries for failing to provide adequate services to small and medium-size firms, there have not been any serious attempts to create mutual banks lending to such firms. The scope for profitable operations by any such banks would clearly be restricted by the ability of low-risk firms to bank with existing commercial banks rather than join in a venture that would end up subsidizing high-risk firms.[8]

---

[8] The structure of market gaps and the interaction of institutions and functions can be seen as examples of the redundancy and complex adaptation of financial networks. For a discussion of the network characteristics of banking and financial systems, see Honohan and Vittas (1996).

In addition to the structure of market gaps, the size and distribution of wealth are also important determinants of scope, not only for thrift deposit institutions, but for all types of financial institutions. Poor people seek a safe place to keep their meager savings. A postal savings bank that maintains the real value of such savings and has a convenient network of post offices would be the ideal institution. But as income and wealth grow, demand for financial services increases and becomes more sophisticated. One of the most recent trends in the financial structure of OECD countries – the growing relative importance of pension and mutual funds – is in many respects a reflection of the growth of the financial wealth of these countries.

The distribution of wealth also affects financial structure. In developing countries, where wealth is highly concentrated, the demand for the services of thrift deposit institutions is very small. The distribution of wealth also has implications for the organization of thrift deposit institutions. For example attempts in Ireland to create rural credit cooperatives with unlimited liability failed because large-scale landowners were reluctant to assume unlimited liability for the debts of small-scale landowners. As seen from the experience of Germany, such cooperatives have a greater chance of success in communities with a more equal distribution of land holdings.

The experience of rural credit cooperatives in Ireland also underscores the importance of cultural factors. As discussed earlier, farmers in Ireland were allegedly reluctant to borrow from credit cooperatives because they did not want their neighbors to know what their financial condition was. In contrast, farmers in Germany were happier borrowing from their local cooperative than applying for a loan from a commercial or savings bank. But a more important aspect of cultural differences was the apparent reluctance of Irish farmers to deposit funds with a credit cooperative because they were afraid that when their neighbors found out about their deposits, the neighbors would ask them for a loan or at least want them to cosign a loan. This reluctance to divulge details about financial wealth appears to be important in poor communities in Africa and Asia.

Another cultural aspect that affected the operation of credit cooperatives in Ireland was the reluctance of members to impose strict discipline on defaulting borrowers. This weakened the benefits of peer monitoring and pressure in maintaining the low level of loan defaults and loan losses that characterized rural credit cooperatives in continental Europe. In this respect it is important to note the emphasis placed on literacy and education by the U.S. commission that investigated agricultural conditions in Europe. A high level of literacy and acceptance of the mutual benefits of peer monitoring and high loan repayment rates are essential for the success of any type of thrift deposit institution. Although most proponents of such institutions emphasize self-help and independence from government interference, they have accepted such support for education and publicity.

Cultural differences probably also explain the emergence of the three-tier structure in most European countries and Canada, where the credit union movement has been strongly influenced by developments in Germany and France, and their absence in Anglo-American countries. One of the great strengths of thrift deposit institutions in continental Europe was the development of the three-tier structure. Over time, this structure created a kind of informal deposit insurance scheme whereby weak links in the network would be rescued from failure but would be subject to strict discipline and the threat of expulsion if internal controls were not acceptable. This behavior was no different from that of the head office and branches of a commercial bank. The main difference lay in the greater autonomy of local institutions to make decisions affecting their local market and therefore their greater identification with and support of local developments. In Anglo-American countries the three-tier structure did not emerge, partly because of the antagonistic behavior of most leading institutions and partly because of regulatory restrictions. Regulatory restrictions were more important in the United States and resulted in a geographic concentration of risk that was aggravated by the failure to prevent the assumption of large interest rate risks by most savings and loan associations. The fear of centralized power was also a factor, especially in the United States, where even today credit union leaders oppose the creation of a three-tier structure.

Despite their differences, thrift deposit institutions were able to gain substantial market shares, not only in the markets in which they specialized, such as mortgage loans or rural deposits, but also in the overall market for financial intermediation services. But they have come under increasing pressure in recent years from four main sources. First, changes in the size and distribution of financial wealth have meant a growing demand for the services of pension and mutual funds. The clear implication of this trend is that even if their size does not decline in absolute terms, thrift deposit institutions are bound to suffer a decline in their relative importance. Although pension funds and mutual funds are similar in many respects – their members share in the returns and costs of their operation – their modes of operation are quite different. Some of the markets that thrift deposit institutions served so well in the past may now be better served by institutional investors, using new securitized instruments that are more suitable to investors' requirements than those of thrifts. Second, the advent of securitization and loss of corporate business by commercial banks has prompted a reorientation toward providing retail financial services to smaller firms and households, thus increasing the competitive pressures on thrifts. Third, changes in technology, both transaction technology and information technology, have reduced, if not completely eliminated, the past comparative advantages of thrift deposit institutions in this area. Fourth, concomitant changes in financial regulation have removed the barriers between different types of institutions. In fact, the right given to thrift deposit institutions to diversify into other financial services has implied an increased demand for external capital, which has been one of the factors motivating the recent spate of conversions into stock ownership. And diversification into new services has further weakened the already flimsy link of mutuality that characterizes modern thrift deposit institutions.

The conversion of mutual savings and loan associations and mutual savings banks into stock institutions has been very extensive in the United States, dating from at least the early 1960s. It has been accelerated by the debacle of savings and loan associations in the 1980s. Demutualization of building societies began in the 1980s and has progressed furthest in Australia, New Zealand, and South Africa, but is now spreading in the United Kingdom. The trend is now also reaching continental Europe (especially Scandinavia) and Japan, where mutual institutions are coming under increasing market and financial pressures.

Relevance for developing countries

Most developing countries have established some type of thrift deposit institution, but achieved mostly unsatisfactory results. For example, postal savings banks have been created in most countries of Africa and Asia. In Africa, postal savings have suffered from high inflation and high, negative, real interest rates, which have eroded the real value of deposits. In Asia, postal savings banks have met with considerable success in some countries, but in other countries their record has been mediocre. Building societies have been established in former British colonies in both Africa and Asia, and savings and loan associations in Latin America. But again their performance has been poor, suffering from the effects of high inflation and low recovery rates. Finally, credit cooperatives and credit unions have been tried in many developing countries, but their performance has been undermined by the availability of external funds – funds not mobilized by their membership – which resulted in poor peer monitoring and low loan recovery rates. Savings banks and credit cooperatives exist in most former socialist countries of Eastern Europe, where their roots date from the precommunist era. But their operations and performance bear little resemblance to the original function of these banks. In most socialist countries, savings banks had monopoly power over household banking, while credit cooperatives operated as branches of a state-controlled central agricultural bank.

Despite their poor record, thrift deposit institutions can still make a positive contribution to financial sector and economic development in developing countries. Thus, provided that macroeconomic policies succeed in lowering inflation to moderate levels, postal savings banks could mobilize deposits from poorer areas where there may be few if any commercial bank branches. Housing finance institutions could still be a useful institution in countries where the commercial banks are oriented toward the corporate sector and mortgage securitization may take some time to develop. Rural credit cooperatives could play a large part in providing financial services and distributing credits to small-scale farmers, again, especially in countries where commercial banks have small branch networks and are unlikely to be successful in accessing these markets.

Many developing countries have created institutions that specialize in lending to the poor, especially in rural areas. Examples include the well-known Grameen Bank in Bangladesh, the Bank Rakyat Indonesia and its Unit Desa network in Indonesia, the Banco de Desarrollo (a bank created and funded by the Catholic Church) in Chile, Finagro in Ecuador, reorganized credit unions in Guatemala, and the *stockvels* in South Africa. But much more needs to be done to increase the effectiveness of such institutions in reaching the poor in rural areas and in helping small farmers, artisans, and traders.

The experience of developed countries with thrift deposit institutions suggests that five elements should be included in any integrated program to build solid and successful institutions. The first element is strong leadership. This implies that support should be given to those groups, such as the church or local administrations, that are likely to attract people with high ideals, integrity, and commitment to the success of these institutions.

The second element is the creation of a three-tier structure: local institutions with small membership and operating in a small geographic area to provide services at the local level and facilitate peer monitoring; regional institutions to provide liquidity management, funding, and auditing services; and national institutions to represent member interests at that level and provide links with national and international markets.

The third element is a strong emphasis on education and dissemination of information about the workings and benefits of these institutions. As was seen from the experience of Ireland, culture can be an important obstacle to the success of thrift deposit institutions.

The fourth and perhaps most important element is the encouragement of active peer monitoring and enforcement of contractual obligations. While the principle of unlimited liability may not be viable in most developing countries, government policies could strengthen monitoring and enforcement processes by providing financial support only to regional units and local institutions that have a good record of loan repayment.

Finally, official policy toward thrift deposit institutions must encourage self-help and avoid total reliance on external funding. External support could be made dependent on the level of resource mobilization attained by each local institution, as well as on its record of monitoring and repayment.

Of course, the recent trends of financial systems in industrial countries – a movement toward securitization, pension funds, and mutual funds; the reorientation of commercial banks toward households and small firms; and new transaction and information technologies – will eventually affect financial systems in developing countries. The new financial, technological, and regulatory environments that are likely to emerge will limit the scope for some thrift deposit institutions. Nevertheless, given the prevalence of poverty and the underdevelopment of a financial infrastructure in most developing countries, the need for institutions that specialize in offering banking services to the poor is likely to persist for a long time.

REFERENCES

Bodfish, Morton, and A. D. Theobald. 1938. *Savings and Loan Principles.* New York: Prentice-Hall.
Bonin, Hubert. 1992. *Le Crédit Agricole de la Gironde, la passion d'une région,* 1901–1991. Bordeaux: Editions L'Horizon Chimerique.
Born, Karl Erich. 1983. *International Banking in the 19th and 20th Centuries.* Leamington Spa: Berg.
Cahill, J. R. 1913. *Report to the Board of Agriculture and Fisheries of an Inquiry into Agricultural Credit and Agricultural Cooperation in Germany.* London: HMSO.
Cleary, Edmond John. 1965. *The Building Society Movement.* London: Elek.
Davis, Lance E. 1960. "The New England Textile Mills and the Capital Markets: A Study of Industrial Borrowing, 1840–1860." *Journal of Economic History,* 20 (March):1–30.
——— 1961. "Mrs. Vatter on Industrial Borrowing: A Reply." *Journal of Economic History* 21 (June):225.
Davis, Lance E., and Peter L. Payne. 1958. "From Benevolence to Business: The Story of Two Savings Banks." *Business History Review* 32 (Winter):386–406.
Guinnane, Timothy W. 1993. "Cooperatives as Information Machines: The Lending Practices of German Agricultural Credit Cooperatives, 1883–1914." Economic Growth Center, Yale University, New Haven, Conn., August.
——— 1994a. "A Failed Institutional Transplant: Raiffeisen's Credit Cooperatives in Ireland, 1894–1914." *Explorations in Economic History* 31:38–61.
——— 1994b. "Diversification, Liquidity and Supervision for Small Financial Institutions: Regional Banks and Auditing Associations for Nineteenth Century German Credit Cooperatives." Department of Economics, Yale University, New Haven, Conn., March.
Honohan, Patrick, and Dimitri Vittas. 1996. *Bank Regulation and the Network Paradigm: Policy Implications for Developing and Transition Economies.* Mimeo, Financial Sector Development Department, World Bank, Washington, D.C.
Krooss, Herman E., and Martin R. Blyn. 1971. *A History of Financial Intermediaries.* New York: Random House.
Lamoreaux, Naomi R. 1994. *Insider Lending: Banks, Personal Connections, and Economic Development in Industrial New England.* Cambridge University Press.
Metcalf, Ralph, and Clark G. Black. 1915. *Rural Credit, Cooperation and Agricultural Organization in Europe: Report to the Governor and Legislature of the State of Washington.* Olympia: Lamborn.
Olsmtead, Alan L. 1972. "Investment Constraints and New York City Mutual Savings Bank Financing of Antebellum Development." *Journal of Economic History* 34 (December): 811–40.
——— 1974. "New York City Mutual Savings Bank Portfolio Management and Trustee Objectives." *Journal of Economic History* 34 (December):815–34.

1976. *New York City Mutual Savings Banks, 1819–1861.* Chapel Hill: University of North Carolina Press.

Snowden, Kenneth A., and Walid Bu-Saba. 1992. *Mortgage Loan Duration before 1940.* University of North Carolina at Greensboro, Mimeo.

Payne, Peter Lester, and Lance Edwin Davis. 1956. *The Savings Bank of Baltimore, 1818–1866: A Historical and Analytical Study.* Baltimore: Johns Hopkins University Press.

Vatter, Barbara. 1961. "Industrial Borrowing by the New England Textile Mills, 1840–1860: A Comment." *Journal of Economic History* 21 (June):216–21.

Vittas, Dimitri, Tim Hindle, Patrick Frazer, and Roger Brown. 1978. *Banking Systems Abroad: The Role of Large Deposit Banks in the Financial Systems of Germany, France, Italy, the Netherlands, Switzerland, Sweden, Japan, and the United States.* London: Inter-Bank Research Organization.

1992. "Thrift Regulation in the United Kingdom and the United States: A Historical Perspective." Financial Policy and Systems Division, World Bank, Washington, D.C., September.

DISCUSSION

Question: I was wondering if developing countries, particularly those in Africa, could make the three-tier structure work. Can it be done on a national scale or should it stay regionalized?

D. Vittas: The regional banks played the most important role in the three-tier structure. The central, or national, institution was mostly concerned with lobbying at the national political level and possibly with providing a link with money and capital markets. The really crucial role of auditing and transferring funds from surplus to deficit areas was played by the regionals. So if strong regionals can be developed, you don't necessarily need a national institution.

Question: You mentioned peer monitoring and pressure as a factor for the success of these institutions. But in the case of Bangladesh, it was peer support rather than peer monitoring and pressure that made the Grameen Bank so successful. Do you recommend lower regulatory standards for thrift institutions? Do you think that the government should place less emphasis on improving the stability of these institutions and on intervening to rescue them in case of failure?

D. Vittas: I would prefer any intervention and support to come from within the institutions, from within the network. This was the experience in Germany after the start of the twentieth century. If one local credit cooperative was in trouble, it would be rescued by the regional or even the central institution. The regional or central institutions would provide deposit insurance facilities. In effect, the local cooperative would be treated as if it were a branch of a large commercial bank. A commercial bank would support the branch; it would not just let the depositors lose money. The advantage of having a three-tier structure instead of a large branch network is the greater autonomy that each local cooperative maintains and the greater link each has to the local market. In this sense I would rather see the support coming from within the cooperative network. But support would be necessary because of the local concentration of risks of individual cooperatives.

Question: It is easy to explain failures when government interventions distort incentives. It is one thing to explain failures by saying that there was fraud, mismanagement, and ineffective reporting, but then the deeper question remains as to why some institutional forms tolerated fraud more than others in a private market system. When the government intervenes, we can always explain failures. We can easily explain the savings and loan crisis in the 1980s, but the banking crises of the 1880s or 1890s are more difficult to explain. There were probably two factors behind these crises. First, commercial banks in New England that failed in the 1890s held mortgage-backed securities on Kansas and Nebraska. It was a one-time bad idea, which receded until the post–World War II period of mortgage-backed securities on real estate. I wonder if these banks were duped into holding these risky securities in their search for lending opportunities. The savings banks also had more restricted entry. Did that contribute to the relative stability of savings and commercial banks?

D. Vittas: Restricted entry did contribute. In Germany, savings banks were connected to local authorities so there was generally room for only one bank in each locality. On the first point, I think I can see why, as an economist, you cannot but attribute failure to some government regulation. My attitude is different: forget about deposit insurance and the banks; look at the securities market. In the 1920s and 1930s some people were using the companies they managed for their personal benefit by awarding business contracts to companies that they controlled. They were awarding contracts at inflated prices, helping their own companies at the expense of the companies that they were managing. Similar practices were prevalent among thrift institutions. When the Liberator failed in 1892 it had 98 percent of its assets in loans to companies controlled by its director. Another example was building societies for blue-collar workers that allocated advances by lottery. These societies were lumbered with onerous contracts offered to companies controlled by their promoters. So, contrary to neoclassical assumptions, the world is not populated by rational human beings and is not governed by rational expectations. Thus, there are many failures among private institutions, even in the absence of the pernicious effects of government regulations.

Comment: You mentioned that countries are increasingly introducing regulatory requirements for new financial institutions to maintain a minimum capital level. Putting a minimum capital requirement on thrift deposit institutions will make the job of the central bank easier, but will discourage the creation of credit unions and other similar institutions that require less capital.

D. Vittas: I think that you could allow small localized institutions to operate with less capital. After all, the world is full of rotating savings and credit associations that operate with virtually no capital. My point is that to encourage growth you could promote the three-tier structure, and in this way the capital requirements of these institutions could be kept low. But once thrift deposit institutions become too large and resemble commercial banks in the structure and range of their operations, they should be subject to the same regulations as commercial banks.

CHAPTER 10

The development of industrial pensions in the United States during the twentieth century

Samuel H. Williamson

Pensions are retirement insurance – they offer protection in case you live long enough to quit collecting a paycheck and are able to head for the links and beaches in Florida. In the United States, pensions are provided by both the public and the private sectors. Private sector pensions are the largest formal financial institution for life-cycle saving, with assets measuring in the trillions of dollars.

Societies have always had to take care of their dependent elderly and disabled. Historically, the United States has honored some of its retired citizens with generous pensions, from Civil War veterans to today's corporate executives. Others have been more or less ignored, and they have fared poorly. Since the turn of the century, occupational pensions have been important providers of retirement insurance.

Creating pensions

In the historical development of pensions, several economic and social issues arose concerning employees, employers, and the general economy. These issues relate to three questions: What do employees want from pensions? What incentives does the employer have to create pensions? What are the desirable effects of company pensions for the general economy?

Employees primarily wanted retirement insurance. If they felt that company pensions provided a better and safer return on life-cycle savings, they would prefer that pensions be provided by employers. In addition, workers did not want to lose their pensions if they left the firm before reaching retirement age. Thus, they wanted pensions that were vested and portable.

Vesting means that after working for an employer for a certain number of years, your pension is guaranteed even if you leave the firm. *Portability* is the ability to take the pension funds that have accumulated when you leave a job and apply them to a pension at another firm. Portability is an issue today in the United States because people who frequently change jobs have lower pensions than workers with long tenure.

Employers have several possible motives for offering pensions, motives that are connected with the rise of internal labor markets. Pensions can entice workers to stay with the firm, thus reducing turnover and saving training costs. They can also help to impose mandatory retirement so that the company can save on the wages of older workers who may have falling productivity. Mandatory retirement also gave the remaining workers a clearer picture of their chances for promotion, since it removed people above them with more seniority and allowed everyone to advance. It was also thought that mandatory retirement would remove older workers whose age was a disability that could lead to accidents. But eventually researchers found that older workers were not more accident prone than younger ones.

Pensions could be used to enforce discipline among workers, by threatening striking workers with the loss of their pensions and by bringing back pensioners to replace strikers. Finally, pensions were established to express appreciation for loyal service, to provide for older workers, and to create goodwill in the public eye for taking care of the elderly.

As the workforce aged, the burden on the state of providing benefits for the elderly rose. A growing occupational pension system would take some of this burden off the state. Pensions would also promote higher labor productivity (consistent with the goals of employers) and a high national saving rate, which is dependent on the method of pension funding.

Funding pensions

Should retirement insurance be financed on a pay-as-you-go basis, or should it be funded as future benefit liabilities are accrued? A pay-as-you-go system would allow for retirement insurance without a financial market. Thus, people often had large families to provide for their "social security." On the other hand, if funded, pensions become an important source of savings.

This dilemma was originally spelled out by Paul Samuelson (1958) when he asked, "Whose chocolates you are going to eat?" In his world people live through two periods. In the first period they worked to produce a chocolate, and in the second period they ate the chocolate. Retirees can eat the chocolates produced by current workers, assuring these workers that they can eat the chocolates of the next generation. In this scenario – that of a pay-as-you-go pension plan – there is no need for a capital market or a place to save the chocolate for retirement.

But one generation's workers may not trust or may decide not to burden their children and so begin to save. They make enough chocolate themselves to support their retirement, and thus a capital market is born.[1] This genera-

---

[1] They may have to produce twice as much in order to take care of their parents and save for their own retirement.

tion's pensions are now funded. In the United States *today* private pensions are largely funded, while public pensions are pay-as-you-go.

Historically, company pensions were financed from current revenue. Workers were not required to contribute, nor did firms set aside funds for future liabilities – these pensions where financed on a pay-as-you-go basis. But today both employees and employers contribute large sums to pensions. Social Security, on the other hand, was always a contributory plan. But it was used to fund retirees from the outset, thus it is a pay-as-you-go plan.

Today there are two general types of private pensions. In a defined contribution, or "money purchase" plan, employee and employer contributions are put into a fund. When the worker retires, benefits are equal to an annuity, which is determined by the value of the accumulated assets and the life expectancy of the worker. In "defined benefit" plans, on the other hand, workers receive a pension determined by a formula based on years worked and average salary.

The Social Security system in the United States is a contributory, defined benefit program. But as presently designed, the system is projected to go bankrupt in the next thirty years. One of the many suggested cures is means testing, in which the amount of social security benefits is based on the financial status of the pensioner. This system is used in most other industrial countries today. There are nearly no means-tested private pensions in the United States.

The historical development of pensions in the United States

Formal pensions evolved from a long-standing historical practice of making transfers to the elderly (Figure 10.1). Farmers, artisans, and merchants passed their means of production onto their heirs in return for support in old age. Often this transfer was accomplished gradually within the family, with older members assigned less taxing tasks in the shop, on the farm, or at home. An important part of this process was the transfer of the farm or business with its productive assets. For those without children, this transfer could be made to neighbors or to the church.

In the post–Civil War period the percentage of the labor force earning wages began to rise, and fewer workers were accumulating a work-connected productive asset to pass on to their children. While average incomes were higher off the farm, they often peaked in mid-career. The falloff in income may have already begun when workers were in their mid-forties, but the trend grew more pronounced when they became superannuated or disabled. These factors created an incentive to find new methods of planning for old age. Most workers had the choice of raising a large family and relying on their offspring to take care of them or accumulating financial assets to live on in their later years. To avoid depending on family or charity, workers had to find new ways of accumulating assets while still at the peak of their earning

1860 to 1900
Babies or bank accounts: the growth of life-cycle saving and the expansion of capital markets.

1900 to 1926
Large companies start pensions as part of the changes in internal labor markets.

1926 to 1930s
Funding and demographic shocks begin to change pension formats.

Depression
Railroads pensions are taken over by the federal government.
A few others fail, but the number of plans continues to grow.
Social Security and the Wagner Act are passed.

1942 to 1945
Wage controls and the tax laws change.

1949
NLRB ruling that pensions are subject to mandatory bargaining is upheld in the courts.

1974
The Employment Retirement Income Security Act (ERISA) is passed.

Figure 10.1. The development of industrial pensions in the United States.

capacity.[2] Many surveys taken before the turn of the century show that a substantial number of workers reported saving more than 12 percent of their prime-year incomes. Overall, the national saving rate was close to 20 percent in the last decades of the nineteenth century.[3] These savings were sometimes invested in bank accounts, but more often were used to finance home ownership or invest in a variety of insurance funds. Hundreds of labor unions,

---

[2] Throughout the nineteenth century the traditional strategy of relying on the support of grown children had fallen from favor (Ransom, Sutch, and Williamson 1992). Between 1870 and 1940 the birth rate in the United States fell from forty-one to eighteen per 1,000.

[3] The national saving rate estimate is based on the work of Gallman (1966). Our earlier work and that of other researchers with household budget data have documented the impressive saving rates that characterized late-nineteenth-century industrial communities. See Ransom, Sutch, and Williamson (1992).

employers, and benefit societies developed saving funds and insurance plans for the benefit of workers.

Tontine insurance

One type of popular policy sold by insurance companies was tontine insurance. A worker's premium payments to the insurance company were split, with one portion covering the cost of simple term insurance and the remaining portion invested in a savings fund that accumulated interest over the life of the policy. The pool of accumulated assets was distributed only to the policyholders who survived to the end of the policy term. Thus, if you died, your funeral was covered. If you lived, you received a lump sum payment that was much greater than what you could have earned from regular savings. This was a good retirement insurance plan. So popular were these policies that by 1905 almost two-thirds of all insurance was tontine insurance, and 9 million policies had been sold to a nation with only 18 million households. But in 1906, after a public scandal of alleged mismanagement and impropriety in the insurance industry and an extensive investigation that exposed abuses in the handling of tontine insurance funds, the State of New York prohibited any further issue of tontine insurance. Other states quickly followed suit, and the individually purchased pension disappeared.[4]

Welfare capitalism

During this period business leaders became interested in different forms of welfare capitalism. Partly in an attempt to counter the rising influence of unions and partly out of benevolence, some larger corporations created their own relief organizations to assist their workers. These organizations provided medical assistance and hospital care, as well as disability, accident, and life insurance.

At this time firms were having a growing problem with the incapacity of older workers.[5] To deal with this problem, many informal pension systems were created within companies throughout the nineteenth century. Minutes of directors meetings refer to long-serving employees and specify pensions as rewards for their faithful service.[6] The next step was taken when compa-

---

[4] For a discussion of the tontine business, the insurance investigation, and the abolition of tontine insurance, see Ransom and Sutch (1987).

[5] It was not unusual for companies to keep their disabled and superannuated workers on the payroll by putting them in positions that were less strenuous. They were also likely to pay them less.

[6] Some companies had rules that pensioned all their superannuated workers, but did not tell the employees to avoid a disincentive to save.

nies realized that it was more efficient for every worker to retire at a certain age with a pension than to try to determine retirement on an individual basis.

The first industrial pension

Although a few plans emerged in the nineteenth century, the major innovation came with a new type of pension created in 1900 by the Pennsylvania Railroad. This new form of retirement insurance was also a new instrument that could be used to deal with older workers. The plan's innovations included universal coverage, mandatory retirement, and no individual contributions – which had never existed in the scope or combination put together by the Pennsylvania Railroad.

Other firms, particularly railroads, had been experimenting with formal pensions. For example, in 1884 the management of the Baltimore & Ohio Railroad created a relief package that included a pension with its life and disability insurance. But this plan was available only for members of its relief organization, who were required to contribute to it to belong.[7] The Pennsylvania plan was very different and set the standard for industrial pension plans; it was imitated for the next twenty-five years by most companies that created their own plans.

The Pennsylvania Railroad, one of the largest employers in the country, also had a relief organization called the Voluntary Relief Department. It was started in 1886 and provided death and disability benefits. At the start of the program, the directors stated that as soon as a surplus had accumulated, they would start paying pension benefits to members of the Voluntary Relief Department when they retired. This practice began in 1900 when retiring members received pensions based on how long they had contributed to the department.

Why, then, would the company create a noncontributory, defined benefit industrial pension when this other plan had just started to pay benefits? Several explanations have been offered, but the primary reason was the desire to impose mandatory retirement on all older workers, who, on average, no longer provided services that justified their salaries. In other words it was thought that most workers older than seventy were earning a wage that exceeded their marginal product, a situation called "wage tilt."[8] But the firm wanted to reward its faithful employees in their retirement.[9] As labor turnover

---

[7] After bitter complaints by the unions, it was changed to a voluntary plan.

[8] "Wage tilt" refers to a pay schedule in which workers are paid less than their marginal product early in their careers and more than their marginal product toward the end of their careers. Theoretically, this wage package is thought to be more efficient; however, it requires mandatory retirement. See Lazear (1979).

[9] Workers received 1 percent of their average wage over their last ten years times the number

in those days was quite high, the company concluded from studying their payroll records that these benefits would not be very expensive. Pensions were paid from current expenses and amounted to less than 1 percent of the wage bill.[10]

This new pension plan was a major departure from the idea of providing a pension only to workers who were members of the contributory, Voluntary Relief Department, where the pension received was based on length of membership.[11] Since not all older workers had also been long-standing members of the Voluntary Relief Department, mandatory retirement would have meant that many would receive little or nothing. Whether motivated by benevolence, public relations, or a desire to maintain labor peace, the railroad felt that it could not retire some of its older workers without providing some income, particularly because up to this point workers may have felt they had an implicit contract to work for the line for life. They had not planned on mandatory retirement.

When the pension was started, it covered all workers seventy and older regardless of their years of service. But the plan also imposed a new maximum hiring age of thirty-five. The firm explained that this upper limit was necessary to ensure that future workers would work long enough for the firm to justify their receiving a pension.

Following the lead of the Pennsylvania Railroad

The Pennsylvania plan was widely imitated by other railroads in the next seven years. By the end of 1905 eighteen U.S. railroads had adopted formal pension plans covering 35 percent of railroad employees in the country. Most railroads in Europe offered pensions earlier than those in the United States, but European railroads were government enterprises and thus provided civil service pensions.

Within a few years pension plans offered by large companies in other industries proliferated rapidly. By 1930 more than 3.6 million workers were covered by formal industrial pensions. Although this number represents less that 20 percent of all industrial workers, the majority of large firms had adopted plans, and pension schemes were widely regarded as part of the package of pay and benefits that a "progressive" employer would offer.[12]

---

of years worked. Voluntary retirement was possible at age sixty-five for those with thirty years of service.

[10] Gratton (1990) presents an excellent description of the creation of the plan and the problems that came up later because the railroad did not anticipate the fall in turnover that took place.

[11] Data that I have collected from a division of the Pennsylvania Railroad show that the average annual turnover of membership in the Voluntary Relief Department was 42 percent between 1889 and 1910. Membership averaged 64 percent of the employees and could not be mandatory because unions had successfully lobbied several states to pass laws forbidding it.

[12] The computation of this number (3.6 million) is available from the author. The figure excludes

Pensions began in the railroads, where growth was rapid, followed by utilities, banking, and manufacturing. Formal pensions were more likely to be found in large firms: 64 percent of covered workers were employed by companies with more than 25,000 employees. Of the 17 firms that held assets worth more than $750 million each, only 2 did not offer pensions at this time.[13] And of the 200 corporations with the most financial assets, 87 had formal pensions.

Nearly all of these plans were noncontributory – they started as pay-as-you-go plans, which gave full credit for past service to all current workers regardless of age. None of the large companies required their workers to contribute to their pensions. Of all workers covered, 95 percent were covered by noncontributory plans.

Most pension plans included all employees. Only 56 plans out of almost 400 excluded some workers, and half of these excluded only officers, "higher employees," or office workers. There appears to have been no exclusions in the larger firms. There were approximately 60,000 pensioners in 1927, more than half of whom were former railroaders. The average pension was $605, although pensions varied widely by industry.[14] Salary data for manufacturing show that the average replacement ratio (pension/worker income) was 35 percent in that industry.

Funding reserves and noncontributory pensions

While many firms were beginning to confront the issue of funding by the time of the depression, there was still much progress to be made.[15] Insurance companies and actuarial organizations were attempting to educate management, but many firms probably underestimated the costs because they underestimated how fast their workforce would age. Latimer (1932) estimated that by 1928 only between 13 and 16 percent of total accrued liabilities of all industrial pension plans were covered.

Most of the early industrial plans were noncontributory, with all of the costs borne by the employer. Employers may have established such a system because they wanted to maintain complete control. The rules of these plans clearly stated that the employee had no contractual right to a pension, the plan could be abolished at any time, and with dismissal or voluntary departure

---

a sizable number of additional workers covered by informal pensions and group annuity plans (Lebergott 1964:513, Table A-4).

[13] General Motors and Standard Gas and Electric were the two exceptions – General Motors because it was too new and Standard Gas and Electric because it offered an informal plan.

[14] More precisely, 21.2 percent of the average pensions by industry were in the $400 to $499 range; 33.8 percent, $500 to $599; and 28.9 percent, $600 to $699 (Williamson 1992:54).

[15] Thirty percent of covered employees worked for companies that had set up a separate trust fund or contracted with an insurance company. The rest of the plans either carried reserves on their balance sheets (19 percent) or paid pensions out of current operating expenses (59 percent, mostly the railroads) (Williamson 1992:55).

workers would forfeit all claim to retirement benefits. Initially, most states prohibited any compulsory deductions from wages.

Another factor influencing this choice was the tontine effect. Firms could keep the expected costs of pensions low if they took advantage of the low probability that workers hired at a young age would stay with the firm until they qualified for a pension. By continually replacing dropouts with young new workers, the firm could expect that it would have to provide pensions for only the small number of faithful workers who stayed.

Firms did not want to collect contributions from workers because firms would be at least morally if not legally obliged to return them if a worker left before retirement. If workers had higher discount rates than the return that firms could earn on these funds, current wages could not be fully adjusted to compensate for the cost. In this case a contributory pension would be a competitive disadvantage.

For workers expecting to stay with the firm until retirement, the noncontributory plan is a nice exchange. They do not want to contribute and thus reduce their current salaries, and they believe that since they have not received any less salary than their co-workers who do drop out, they will receive a "free" annuity when they retire.

Where did the unions stand?

At the beginning of the century labor leaders had been either neutral or antagonistic toward company pensions. They saw pensions as a means to confiscate workers' wages, which would be returned only if workers were loyal to the firm and, therefore, reluctant to follow the policies of the union. Although it is difficult to find evidence that workers pressured their employers to create pensions, there is also no evidence that the rank and file opposed pensions. But once firms began providing pensions, ample evidence shows that workers were interested in pension survival and expansion.

At this stage unions chose to compete by setting up pensions of their own, and by 1930 more than one million union members were covered by union pension plans. Unfortunately, many of these failed during the depression because they were pay-as-you-go plans, and the young workers dropped out (Williamson 1992).

Cycles between contributory and noncontributory plans

All large pension plans and most other plans were noncontributory until 1926. Following this date and until World War II, most new plans required workers to contribute.[16] From 1942 through the 1950s, noncontributory plans domi-

---

[16] Eighty percent of the newly covered workers, even in this later period, were covered by a

Table 10.1. *Number of pension plans by type, 1900–46*

Period in which plans became effective	Contributory plans (%)	Noncontributory plans (%)	Total
1900–25	75 (16)	406 (84)	481
1926–29	69 (73)	25 (27)	94
1930–39	425 (82)	92 (18)	517
1940–September 1, 1942	526 (62)	317 (38)	843
September 2, 1942–1944	1,101 (26)	3,107 (74)	4,208
1945 and 1946	43 (37)	750 (63)	1,189

Sources: Williamson (1992), Robbins (1949).

nated. And for the past thirty years contributory, defined contribution plans have been more prevalent (Table 10.1).

One possible explanation for the change in 1926 was the impact of the court case involving the sale of the packing firm Morris and Company to Armour and Company. Morris and Company had set up a contributory pension in 1909 that was so generous that employee contributions would not cover its cost. When the company was near bankruptcy in 1923, it was sold to Armour. The amount of money in the pension trust fund was $7 million less than the estimated liabilities. Armour refused to make up the difference, and the employees sued. The Illinois Supreme Court ruled against the employees in 1925, and the surrounding publicity caused a reexamination of pension funding.

After the bad publicity died down, employers had a new attitude toward establishing pensions:

- Pensions were seen more as an employee fringe benefit. Firms could no longer think of pensions as a luxury that they could discontinue any time without damaging company reputation and incurring high legal costs.
- Some workers wanted a system in which funds were more secure financially and in which they could count on receiving their contributions back at any time.[17] Because, after 1921, interest earned on pension trusts was tax free, high-wage-earning workers would see pensions as a superior way to save. And since contributions were usually matched by employers and could be received only at retire-

few large noncontributory plans. Most contributory plans were not defined contribution or money purchase plans, but defined benefit plans to which employees contributed.

[17] Most contributory pensions returned contributions when a worker left. Withdrawal rights varied from none to promises to return everything the worker contributed plus 6 percent. A majority of withdrawal rights promised to return contributions plus 4 percent. Partly because current workers were given credit for previous service when plans were started, these plans were often no better funded than some of the noncontributory plans.

ment, there was a strong tontine effect, desirable to both worker and employer.

• Many of these new plans were voluntary, so employers could encourage those workers that they wanted to keep and not have to worry about the rest.

• Some of these new plans were "money purchase" plans, or what is known today as "defined contribution" plans. Such plans reduce employers' risks of uncertain turnover and mortality rates, as well as financial market variations.

The Depression and the railroads

Most private pension plans survived the Depression. Company-provided railroad pensions were the exception. Railroad employment had been declining in the twenty years leading up to the Depression. Because of the Depression and the effectiveness of efficient wage contracting, worker turnover had fallen considerably. Thus, the average age of railroad workers was much higher than that of workers in many other industries.

Partly because of Interstate Commerce Commission accounting rules, nearly all railroads were running pay-as-you-go pensions, paying benefits out of current expenses. By 1932 most lines had cut pension benefits, but the decrease in expenses was usually about the same as the fall in railroad worker wage rates.

Railroaders were heavily unionized and had strong political allies. After years of lobbying, they convinced Congress to create a public pension for railroad workers with portability and vesting after ten years. Workers could thus get credit for all their railroad work, regardless of rail line and whether or not they were still working on the railroads at age sixty-five.

When the Railroad Retirement Act was finalized in 1937, the government took over an industrial pay-as-you-go system. The railroad lines did not give the government any funds based on past services of these workers. I see no reason why the railroad pensions would have failed if the government had not taken them over. Freight and passenger rates were controlled by the Interstate Commerce Commission and were set on a cost-plus basis. In principle, rates could have been raised to cover rising pension costs.

Social Security

Social Security began as a funded system; that is, participants had to contribute for several employment periods before qualifying to receive benefits. This system was different from industrial pension systems at the time. In particular, the soon-to-retire worker did not get full credit for past years of work, as railroad workers did under the Railroad Retirement Act; nor did those with most private plans begun thirty years earlier. The U.S. government

plan was also different from those in many other countries in that benefits
were not means-tested. Social Security was not designed to bail out the private pension system as much as to cover the rest of the workforce. Although
some plans revised their benefits so that they were tied to the Social Security
system, *many did not*.

World War II and afterward

The Wage and Salary Stabilization Regulation Act of 1942 is often regarded
as the origin of favorable tax treatment of pensions. But its main intention
was to tighten up coverage regulations, particularly to prevent discrimination
in favor of a minority of employees that might be, for example, just officers
and shareholders. The act mandated that a qualified plan had to cover at least
70 percent of employees or 80 percent of eligible employees. But this act
did not have a vesting rule:

> A very serious effort was made in the suggested 1942 legislation to require
> vesting of pension expectations as a condition for deductibility of employer
> contributions. . . . employer threats to discontinue non-vested plans brought
> to Congress an avalanche of protests from older workers who saw their
> pension prospects endangered. (Robbins 1949: 15)

On the surface this act should have reduced the incentive to create new
contributory or noncontributory pensions. It offered no new tax advantages
and tightened the rules for awarding tax-exempt status. But two other factors
were far more important, both results of World War II: the large increase in
corporate and income tax rates and the freezing of wage rates in the tight
labor market.

In 1942 wages and salaries were frozen to contain inflation during the
war, creating a strong incentive to find ways to pay a deferred wage, that is,
a pension. Employers saw the pension as an alternative inducement to keep
employees from leaving in search of higher wages elsewhere. Employees
were happy with this arrangement because they would receive their deferred
wages after the war, when personal tax rates would be lower. There was little
incentive to make workers contribute from their after-tax income, since employers' contributions reduced tax liability at the high war rates by as much
as 80 percent. Thus, employers could pay a dollar in deferred wages that cost
as little as 20 cents.

In 1946 wage controls were lifted and a trend toward contributory plans
began. By now, however, organized labor had changed its attitude about
pensions. Also in 1946, a union of Inland Steel filed a grievance with the
National Labor Relations Board over the company's compulsory retirement
policy. In 1949 the courts ruled that the terms of a pension plan are subject
to mandatory collective bargaining, on the grounds that although they are not
wages, they do constitute "other conditions of employment." With court

backing, unions now preferred that the employer bear all the risk, and because worker contributions were *not* deductible, noncontributory plans offered a clear advantage to both sides.

The Employment Retirement Income Security Act of 1974

Until 1974 most regulations on pensions were intended to protect the Treasury from lost tax revenue. The Employment Retirement Income Security Act (ERISA) was passed to protect the employee and the pensioner. The main components of this act imposed rules requiring full vesting in a maximum of fifteen years, encouraging actuarial soundness, and imposing fiduciary responsibility.

Corporations had to be more financially responsible for their pension liabilities. They had to join the Pension Benefit Guaranty Corporation (PBGC), which, within limits, insured underfunded plans against termination. If a plan terminated, the PBGC could claim the assets of the firm's pension fund and up to 30 percent of the corporation's net assets to settle the costs.

Recently, many employers have moved away from defined benefit plans. Several factors have contributed to this trend, among them increased benefits from Social Security and a more rapid increase in life expectancy of older workers.[18] This development increased costs, which employers preferred to share with employees. Other factors included the continued increase in the number of regulations governing the establishment of a defined benefit plan and the creation of 401(k) plans, which allowed employees' contributions to be tax deductible.

Conclusions

Historically, industrial pensions have been used by employers to influence the behavior of their employees. It is not surprising that many of the first pensions were in capital-intensive industries where many workers had accumulated valuable industry and firm-specific human capital. Examples are the railroads and the public utilities. These employers wanted to create a stable, experienced workforce that was reluctant to leave prematurely and thus had an incentive to create a deferred wage to reduce turnover. These industries would also be concerned about shirking; that is, a worker's negligent behavior might lead to expensive losses. This is another reason to have a pension as part of the deferred wage that would not have to be paid if the worker was fired.

Employers also wanted to retire senior workers whose productivity was no longer sufficient to justify their wage. Rather than suffer the public rela-

---

[18] Life expectancy at age 65 increased from 11.9 years in 1900 to 14.3 years in 1960 and 16.7 years in 1985.

tions embarrassment of putting old and faithful workers out with nothing, the pension was regarded as an inexpensive solution to a growing problem of the superannuated worker. On the demand side, workers wanted retirement insurance. Industrial pensions grew at a time when more traditional forms of life-cycle saving became more difficult to carry out, job tenure increased, and there was a movement away from the spot labor market. Since more workers felt there was an increased probability that they would spend their entire careers as employees of one firm, pensions became a more desirable form of saving. If they left in mid-career for a better opportunity, then they lost their chance for pensions. If, however, they did end up working most of their lives for a firm with pensions and made it to the qualifying age of sixty-five or seventy, they then qualified for the pensions.

By the turn of the century, labor relations had improved substantially and corporations were more financially secure, so there was more faith that firms would honor their commitment to long-term employment and to the pension. Among the alternatives, private saving had become more difficult with the abolition of the tontines, the securities markets were unregulated and suffered from the effects of frequent business cycles, and state and federal governments were not yet thinking about universal pensions.

As the workforce ages in developing countries, firms will employ workers who will have longer job tenure and will want secure and substantial pensions. Which institution can best provide pensions: the employer, a financial intermediary, or the government? If markets fluctuate because of financial instability, workers will prefer defined benefit plans, and they will choose the institution that they have the most faith in to provide them. The problem is that in today's world there may be less confidence in the long-term commitments of employers and the fiscal viability of governments.

Funding is important in the long run. Sound accounting practices would dictate that the accumulated reserves match pension liabilities as they accrue. The regular contribution to these funds would be the deferred part of the wage. But historically, in the United States pensions were funded only when profits were high or tax incentives or regulation dictated. Developing countries will need a sound corporate tax structure and be willing to forgo some immediate tax revenue to create a large pension savings fund.

REFERENCES

Gallman, Robert E. 1966. "Gross National Product in the United States, 1834–1909." In National Bureau of Economic Research, *Output, Employment, and Productivity in the United States after 1800.* Studies in Income and Wealth, vol. 30. Princeton, N.J.: Princeton University Press.
Gratton, Brian. 1990. " 'A Triumph in Modern Philanthropy': Age Criteria in Labor Management at the Pennsylvania Railroad, 1875–1930." *Business History Review* 64 (Winter):630–56.

Latimer, Murray W. 1932. *Industrial Pension Systems in the United States and Canada*. New York: Industrial Relations Counsellors.

Lazear, Edward P. 1979. "Why Is There Mandatory Retirement?" *Journal of Political Economy* 87 (December):1261–84.

Lebergott, Stanley. 1964. *Manpower in Economic Growth: The American Record since 1800*. New York: McGraw-Hill.

Ransom, Roger L., and Richard Sutch. 1987. "Tontine Insurance and the Armstrong Commission: A Case of Stifled Innovation in the American Life Insurance Industry." *Journal of Economic History* (June):379–90.

Ransom, Roger L., Richard Sutch, and Samuel H. Williamson. 1992. "Inventing Pensions: The Origin of the Company-Provided Pension in the United States, 1900–1940." In K. Warren Schaie and W. Andrew, eds., *Societal Impact on Aging: Historical Perspectives*. Achenbaum, N.Y.: Springer, pp. 1–38.

Robbins, Rainard B. 1949. *Impact of Taxes on Industrial Pension Plans*. New York: Industrial Relations Counselors.

Samuelson, Paul A. 1958. "An Exact Consumption-Loan Model of Interest with or without the Social Contrivance of Money." *Journal of Political Economy* 66 (6):467–82.

Williamson, Samuel H. 1992. "United States and Canadian Pensions before 1930: A Historical Perspective." In U.S. Department of Labor, *Trends in Pensions, 1992* Vol. 2, pp. 34–45

DISCUSSION

Question: Do you agree that by reducing, if not eliminating, the tontine effect of company pensions, the ERISA also undermined the incentive effects and the use of pensions as an internal labor market tool?

S. Williamson: Yes. Although some companies provided formal vesting, others didn't. By setting minimum vesting and financial responsibility standards, the passage of the ERISA meant that workers became less worried about leaving a firm. I would say that the ERISA definitely undermined the internal labor market effect.

Question: Throughout this period, total factor productivity grew in the United States by about 1.5 percent. Manufacturing probably led in terms of productivity growth. Do you think that the company pension systems contributed to this growth?

S. Williamson: Pension plans were part of personnel policies that aimed to create an experienced and stable labor force, but with mandatory retirement to induce older workers to leave. The deferred wage provided a strong incentive for higher efficiency and productivity, but it was only one factor behind the large increase in total factor productivity.

Question: Several times you touch on the issue of portability and pension vesting. Did the system encourage mobility and portability in some sectors but not in others?

S. Williamson: It depended on the industry. In the construction industry there were not many employer-provided pensions. The construction unions provided pensions. In this sector the unions were usually larger than the employers. After 1949 the multiemployer pension plans became a much stronger force, and they developed in those industries that were less interested in creating firm-specific human capital by promoting from within. I think that you need to look at the issue on a case-by-case basis. Which industries are better off with mobility and portability and which industries aren't?

Question: You mentioned that pension plans are a way of removing older workers from the workforce. I guess the alternative is to fire them, but that could be bad for the morale of the younger workforce. But in the current climate, in which there are a lot of cutbacks, the effect on morale doesn't seem to be in the minds of corporate managers. Maybe you have some background on the economics of firing people compared with the economics of retiring people.

S. Williamson: Before the 1930s there was no Social Security, and I think that's an important factor. Also, this was a period of long-term tenure. Employees had worked for twenty or twenty-five years and then had to be turned out. That was different than firing a person who had worked for only three years. There was no vesting. So if you fired workers at sixty-four, they had nothing. Today the person who is let go at sixty-four is usually a buyout or at least has a defined contribution plan or is vested in the defined contribution plan. The morale effect is quite different because of vesting.

Question: The investment policies of these plans are no doubt very heavily regulated since the ERISA. But in the period, say, between World War II and 1974, what did the pension funds invest in? Were they allowed to invest in the stock of their own company? Were pensioners buying a piece of the company or were they buying something that was part of the stock market?

S. Williamson: I'm not familiar with all the rules. As far as buying part of the company, in a sense that is what a pay-as-you-go system is. The worker gives up some current wage for a "dividend" in the future, that is, the pension.
　　A few companies had independently funded reserves against at least part of their pension liabilities. Others only kept the pension liability as part of general liabilities, so pensions were no more secure than the ability of the company to pay benefits out of future revenue. It is an important point that a pension fund or trust has a very predictable payoff period because you know the age of your workers and when you're going to need those benefits. Also, since pensions are long-term payoffs, pension reserves can be a source of long-term capital investment. The treasurers of the corporation usually were the trustees of the pension plan, and their stock holdings were probably greater than the workers who contributed to the plans would have preferred; that is, the workers were perhaps more risk averse than the trustees. The funds should have focused more on long-term investments in bonds, mortgages, and stocks because of their nature, but I'm not an authority on this.

Question: One chart from your presentation shows that the companies paid a very low cost for the pension schemes, which at its highest was less than 1 percent. I suppose that had to do with the lack of vesting and the tontine effect. Do you have any information on how this cost rose over time? How high was it in the 1950s? Before the ERISA? A related question regards the coverage of company plans. In the United States this coverage is estimated at less than 50 percent of the labor force. Do you have any information on whether the workers that were not covered relied only on Social Security or did they have other savings?

S. Williamson: Regarding the first question, I don't have statistics on that period. The cost did rise somewhat, but I don't think substantially. I don't think the lack of vesting was the main problem addressed by the ERISA. I think the main problem that the ERISA tried to tackle was underfunding.

What did workers do who had no pension coverage? Most current statistics indicate that those with pensions have also saved more. Social Security is 80 percent of the income of the lowest quintal of retirees.

Question: You mentioned that earlier on most pension plans were underfunded. Why did it take the companies and the regulators such a long time to realize the dangers of underfunding?

S. Williamson: The railroads were not the only corporations that were underfunded during the Depression. Other large corporations went right through the Depression underfunded, although they did start to increase their funding during this period. One reason for the underfunding before the Depression was the low cost caused by the tontine effect. The actuaries were calculating that only one in fifty workers would qualify for a pension, and thus the plans were not very expensive. The Depression greatly reduced turnover, and the cost of the plans started to rise as fewer workers quit. I don't think that the fall in turnover created the need as much as new regulations did.

Question: Is there evidence from the historical records that you examined that these schemes had difficulty because of instability of the financial markets? Was there evidence that corporations or insurance schemes just couldn't deal effectively with the volatility of the financial markets?

S. Williamson: I don't think that the volatility of the financial markets was the main reason for abolishing tontine insurance. But the abolition took away that avenue for the individual, so insurance companies began offering group life insurance, which again was able to take advantage of self-selection. I don't think that instability in the financial markets was important. But to go back to your point, if I am a worker in a country with political instability, perhaps financial market instability, I may decide that the best institution to care for me in my old age is my employer. If I have been with an employer for a long time and I know that this employer is taking care of old workers, that's where I want my social security to come from.

Comment: That means that if it accumulates reserves, the firm would be able to invest in a relatively diversified financial market or at least have the capacity to invest abroad. This would seem to me to be a critical element – that there is an open capital account scheme that can be diversified.

S. Williamson: The transformation from a pay-as-you-go to a funded program is extremely important. It requires institutions that are stable and encouraging.

CHAPTER 11

The rise of securities markets: What can government do?

Richard Sylla

What role do securities markets play in economic development? How do they emerge in the development process? And how can regulation make them more effective? Like many a business school professor, I will use a case study to explore these issues. The case is the history of U.S. securities markets, a history that I believe is very relevant to policy makers and financial reformers concerned with developing countries today.

Some might doubt that lessons of financial history from the United States could be relevant to developing and transition economies. I would remind these doubters that two centuries ago the United States was a small and undeveloped country with serious financial problems. But it confronted those problems and creatively reformed its financial system, which then became a foundation of the U.S. economic infrastructure and a bulwark of the country's long-term growth. Several background papers – Smith and Sylla (1993), Sylla, Wilson, and Jones (1994), and Sylla and Smith (1995) – examine this history in great detail. Here I will mention only the most interesting points and add some additional evidence regarding the importance of foreign investment in U.S. history and the role of securities markets in promoting foreign investment.

Securities markets in U.S. history

Securities markets in the United States have a long history. The bond and stock markets date back to the first presidential term (1789–93) of George Washington. At that time, as will be discussed in more detail later, the debt hangover from the American Revolution was restructured, and shares of newly founded banks and other enterprises began actively to be traded.

As an economist and financial historian I have been interested in such questions as what can we learn about early U.S. economic growth from financial data? Aggregate data on production are too sketchy to allow for good estimates of gross product before the mid-1830s. And by that time the U.S. economy was already growing at high, modern rates. But U.S. financial markets generated price, yield, and asset-return data much earlier, starting in the 1790s. These data indicate how well the U.S. economy did in its earliest years and when, perhaps, it began to expand at the high rates characteristic of modern economic growth.

Just when did modern economic growth begin in the United States? Sylla, Wilson, and Jones (1994) explore this question in some detail using the data generated by early U.S. financial markets. Although the available data are not altogether inconsistent with an earlier upsurge, the returns that investors in the United States earned on stocks and bonds suggest that a great upsurge of economic growth began sometime around 1815 (see Figure 11.1). The financial returns data show a cyclical downturn around 1824, but on closer inspection this drop seems to be an interruption in very rapid growth: returns grew to be extremely high by 1824 and then fell to a "mere" 10 percent in succeeding years. Even in the depression of the 1840s the real return on stocks was 5 percent on a ten-year moving average.

Economic historians debate when modern economic growth really took off in the United States. From the financial returns evidence, my collaborators and I conclude that sometime after the second war with Britain, the War of 1812, there was a great upsurge, a great bull market, which lasted until about the middle of the nineteenth century. This trend is seen in both the stock (equity) and bond markets. As I note later, stocks and bonds tend to deliver better long-run returns when stable, effective government is in place and peace is not threatened. That is one lesson of U.S. economic history.

Securities markets and economic development

What role can securities markets play in economic development? Like all financial markets they link "deficit units" – people, enterprises, or governments – which want more funds than they currently have, to "surplus units," which have more funds than they currently need. In more colorful, if less comprehensive, terms, securities markets provide a meeting place for investors and borrowers who want to invest money in business (real productive assets) and the savers and lenders who seek financial returns. The users of capital – government and businesses – are the issuers of securities, whereas the providers of capital are the buyers of securities.

Banks, of course, provide another meeting place for borrowers and lenders. Historically, in countries that witnessed the rise of securities markets, a division of labor in finance emerged with banks dealing in relatively short-term loans and the securities markets providing long-term funds. But there were many gray areas between and overlaps among the long- and short-term financial markets. Today the distinctions are even less clear as banks increasingly take long-term investment positions in nonbank enterprises and

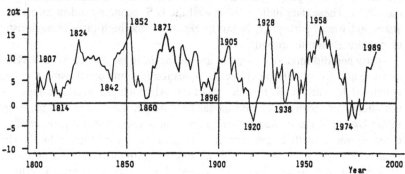

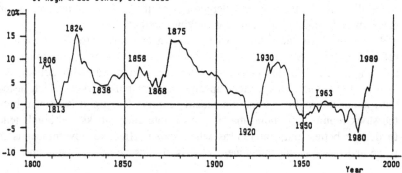

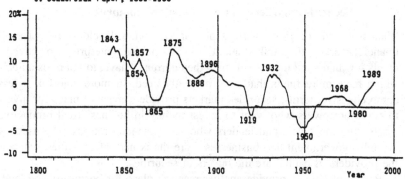

Figure 11.1. Real returns of common stocks, bonds, and commercial paper, 1789–1989 (ten-year moving averages). Notes: Since the data charted are ten-year moving averages, the initial dates of the charted series are 1800 for stocks, 1805 for bonds, and 1840 for commercial paper. Dates of major peaks and troughs are noted on the charts.

as the securities markets "securitize" many types of short-term loans. Banks and securities markets compete, but they also cooperate with and complement each other. A well-developed financial system features both banks and securities markets. The trend of financial history nonetheless seems to favor an increasingly important role for securities markets and a lesser role for banks. Regional, national, and world financial centers tend to be characterized more by the presence of developed securities markets than by that of large banks.

Securities markets have two broad components: primary and secondary markets. The primary securities market is the new-issue market where securities originate, that is, where bond and stock issues are born, typically with the assistance of midwives called "investment or merchant bankers." The secondary markets, the markets we read about in the papers everyday and whose results are regularly reported on radio and television, are the trading markets where stocks, bonds, and other securities are bought and sold by investors after they are issued.

Many people, including some economists, do not think that secondary markets are important in a fundamental economic sense because they only shuffle assets (or the ownership of assets) from one owner to another. This view is incorrect for at least two reasons. First, the primary, new-issue markets would probably not exist or would be much smaller than they are if the secondary markets did not exist to give liquidity, or shiftability, to securities after they are first issued. When I exchange some of my money for a twenty-year bond or 100 shares of common stock, one of the most important reasons I do so is because if I change my mind tomorrow (or next month or next year), I can sell the stock or bond to someone else in the trading market and turn it back into money.

Second, secondary trading markets produce an extremely valuable commodity: information. Information and liquidity are really the products of secondary markets. Although many people think that there is too much information in our world today, that we are in danger of suffering from information overload, when it comes to investment decisions there never seems to be enough information. The social function of secondary securities markets lies in their generation of tremendous amounts of information on the value of government debts, on the value of corporate bond and stock issues, on the trade-offs between present and future income and consumption, and on the yields and returns of different investments. All of this information is extremely important for efficiently allocating the world's capital.

Securities markets contribute to development because they increase savings and investment flows and make the allocation of these flows more efficient. In doing so, they reduce the cost of funds to borrowers and investors in real productive assets while increasing the returns to savers, lenders, and financial investors. They accomplish this by creating liquidity and generating information, thereby encouraging people to save and invest more.

Securities markets and public finance

Let me anticipate some of the lessons I will draw from the evolution of securities markets. The first lesson is that it is important to take a holistic view in thinking about finance and the financial system – we must recognize that each component of this system is related to every other part. Trying to reform or fix just one part of a financial system in a country is probably not going to be very useful to its citizens if other parts are defective. Instead, one should consider every part – the monetary system, the banking system, the securities and other capital markets, and, possibly most important of all, the public finance system.

The public finance system teaches a second lesson. As I read history, I see that public finances are often crucial to the development of an effective financial system. Effective public finance can set the tone for and tie together all parts of a fully articulated system of public and private finance. The public finance aspects of financial systems are much more important than one would discover today by studying in a typical economics or finance department at a college, university, or business school. We live in an age of academic specialization. Public finance economists pay little or no attention to private finance, and finance specialists pay no attention to public finance, other than to assume that it is in place and generates safe assets, such as treasury bills, to include in efficient portfolios. But historically, public and private finance were much more closely intertwined. In fact, history teaches that if a country gets its public finances right, other components of a financial system such as securities markets naturally emerge. The U.S. case is discussed herein; for the case of Britain, see Dickson (1967).

How can we apply these lessons to today's developing countries? Clearly, before trying to reform banks and establish securities markets, pension funds, or deposit insurance, governments and their financial advisors must get public finances in order. If they do so – and it is seldom a simple task – then many other facets of the financial system will tend to fall into place.

A third lesson applies directly to securities markets. Because securities markets are essentially markets in information, regulation can improve them by increasing the amount of information that they receive and process, and then disseminating this information among actual and potential investors. Many people hold that if information is really worthwhile, it will come out automatically through market processes. But historically, capital markets did not automatically generate needed information. Information certainly has value, but in capital markets people who have had inside information have wanted, as a matter of self-interest, to retain it for their own use. Some of the great figures in financial history were people who had inside information and made a lot of money controlling that information. Therefore, the kind of regulation that the Securities and Exchange Commission (SEC) enforces in the United States, especially in the area of corporate disclosure, is good overall because it spreads information widely and thereby serves to expand financial markets while making them fairer. Although SEC regulation was widely resented when it was first implemented, some of the more knowledgeable and thoughtful financial market practitioners on Wall Street now recognize that the huge, innovative, and highly successful capital markets in the United States owe much to the confidence in their openness, honesty, and fairness that participants gained as a result of SEC regulation.

Case study: Alexander Hamilton and the formation of the U.S. financial system

Just over two centuries ago the United States was a developing economy. It was populated with only 3.9 million people in 1790. In a very short time, largely because of the financial acumen of one leader, the United States got its public finances in order, and consequently, private financial institutions and markets developed in short order. Because a good financial structure developed, the United States had from the outset a critical piece of economic infrastructure that facilitated all subsequent development. Thus, before there were more than a handful of isolated banks, before the industrial revolution came to a nation where 90 percent of the people worked in agriculture, before the great transportation improvements of the nineteenth century, and before the westward movement across the North American continent, the basis of a resilient financial system grounded in strong public finances suddenly emerged in the United States.

What was the financial problem at that time? The American Revolution of 1775–81, financed largely by paper money and loans, led to inflation and monetary depreciation plus a huge overhang of domestic and foreign debt. In the 1780s, after the war was over and independence achieved, economic conditions were depressed, and both the states and the national government struggled with their debt overhangs; for a detailed account, see Perkins (1994). The states made some progress in handling their debt problems. The national government made no progress because it did not have any taxing power. The U.S. revolutionaries had fought a war against a strong British government, and they naturally set up a weak government under the Articles of Confederation, the original U.S. governmental compact. Under the Articles, the Congress could requisition financial support from the states, but given the depressed conditions in the 1780s, the states were not inclined to respond favorably to the national government's calls for assistance.

At the same time, because of the depression, some states began printing more of their own paper money and putting tariffs on imports from other states. Other states retaliated with tariffs of their own. These were not strong signs of unity in the newly established United States. Some of the states raised taxes to try to service and pay off their debts. Massachusetts was an example with notable consequences – Shays's Rebellion of 1786–87, an early

U.S. taxpayers' revolt. This was an armed revolt, not a revolt at the ballot box, and also not a sign of unity.

Clearly, a fundamental problem under the Articles of Confederation was the absence of taxing power at the national level. When states failed to meet the requisitions of the Confederation congresses, the principal and interest on the large national debt that had been incurred to gain independence was not paid. More debt was therefore incurred to pay interest on the old debt. Does this country sound like a transitional economy with serious financial problems? Possibly.

Controversies over tariffs between states and other commercial difficulties led to a convention in Annapolis in 1786. That convention led to a call for another convention in Philadelphia in the spring and summer of 1787 to revise the Articles of Confederation. The Philadelphia convention instead drafted a new constitution, giving the new federal government powers of taxation and, more important given the problems at the time, the power to regulate trade between the states. That decision was fundamental because it established the potential for a large, internal free-trade area more than 200 years ago – potential soon realized. The Constitution of 1787 also gave the federal government monetary powers, taking from the states the power to print their own paper money. The weak national government defined by the Articles became a strong federal government of the Constitution. After much debate between Federalists – supporters of the Constitution – and Antifederalists, the Constitution was adopted. George Washington was elected to be the first president and took the oath of office in April 1789 – opposite what today is the New York Stock Exchange in Wall Street. The first congress under the Constitution passed the Tariff Act of 1789, and on July 4 the new government's first tax became law.

Now entering the picture was Alexander Hamilton (1757–1804), the financial expert who would get U.S. public finances right. Hamilton, of course, enters now only in the context of this chapter: he was, in fact, a leading participant in most of the key events between 1774 and 1801. Hamilton had written revolutionary pamphlets as a teenager on the eve of the Revolution, and as a soldier had crossed the Delaware with Washington, spent the winter at Valley Forge as Washington's aide-de-camp, and stormed the last British redoubt at Yorktown in 1781. He had called for a constitutional convention as early as 1780, had participated at Annapolis in 1786 and at Philadelphia in 1787, had written much of *The Federalist* to defend and explain the new Constitution in 1787–88, and had led the successful fight for its acceptance in New York's ratification convention in 1788. Yet he was only thirty-two years old when he became the first secretary of the Treasury in 1789. Hamilton's achievements, before and after 1789, would lead the wily French diplomat Talleyrand, himself a major player on the world scene in the late eighteenth and early nineteenth centuries, to write that Hamilton was the greatest statesman of that era, with only Napoleon in France and Pitt in Britain being in his league.

Funding the Revolutionary War debt

Hamilton's first task was to draw up a plan to fund all the outstanding debts connected with gaining independence. "Funding" in this context meant restructuring the debts, funding interest payments right away, and eventually making provisions to redeem the principal. In January 1790, Hamilton, just four months in office, came up with a plan for funding all national debts and those of the states that had issued their own debts in the cause of independence. Because the states had issued debts for a common cause, Hamilton argued that the national government should assume those debts and fund them with long-term U.S. government bonds, paying interest and principal in gold and silver. For detailed accounts of the background, execution, and results of Hamilton's debt-restructuring program, see James and Sylla (1980), Garber (1991), and Perkins (1994).

How was Hamilton able to claim that the United States could pay the interest and principal in gold and silver? Precisely because the new government had the power to tax imports. These taxes were important for raising revenue, rather than for protectionist purposes, and were to be paid in gold and silver money. Hamilton could promise to pay U.S. creditors in gold and silver provided that U.S. revenues were sufficient. To ensure that they were sufficient, he also added to his plan an excise tax on whiskey, a domestic tax that was enacted to help pay for the assumption of state debts. Other domestic excise taxes soon followed. In 1790 the federal debt, including arrears of interest, was estimated to be $54 million and the aggregate state debts to be $25 million. Congress vigorously debated Hamilton's plan for several months and finally adopted it. An interesting by-product was a compromise that Hamilton, a New Yorker, struck with southern political leaders, particularly the Virginian opponents of his plan. In return for their support, the U.S. capital would be moved from New York City to Philadelphia for ten years, and then to the banks of the Potomac in what became Washington, D.C.

The impact of Hamilton's program on the value of U.S. debt was dramatic. What were junk bonds in default in August 1789, when Hamilton was about to become secretary of the Treasury, quickly became prime paper. The main issues of revolutionary war debt were selling at 25 percent of par in the summer of 1789, but a year later, just after the bill embodying Hamilton's proposals had been enacted by Congress, their price rose to 60 percent of par. In August 1791, when the main federal debt issue started to carry interest in gold and silver, the price was 100 percent of par. In September 1792, toward the end of President Washington's first term, these bonds were selling at 120 percent of par. The junk bonds of 1789 became prime low-risk bonds by 1791–92 as a result of Hamilton's funding plan and its execution. The implementation of the plan created a lot of new securities – nearly $80 million of them – and active trading markets for these securities quickly emerged on Wall Street in New York and in a few other cities. The United States suddenly had an organized bond market.

Creating the Bank of the United States

The next task in Hamilton's financial plan was to create the Bank of the United States, which would serve as the government's fiscal agent as well as in other capacities, as the Bank of England did for the British government. Hamilton's bank proposal was introduced late in 1790, and again the southerners resisted. The origins of political parties in the United States are found in the debates that took place over Hamilton's bank; see Beard (1915). Jefferson and Madison contended that Hamilton's plan for the Bank of the United States was unconstitutional because the Constitution did not explicitly grant the new government the power to charter such an institution or, in fact, even mention the word *bank*. Hamilton, however, persuaded Congress to pass his bank bill and then persuaded President Washington, against the advice of other members of his cabinet, to sign the bill, by arguing effectively that the Constitution contained implied as well as explicit powers. Hamilton contended that the Constitution was designed to promote the nation's welfare and therefore implied that the government could create a bank if it would help to accomplish this. The legal principle of implied powers, developed by Hamilton to secure his bank, subsequently became a pillar of constitutional law everywhere.

Soon after the bank bill was enacted in 1791, scrip (rights to subscribe to bank shares when they became available) was issued and became an object of frenzied trading. Not long afterward the bank itself issued equity shares – $10 million worth, of which one-fifth was subscribed by the U.S. government – and the trading in these shares commenced. By 1791 the United States thus had active stock markets for bank and other shares, especially on Wall Street.

Hamilton demonstrated his financial acumen as well as statecraft in making much of the bank's stock available for purchase by tendering the U.S. bonds created from his funding plan. Thus, the bank supported the national debt, the debt supported the bank, and the federal revenue system supported both the debt and the bank. And perhaps most important of all, the holders of U.S. bonds and bank stock had strong reasons to support the fledgling, untested federal government.

Hamilton's debt and bank bills, as well as his mint bill and Report on Manufactures that soon followed, were all completed within two years. They essentially created the U.S. money and capital markets, and charted the course of subsequent U.S. economic development. The federal government collected its revenue, minted coins, paid interest on a large national debt, and was able to borrow from the Bank of the United States. The Bank of the United States helped to manage the government's finances and practiced private banking as well. The securities markets traded U.S. bonds and bank stock, and with these issues at their base, they extended their scope to include other securities issues. Both the federal government and the U.S. economy emerged stronger.

Hamilton's plan to align the interests of government, business, and investors also attracted foreign capital. He predicted that if his program were adopted, the United States would export securities. And that is exactly what happened. By 1795, of a national debt totaling about $70 million, $20 million was held abroad. This figure rose to $33 million in 1801 and to $50 million in 1803. The Bank of the United States was capitalized in 1791 at $10 million, and by 1803, barely a decade after its birth, about 60 percent of its shares had been purchased by foreign investors. Largely because of Hamilton's system, U.S. credit had risen in the world. A decade after his plans were conceived and implemented, a huge amount of U.S. securities were held overseas, meaning that capital had been transferred to the United States. Ironically, Thomas Jefferson, who had so often opposed Hamilton's plans, became a beneficiary of Hamilton's system. When Jefferson, as president in 1803, was offered the Louisiana Territory by Napoleon (a purchase that would double the size of the United States), he was easily able to borrow the purchase amount in Europe because of the prime credit status the United States had attained as a result of Hamilton's program. Such an outcome would have been unthinkable only fifteen years earlier, when the United States was unable even to service its debts to France.

Hamilton's legacy

Once securities markets are established with firm grounding, as they were early in U.S. history, they remain important in a country's long-term development. When Hamilton's program established public credit and securities markets in the early 1790s, U.S. citizens were immediately able to borrow from older, richer countries. And these effects persisted for more than a century as the United States financed its rise to become the world's largest economy with the help of foreign capital. By the end of the nineteenth century the United States had become so developed and wealthy that U.S. residents began for the first time to lend and invest more abroad than they borrowed.

During the 1820s and 1830s the United States – usually state governments – borrowed large sums from foreign investors to build roads, canals, and early railroads; make other transportation improvements; and capitalize state banks. From the 1840s to the end of the century, still larger sums from overseas went into private U.S. railway companies that provided a continental economy with cheap transportation. Much of this borrowing took the form of state and corporate bond sales to overseas investors. The pristine federal

Table 11.1. *Foreign investments in the United States, 1853*

Type of security	Value held by foreigners (in $ millions)	Percentage of total securities outstanding held by foreigners
U.S. government stock (mainly bonds)	27.0	46
State stock (mainly bonds)	111.0	58
113 cities and towns (bonds)	16.5	21
317 counties (mainly bonds)	5.0	36
985 banks (stocks)	6.7	3
75 insurance companies (stocks)	0.4	3
244 railroad companies (stocks)	8.2	3
244 railroad companies (bonds)	43.9	26
16 canal and navigation companies (stocks)	0.5	2
16 canal and navigation companies (bonds)	2.0	9
15 miscellaneous companies (stocks)	0.8	5
15 miscellaneous companies (bonds)	0.3	11
Total	222.2	19

Source: Adapted from Wilkins (1989:76).

government credit established by Hamilton thus rubbed off on U.S. state and corporate debt.

The U.S. stock market developed more slowly than the bond market, but it both aided and benefited from foreign investment in U.S. bonds. It was only natural that foreigners who invested in a country, particularly a young but promising country, would prefer safe debt securities to speculative equities. Yet equity securities are good for a country – or for the corporate enterprises of a country – in part because they create a safety margin for bondholders, who, because of this margin, are more willing to purchase and hold bonds. Data for the United States in the 1850s indicate that outstanding securities totaled between $1 and $1.5 billion and were about evenly divided between bonds and equities. Other data for the same period show that about one-fifth of U.S. securities were held by foreign investors (Table 11.1). Foreign holdings of U.S. securities in 1853 were mostly bonds (about 93 percent) with only about 7 percent in stocks (equities). In other words, foreign investors had a much stronger preference for bonds compared with U.S. investors, who, after they exported bonds, held more stock than bonds at home.

It is clear from the record that foreign investors in the United States preferred to hold bonds rather than equities. But why were U.S. investors willing to hold almost all of the outstanding U.S. equities? The answer to this question reveals why secondary trading markets for securities are important. Because good stock markets permit the conversion of equity securities into cash, more people become more willing to invest in equities. This is one of the benefits of a good stock market for a developing country: the country will

Table 11.2. *Corporate stock as percentage of national assets, six countries, 1800–1978*

Period	Gt. Britain	USA	Canada	France	Germany	Japan
1800–15	1.1	2.3	—	—	—	—
1850	4e	5.5	—	1.0	0.5	—
1875–80	6e	9.2	—	2.7	1.7	—
1895–1900	16.1	9.2	—	—	2.7	3.8
1912–13	14.0	12.5	—	5.1	3.2	4.7
1929–30	15.7	19.4	—	2.7	3.0	6.8
1937–40	17.6	11.5	—	—	2.5	11.8
1948–50	12.3	8.0	—	5.1	2.4	—
1965	10.4	15.8	5.7	—	—	5.0
1976–78	6.0	7.3	4.6	5.4	3.0	4.2

Note: For the years 1850 and 1875–80, e means estimated.
Source: Goldsmith (1985). For Great Britain in 1850 and 1875, Goldsmith reports a combined percentage for corporate bonds and stock. I make a rough estimate for the stock share based on the 1895 and 1913 data, which give corporate bond and stock shares separately.

find it easier to sell bonds to foreign investors. That, at least, was the U.S. experience more than a century ago.

A final point I would make about historical securities markets concerns the size of corporate stock holdings as a percentage of national assets (Table 11.2). U.S. residents, relative to their economy's total assets, had the biggest stock market in the world in the early nineteenth century, even though they were mainly a nation of farmers at that time. The United States maintained a stock market relatively larger than that of Britain, a country whose economy then was more developed and diversified. Britain's earlier legislation – the Bubble Act and other laws dating from the early eighteenth century – made it difficult to establish corporations. Thus, it is not surprising that Britain lagged behind the United States in equity market development, as the United States had no such constraints. By the middle of the nineteenth century the United States had outpaced other countries, such as Germany, by even more in terms of the ratio of corporate stock to national assets. But the British did manage to catch up. And by the beginning of the twentieth century Britain surpassed the United States in corporate stock relative to national assets.

Why did Britain catch up with and pass the United States in terms of this measure of stock market development? One important reason is that the British, beginning in the mid-nineteenth century, began to develop stock market regulation, requiring corporations to issue prospectuses, to place audited reports in the hands of investors, and to make other disclosures to investors; see Sylla and Smith (1995). This regulation was firmly established by the early twentieth century. The United States, on the other hand, did not require companies to publish audited reports, they did not require registration of

210   **Richard Sylla**

securities issues, and there was no federal securities regulation. With limited information in the hands of investors, insider trading flourished in U.S. equity markets and worked to stifle equity market development, at least in comparison to Britain. During the 1930s and 1940s, however, the United States, with its SEC-mandated disclosure and other forms of securities market regulation, caught up with and passed the British. Since that time U.S. stock and bond markets have remained world leaders in many respects, with their operating practices and regulatory structures widely copied.

Thus, we can conclude that what many developing and transitional economies need today is another Alexander Hamilton. But such individual ability is rarely encountered in history. The modern age, fortunately, has institutional substitutes. If the World Bank and other modern institutions are interested in stimulating securities market development in developing and transitional economies, they would do well to remember some lessons of U.S. history: put fiscal, monetary, and banking practices on a solid ground and then mandate disclosure of pertinent financial information to investors. These measures will stimulate both the emergence of securities markets and the demand for securities. Once they are in place, the authorities need only to get out of the way – securities markets will continue to develop on their own and enhance economic development.

REFERENCES

Beard, Charles A. 1915. *Economic Origins of Jeffersonian Democracy*. New York: Macmillan.
Dickson, P. G. M. 1967. *The Financial Revolution in England: A Study in the Development of Public Credit, 1688–1756*. London: Macmillan.
Garber, Peter M. 1991. "Alexander Hamilton's Market-Based Debt Reduction Plan." *Carnegie-Rochester Conference Series, Public Policy* 35 (Autumn): 38.
Goldsmith, Raymond W. 1985. *Comparative National Balance Sheets*. Chicago: University of Chicago Press, Appendix A.
James, John A., and Richard Sylla. 1980. "The Changing Nature of American Public Debt." In *La dette publique aux XVIIe et XIXe siecles son developpement sur le plan local*. Brussels: Credit Communale de Belgique, pp. 197–228.
Perkins, Edwin. 1994. *American Public Finance and Financial Services, 1700–1815*. Columbus: Ohio State University Press.
Smith, George David, and Richard Sylla. 1993. "The Transformation of Financial Capitalism: An Essay on the History of American Capital Markets." *Financial Markets, Institutions & Instruments* 2 (2).
Sylla, Richard, and George David Smith. 1995. "Information and Capital Market Regulation in Anglo-American Finance." In Michael D. Bordo and Richard Sylla, eds., *Anglo-American Financial Systems: Institutions and Markets in the Twentieth Century*. Burr Ridge, Ill.: Irwin, pp. 179–205.
Sylla, Richard, Jack W. Wilson, and Charles P. Jones. 1994. "U.S. Financial Markets and Long-Term Economic Growth, 1790–1989." In Thomas Weiss and Donald Schaefar, eds., *American Development in Historical Perspective*. Stanford, Calif.: Stanford University Press, pp. 219–37.

Wilkins, Mira. 1989. *The History of Foreign Investment in the United States to 1914.* Cambridge, Mass.: Harvard University Press.

DISCUSSION

Question: To what extent can one compare the U.S. and German systems? One argument concerning the late development of German stock markets explains that it has been fragmented, as the regulations of the leading states and exchanges are not all the same. Should this system be recommended in other countries?

Prof. Sylla: The German stock market is a lot smaller relative to its economy than the U.S. stock market, and a key difference between the two is the universal banking system. In the German system the banks are big and the stock and bond markets are small, whereas in the U.S. system banks are not large relative to the size of the U.S. economy, but the open capital markets and the stock and bond markets are big. Why do these differences exist? Historically, the German banking system had played a much larger role in company finance and much of the stock was held by banks; this outcome was hastened by German taxes and regulations on stock trading. In the United States there were all kinds of experiments and restrictions on banks, including the fragmentation of banking right through the Glass–Steagall Act of the 1930s, which is now under attack. The U.S. government tried to make it tough for bankers to do what they might be led to do on their own: it prevented interstate branching and frowned on the idea of investment and commercial banks getting together. But it didn't regulate the stock and bond markets very much until the twentieth century, allowing them to develop in relative freedom. And when the government did regulate them, it did so in an enlightened way that encouraged further development. About both Germany and the United States we can say that one part of the financial system is free from onerous government regulations and the other part is highly regulated. Which one can be expected to do well? The unregulated part is going to chip away and steal from the more regulated part.

The Germans levied heavy taxes on stock trading in the 1890s. As a result their stock markets shrank and a lot of the stock trading in Germany went on inside the banks – the banks developed something like an internal stock market. Germany didn't regulate its banks to anywhere near the extent that the United States did, but it did get tough on its stock markets. That is how these two systems differ.

Prof. Calomiris: I think that explanation overemphasizes the taxation of stocks. A better way to explain the difference is that the secondary market may serve a very different function in the United States, a function that's not necessary in Germany. Given the reserve pyramid in New York City, with liquidity, shocks and seasonal shocks that may require people to dump securities very quickly, it is crucial to have that secondary market in New York. In Germany, with nationwide branching, there is no reserve pyramiding. So, the tax story doesn't wash. Rather, reserve pyramiding is really what accounts for major differences. The taxation of securities may be part of the story later on. Look at the primary market: even in the United States today and since the postwar period, actual stock issues are about 1 percent of corporate finance on average. Two-thirds are retained earnings. Looking at Table 11.2, I don't like the numerator or the denominator. The denominator is national assets, a questionable denominator in a corporate finance program. But the numerator is even worse – it is corporate stock, most of which is accumulated retained earnings. To answer which is the more attractive technology (focusing on the primary stock market), we must look at primary stock issues, and in this area the United States is far behind. However, I think your story describes the first industrial revolution. My story, and I want to be very clear, is about the second industrial revolution.

Question: I agree that the public finance problem is a big problem in terms of getting the system right at the start. Certainly in African countries the problem of establishing the creditworthiness of the government is important. It is very difficult to make the system work when governments aren't creditworthy. But then you asked the question, Why Alexander Hamilton? Was he the cause or the effect? Certainly he can propose a system, but politically he had to sell it. And what disposes a country to accept such a system? In the United States public finance ideas transplanted from the English culture may have been responsible. How does a country develop the sense that the government has to be creditworthy? Also, what was the mechanism, between 1789 and 1792, that made these bonds increase toward par value? Was it because the government was able to collect enough tax revenue to start paying off the debt?

Prof. Sylla: The old debt was a collection of securities that said the U.S. government owes a given amount of money, on which it will pay interest. These securities were collected – people had to exchange them for new issues of long-term bonds paying 6 percent interest. It's an interesting debt restructuring deal. All of the face value of the debt was funded into new bonds, but some of them didn't pay interest until 1800 (ten years later), and some of them paid only 3 percent interest instead of 6 percent. When the new securities were announced, they were considered so much more attractive than the old, probably because the government's commitment was now credible, that both old and new securities, for which the old could be exchanged, rose in market value.

As for why Hamilton, who knows. How can one account for extraordinary ability whenever and wherever it arises? One can say that the United States was very fortunate to have such a talent present at the start. Certainly Hamilton was familiar with British and French financial practices. But a key part of his genius was not only to realize and say, in the U.S. context, what should be done, but also to sell it politically against strong opposition, and then implement it with administrative talent of the highest order.

Comment: Underlying the ability to pay back debts is the promise of future revenue. The establishment of the revenue base must be fundamentally important.

Prof. Sylla: Agreed. Establishing the revenue base was the initial element of financial reform. Hamilton pushed for the tariff act and probably would have liked to have made tariffs a little higher to maximize revenue. He also argued for internal taxes. Congress enacted the whiskey tax and other taxes later on.

The Jeffersonians didn't like that a bit, but Hamilton persuaded Congress that the country had to have a strong revenue system to underpin the debt funding program.

One favorable factor was that the United States in the eighteenth and nineteenth centuries was the most rapidly growing economy in the world. And it was taxing imports. When an economy grows, what happens to imports? They grow. Import tax revenues can become very large, even with low tariff rates. Between 1816, when tariff rates were raised, and the 1830s so much money came in, which the Jeffersonian and Jacksonian governments didn't want the federal government to spend, that they simply paid down the debt. By 1835 all of the U.S. national debt was paid off. This occurrence was unique in history, before and since. Now, what does paying off your entire national debt do for your credit rating overseas? Europeans started shoveling their money to the United States!

It seems to me that Jefferson, Madison, Hamilton, and most of the U.S. leaders agreed on the necessity of retiring government debt, if possible, even if they may have differed on the rate of retirement. It was perceived to be not just honorable, but also practical for a sustainable government. Repaying now would allow more borrowing in the future, if that became necessary.

Question: Then the explanation is that the U.S. authorities – fortunately – inherited their ideas from the British. And Hamilton was the instrument for making that state of mind work effectively. But the question remains, What does that mean for the rest of the world? Do countries have to model themselves after the British? How will you persuade anyone to do that?

M. Shirley: Well, I think the answer to that question is that Hamilton also made many side deals with business elites, at least to give them a stake in the system he was creating. Unfortunately, outside advisors often come along, even when there is an Alexander Hamilton, and say, ''You cannot be making these deals because we need level playing fields and transparency.''

Prof. Sylla: The British precedents were there, but it is easy to exaggerate their influence in the United States. The British issued consols, perpetual debt, and were far less committed than the United States to retiring government debt. But creating stakes in a government is important. Today you still could try to align the interests of the business classes in, say, Poland, with those of the Polish government. That's what Hamilton wanted to do and did, and that's what the British did. It is difficult, but it can be done.

Question: You establish that government creditworthiness sets the anchor for the whole system. But there are a lot of countries in the world where that isn't true. Some countries don't pay any bills, not even public sector salaries, and nobody lends them resources.

Prof. Sylla: Such countries probably don't have well-functioning stock and bond markets either.

Question: But how do you solve their problems? Should you try to sponsor a capital market when the needed conditions are absent? One of the elements of success in the United States was the capacity of the U.S. government to raise revenue. As you said, the economy was growing very fast, and most of the revenue was coming from imports. So, essentially, the government's fiscal ability was based on import taxes. This historical fact is very interesting because most of the time we propose a decrease in import taxes.

Prof. Sylla: We propose a decrease because we are all supposed to be free traders. I've been taught by economic theory to be a free trader too. But in the 1780s and 1790s in the United States it was very important that the government be financed. The tax on imports may have been the most efficient tax for the government to implement, overriding the usual free-trade arguments against tariffs. In a country that doesn't have a lot of market transactions or in which it's hard to implement an income tax system, collecting taxes at a few ports can be very efficient. Hamilton's administrative ability made it efficient – there were surprisingly few complaints or controversies about a new, large tax system. So I would argue that the early U.S. tariffs were an efficient revenue raising measure. And the rates were only 5 to 10 percent, hardly protectionist and not intended to be protectionist. Many state and local sales taxes today are in that range, but free traders do not seem incensed.

Comment: In a sense Hamilton was doing something very simple. There really are only two options. One option is arranging things so that you can pay the interest. The other option is hoping that something will crop up. The first is generally acceptable to any thinking person. We can survive with such a rule. With the other rule we probably won't survive. I think simple rules do tend to attract adherents.

Prof. Sylla: And you must sell it, as Hamilton did. Go out to countries and sell such rules. The problem is that governments often have difficulty following them.

Response: The leaders who function in economies that are performing so badly are probably trying to grab as much as they can in a short time before they get knocked out of power. That's very common thinking. They're not planning for a long ride; they're planning for a short ride.

Prof. Sylla: If you follow good rules, you'll be able to maintain a governmental system for a long time. In 1790 the United States was the newest country in the world. Now, 200 years later, with no fundamental change in government, it's the oldest country in the world, politically speaking. If that sort of stability appeals to people and national leaders, then I don't think it would be hard to sell the ideas, the rules. What's difficult is to implement them, and I think that's where you really have to give Alexander Hamilton credit. His contribution was not only in selling ideas, but in setting up the revenue collection system and persuading the majority of people in Congress that they should follow his plan.

Comment: I think the initial conditions in a lot of our countries are quite different in a number of respects. Look at our expenditures compared with those of the United States 200 years ago. A lot of our governments are supporting public enterprises, sometimes explicitly on budget. They're trying to finance education, health, and transportation, and they're trying to establish social safety nets and a social security system. They're doing far more than the United States was doing 200 years ago. So just looking at expenditures, they're in worse shape. And on the revenue side, a lot of the economies are not growing, and they may not have a lot of potential for growth. In terms of their ability to tax and raise revenue, they're in worse shape. To start out with, they don't have the potential for financing the public deficit.

Prof. Sylla: If you could total up their national debts and compare it with their GDPs, what ratio would you get? It turns out that the U.S. debt at that time had about the same ratio to GNP as many countries have today. So in fact there was a large obligation in the United States in 1790. You're saying that this obligation is complicated by the fact that modern governments have many expenditure programs. I agree, that's a problem. But revenue capacity has advanced substantially as well.

To conclude, without addressing the public finance problem, it is difficult to see how security markets can develop. So why not fix the public finance problem first?

Index

adverse selection: with contingent liability systems, 107–9; pre-FDIC deposit insurance, 88–90
Akerlof, George A., 10
Aoki, Masahiko, 129
Ayr Bank collapse, 50, 56, 62

Bade, R., 29
Bagehot, Walter, 27
Banco de Desarrollo, Chile, 176
Bank Act (1900 revision), Canada, 76
Bank Charter Act (1844), United Kingdom, 52
Bank chartering, United States, 103
bank failures: Canada, 8; need to prevent, 25–6; in pre- and post-World War II Japan, 128, 140; reasons for, 8; role of fraud in, 10; United States and Canada (1870–80), 67–78; U.S. banking system, 8, 91–2
Bank Holding Company Act (1956), U.S., 120
Banking Act (1844), England, 44–5
Banking Act (1765), Scotland, 48–9
Banking Act (1933), United States: deposit insurance provisions, 87–8, 93; fragmentation of banking under, 211; repeal of double liability, 105; restrictions on commercial bank equity underwriting, 120
Banking Act (1935), United States: increase in amount insured, 93; repeal of double liability, 105
banking system: See also branch banking; universal banking; before central banks, 4; comparison of U.S. and Canadian (1870–1920), 71–8; comparison of U.S. and Canadian (1920–1980), 67–71; English compared to Scottish, 53–5; with limited liability, 106; as precursor of central bank, 24; role of central bank in, 24; role of German, 211; Scottish bank notes, 45–9;

solvency problems, 8–9; with and without central bank, 37–8
banking system, Canada: bank failures and performance (1870–1920), 8, 65–6; pre-1920 instability, 76; stability and performance (1920–1980), 66–8
banking system, Japan: See also zaibatsu banks; firm–bank relationships, 128–30, 139; interwar, 134–6
Banking system, Scotland: exchange and clearing system, 49–52
banking system, Scotland: compared to English system, 53–5; note issue, 45–9; post-1862 limited liability, 102; pre-1862 unlimited liability, 101–2
banking system, United States: bank failures (1933), 91–2; compared to Canadian banking system (1920–1980), 67; contingent liability among national banks, 104–5; double liability experiment, 101, 103; dual, 66, 72; effect of regulation on, 85–6; national, 104; post-World War I consolidation, 123; real bills doctrine (nineteenth century), 86
bank notes: Ayr Bank overissue, 50, 56; free banking era in Scotland, 45–6; option clause, 46–9, 51; replacement by Federal Reserve notes in United States, 104–5; restraint of note growth in Scotland, 50–2; as Scottish bank liability, 102; Scottish clearing and exchange system, 49–52; Suffolk system of clearing and exchange, 50; as U.S. bank liability, 104; value of central bank, 25
Bank of England: established (1694), 24; formal control of Scotland's free banking system (1844), 44–5; independence of, 4–5; as lender of last resort, 29; note issue dominance, 51–2; post-World War I independence, 31; responsibilities as central bank (ca. 1800), 29, 36–7; use of open market operations, 27–8